St. Louis Community College

Forest Park
Florissant Valley
Meramec

Instructional Resources
St. Louis, Missouri

UNDERSTANDING
PIAGET

Books by Mary Ann Spencer Pulaski, Ph.D.

UNDERSTANDING PIAGET
An Introduction to
Children's Cognitive Development

YOUR BABY'S MIND AND HOW IT GROWS
Piaget's Theory for Parents

STEP-BY-STEP GUIDE TO CORRECT ENGLISH

Verne N. Rockcastle, 1964

JEAN PIAGET

IN MEMORIAM

August 9, 1896—September 16, 1980

UNDERSTANDING
PIAGET

An Introduction to
Children's Cognitive Development

REVISED AND EXPANDED EDITION

Mary Ann Spencer Pulaski, Ph.D.

1817

HARPER & ROW, PUBLISHERS, New York
Cambridge, Hagerstown, Philadelphia, San Francisco,
London, Mexico City, São Paulo, Sydney

Designer: Robin Malkin

Library of Congress Cataloging in Publication Data

Pulaski, Mary Ann Spencer.
  Understanding Piaget.

  Bibliography: p.
  Includes index.
  1. Piaget, Jean, 1896–   2.   Cognition in
children.   I. Title.
BF723.C5P85   1980   155.4'13'0924   80–7595
ISBN 0–06–013454–2

89 90 91 10 9 8 7 6 5

To my children
SANDY and BETSY
and to all children growing up today

Contents

Introduction

Why should one wish to read about the psychological theory of Jean Piaget? Because he is one of the most influential of living thinkers. His ideas about the development of cognition in children are affecting research, preschool programs, methods of parenting, curriculum planning, and many other areas of psychology and education today. Just as Freud opened our eyes to children's emotional growth, so Piaget is casting new light on our understanding of children's intellectual growth. Thinking, knowing, imagining, perceiving, remembering, recognizing, abstracting, generalizing—all these processes are included in the term *cognition*, which refers to all the intellectual activities of the mind. Piaget's studies of human cognitive development help us to understand what to expect of children, how they perceive the world around them at different ages, and why they ask questions and interpret information in ways that may seem strange to adults.

Piaget is a Swiss psychologist who has been working with children for over half a century. He is interested in how children learn to know, how they organize their thinking. How does a baby come to recognize his mother, for example, and to know who are strangers? How does a child develop language? When and by what steps does he learn to add and manipulate numbers? What is the relation between maturation and learning? These are questions Piaget has tried to answer, with results that have had a growing impact on present-day psychology. His early works, translated into English in the 1920s, were received with astonishment and disbelief. A good deal of criticism followed because of the small number of subjects studied and the lack of statistical validation; in his early work Piaget ignored most of the accepted methods of scientific research. Moreover, his theoretical views were in direct conflict with the basic American psychology of behaviorism, which still permeates our thinking. As a result, Piaget's contributions were largely neglected in this country for many years, but since about 1950 there has been a tremendous revival of interest in his work. Most of his numerous books have now been published in English, and a growing body of research is developing, based on his findings. In the past decade alone, so much has been written and translated as to make necessary this revision of the 1971 edition of *Understanding Piaget*.

If Piaget's thinking is so important, why not read it in the original? Because Piaget has been publishing prolifically ever since he was eleven, and it has become a monumental task to keep up with all his productions. He is the author of at least fifty books and innumerable articles. Moreover, his ideas, like Freud's, have grown and changed with the years, so that his later theories are more developed or have different areas of emphasis from those of his early works. In addition, Piaget writes in French, and his terms are sometimes translated differently by different scholars. This makes it difficult to follow his thinking from one book to another.

Even if all Piaget's work were available in one volume by one translator, the uninitiated would find it hard to understand. Piaget uses very difficult terms, such as *reciprocal assimilation* and *genetic epistemology*. Furthermore, he employs familiar words such as *conservation* and *egocentrism* with shades of meaning that are different from their usual connotation. In this book I have attempted to avoid such terminology as much as possible, in an effort to make Piaget's thinking and research understandable to everyone interested in children. I hope readers will share my enjoyment of his deep insight, his warm empathy for children, and his quiet sense of humor. The mark of Piaget's greatness is that his ideas are so fruitful and have generated so much interest and research among others. He has broken fresh ground and gleaned a rich harvest of knowledge. There are many who feel that Piaget will eventually be as well known as Freud. Already his influence has been so profound that today no knowledgeable person can afford to be unfamiliar with his ideas.

Piaget's research is so comprehensive and so fully developed that a guide is needed in approaching it. This book attempts to fill that need. First, it reviews the theoretical rationale behind Piaget's work and sets forth his basic principles of development. Then comes an overview of developmental stages of intellectual growth from infancy to adolescence. Next, there follows a more detailed presentation of Piaget's work in many areas as diverse as play, morality, perception, time, numbers, and emotions. Three new chapters have been added to this revision; it has been extended to include not only Piaget's work but that of some of his associates who make up what is now called "the Genevan school." It reviews Inhelder's important studies of learning and Sinclair's work on language, and makes brief references as well to American research such as Kohlberg's on morality and Liben's on memory. There are references to a number of books based on Piaget's theory, such as those by Gallagher and Reid on learning and Kamii and DeVries on preschool education. New research is constantly appearing in the journals of child development and genetic psychology; much of this literature is reviewed in the newsletter of the Jean Piaget Society (Temple University, Philadelphia, Pennsylvania) and the proceedings of the annual conferences on Piagetian Theory and the Helping Professions (University Affiliated Program, Childrens Hospital, Los Angeles, California).

For those who wish to read Piaget's own works, a chronological listing by French publication dates is included. Such a chronology is necessary because the English translations do not correspond to the time or order in which the originals were written. The first five books belong to Piaget's early period, when he was interested in the conversations, questions, and reasoning of young children such as those he saw at the Maison des Petits in Geneva. Then come the books based largely on Piaget's own children. They study the very beginnings of intelligence in babies and show how children develop their earliest notions of space, time, causality, and object permanence during the sensory-motor period. Since about 1940, Piaget has been developing his theories of mathematical groups and the logical expression of cognitive structures. His works on logic, time, speed, and number are all characterized by these logical-mathematical formulations. In the past decade, Piaget's thinking has come full circle back to the biological basis for behavior, the "embryology of intelligence" he has been mulling over since before the 1920s. His seminal books *Biology and Knowledge* and *Behavior and Evolution* sum up his lifetime of thinking on this subject.

We have reviewed all of these books, as well as most of the earlier ones that are better known and more easily read. In addition there are a number of articles that have appeared in journals such as *Scientific American,* or in edited collections. Some of these, such as "Children's Philosophies," are delightful reading. The reader, however, must be aware of the time sequence of Piaget's work. In a recent contribution (to Mussen [ed.], *Carmichael's Manual of Child Psychology*) Piaget explains that his theory has never been completed and that he considers himself one of the chief "revisionists of Piaget."

Reading Piaget over the years, one notices major changes. Instead of the earlier, rather mechanical formulation of stages and substages, he has developed an increasing awareness of the complex interactions taking place between the child and his environment. Out of this interaction develop the structures of thought, each one richer, more complex, and qualitatively different from the one before it. This recapitulation of intellectual development at each succeeding stage is a fascinating aspect of cognitive growth; Piaget calls it "the spiral of knowing." In addition, the concept of equilibration, the self-regulating process of seeking a "steady state" of equilibrium at different stages, has gained added importance in Piaget's thinking, enriched by the work of such modern biologists as C. F. Waddington.

Such changes are reflected, insofar as is possible, in this admittedly simplified interpretation of Piaget's theory.

In the writing and rewriting of this guide to Piaget's work, I have been indebted to many people. First and foremost, of course, is Jean Piaget himself, whose keen mind and sense of humor delighted me first in his books and then in listening to him during a visit to his International Center for Genetic Epistemology. John Flavell's scholarly *Developmental Psychology of Jean Piaget* was my first introduction to Piaget, in a graduate course taught by Professor Wayne Dennis, who encouraged me in this effort. Many members of the Jean Piaget Society—among them, Gilbert Voyat, James Magary, Millie Almy, Marilyn Appel, Rheta DeVries, David Elkind, Howard Gruber, and Deanna Kuhn—have helped me, either with direct suggestions or indirectly through their publications. My thanks go also to Joy Gentry, Fred Skinner, and all the teachers whose classrooms I visited in the British "infant schools" of Kent.

I am especially indebted to Professor Bärbel Inhelder for graciously welcoming me to the University of Geneva during my sabbatical leave; she and all her associates, especially Professors Hermine Sinclair and Marianne Denis-Prinzhorn and the librarians at the Jean Piaget Archives, were generous in their assistance to me. I owe a very special debt to Jeanette Gallagher, who read and criticized several chapters, and to Constance Kamii, who helped me work through some difficult ideas. I am also grateful to the Herricks School District for giving me a sabbatical leave, and to Eugene T. Goldwasser, my principal, who offered suggestions for the chapter on education.

Mrs. Ann Harris, my editor at Harper & Row, has become a trusted adviser and friend over the past ten years. Mrs. Margit Breakiron put aside her portraits of children to do many of the illustrations for this book. My faithful typists Aline Smith and Rita O'Toole have made order out of a sometimes chaotic manuscript. Finally, my gratitude goes to my family and friends for helping, encouraging, and putting up with me as I have written and rewritten these chapters. To all of these people I owe my heartfelt thanks.

M.A.P.

1. Piaget: A Profile

Jean Piaget was born on August 9, 1896, in Neuchâtel, Switzerland. His father was a scholar of medieval history, "a man of a painstaking and critical mind"[1]* who passed on to his small son the habit of systematic thinking down to the least detail that is so apparent in Piaget's writings. His mother was very intelligent and devoutly religious. Piaget reports in his autobiography that "her rather neurotic temperament . . . made our family life somewhat troublesome."[2] As a consequence of the atmosphere at home, Piaget reports that he early became a serious little boy, interested in mechanics, birds, fossils, and sea shells. He was barely eleven when he published his first paper, on a partly albino sparrow he had seen in the park. Then he asked the director of the natural history museum in Neuchâtel if he might assist him after school hours. This kindly man put the boy to work labeling his extensive collection of shells. The director was a specialist in mollusks, and he taught the eager youngster a great deal,

*Notes begin on page 221.

as well as giving him rare specimens for his own collection. After four years of this association, the director died; but Piaget had learned enough to begin publishing articles on malacology (the branch of zoology dealing with mollusks) in zoological journals. As a result of these papers, he was offered the position of curator of the mollusk collection by the director of the natural history museum in Geneva—a position he was forced to decline because he was still a schoolboy. Piaget went on to take his degree in the natural sciences at the University of Neuchâtel, and in 1918 he was awarded a doctorate for his thesis on malacology. His childish curiosity about mollusks had developed into an abiding interest in biology, which was to influence his thinking for the rest of his life.

During his adolescent years, Piaget read extensively in philosophy, religion, sociology, and psychology. His godfather introduced him to Henri Bergson's philosophy of creative evolution, and Piaget reports, "The identification of God with life itself was an idea that stirred me almost to ecstasy because it now enabled me to see in biology the explanation for all things and of the mind itself."[3] The young scientist decided at that moment to consecrate his life to the biological explanation of knowledge.

The study of knowledge—of how we come to know and what it is we know—is called epistemology; it deals with a problem that has challenged philosophers down through the ages. The ancient Greeks, and later on the 17th century philosophers such as Descartes, believed that ideas were innate in the mind of man. Others, like Locke, insisted that the baby's mind was a "tabula rasa" and that all knowledge came from the environment through the senses. This is close to the behaviorist position of many American psychologists of today, who believe that knowledge stems from the response of an organism to a stimulus from the environment.

Piaget has always firmly rejected both of these positions. He does not believe in innate ideas, but in knowledge that is constructed by each individual in interaction with his or her environment. Nor does the individual come to know by passively receiving and copying knowledge from the environment; he seeks it out, organizes it, and assimilates it into his or her previous state of knowledge. Thus Piaget is neither a nativist nor an empiricist, but an *interactionist.* Knowledge, for him, develops during a long, slow process of relating new ideas and activities to earlier ones. The key to the study of knowledge, he believes, is a developmental approach. Long ago he coined the term *genetic* (developmental) *epistemology* to describe his unique approach to the study of knowledge.[4] He was searching for an "embryology of intelligence" that would throw light on the problem of the relation between the acting or thinking subject and the objects of his knowledge.

This search led Piaget from biology to psychology, the study of the human mind. As such, he felt that psychology would provide the missing link between the philosophical problem of epistemology and its biological substrate. Having completed his studies in Neuchâtel, Piaget left for Zurich, where he worked in two psychological laboratories as well as in Bleuler's psychiatric clinic. Because of his mother's poor mental health, Piaget had become intensely interested in psychopathology and the theories of Freud. In the fall of 1919 he moved on to the Sorbonne in Paris, where he took courses in psychopathology as well as in logic, epistemology, and the philosophy of science. There he learned the art of clinical interviewing by questioning mental patients in a flexible, open-ended way that allowed him to follow the patient's own line of thought without imposing direction or standardized procedures on it.

Piaget soon had a chance to put this "méthode clinique" to good use. Looking around for an area of experimentation, he was fortunate enough to be recommended to Dr. Théophile Simon, who with Alfred Binet had developed the first intelligence test. Binet had died, and his laboratory in a Parisian public school was standing empty. Simon suggested to Piaget that he work there, standardizing on French children some of Sir Cyril Burt's English reasoning tests for use in the Binet scale.

These tests consisted of questions involving part-whole relationships, such as: "Some of my flowers are buttercups. Does my bouquet contain (1) all yellow flowers; (2) some yellow flowers; (3) no yellow flowers?" Questions like these, Piaget discovered, were very hard for young children because they have difficulty understanding the relationship of the part (yellow flowers) to the whole (bouquet). He found himself becoming increasingly more interested in why children fail tests such as these than in establishing norms for success. By what paths did children reach their answers? What thought processes led them astray? What factors did they fail to grasp in their search for solutions? To answer these questions, Piaget began to study the reasoning of children. He presented them with open-ended questions about relationships or problems of cause and effect. The children responded well to the tall, friendly young "M'sieu" who was so interested in their ideas. Soon he had enough material to publish a series of articles.

One of these articles drew the attention of Dr. Edouard Claparède, director of the Institut Jean-Jacques Rousseau in Geneva, a school formed for the scientific study of the child and the training of teachers. Claparède offered Piaget the position of director of research at this institute. He accepted, and in 1921, at the age of twenty-five, the young biologist, now become a psychologist, embarked on the research that was to be his life's work.

During the next decade Piaget published five books based on his research with Genevan schoolchildren, as well as those at the Maison des Petits, the school attached to the Institut Jean-Jacques Rousseau. He thought of them only as preliminary studies, published partly to stimulate further research. Instead, he found they brought him worldwide attention and made him famous before he was thirty. Meanwhile, he had married one of his students at the Institute, and in time they had three children—Jacqueline, Lucienne, and later a son, Laurent. With his wife's help, Piaget studied their cognitive development in meticulous detail; on these observations he based his later books on the development of intelligence during infancy and toddlerhood.

As he extended his studies into childhood and adolescence, Piaget collaborated with others, notably Alina Szeminska and Bärbel Inhelder, on books on the development of logical thinking in regard to quantity, numbers, geometry, space, time, movement, and speed. Piaget also became very much interested in the development of perception in children and published a whole series of experiments on this subject, followed by studies of mental imagery and memory. During this period, he modified his method of free verbal questioning to include tasks using concrete manipulative materials, which were followed by questions which forced the subject to justify his or her response. Critics had complained that conversations with small children may have given undependable results. This new, task-oriented approach is called "the method of critical exploration"; students in developmental psychology at the University of Geneva receive a year's training in working with children, combining the tasks given the children with specifically focused questions, even though they may be individually phrased.

Over the years Piaget has taught courses in philosophy, psychology, and sociology at the Institute and at the Universities of Geneva, Neuchâtel, and Lausanne, as well as the Sorbonne. In 1929 he was appointed a director of the International Office of Education; his activity increased after the war, when he gave generously of his time to UNESCO and became a member of its executive council. In the thirties the Rousseau Institute became merged with the University of Geneva. After Claparède's death in 1940 Piaget took over as its head, as well as becoming director of the Psychology Laboratory. He was also the first president of the Swiss Society of Psychology.

In 1955, with aid from the Rockefeller Foundation, Piaget organized his own International Center for Genetic Epistemology in Geneva, where scholars of different disciplines come from all over the world to discuss contemporary issues in cognitive development. Although Piaget retired from active teaching in 1971, he continues his research, publishes constantly, and still supervises the weekly meetings of the Center. These are characterized by lively interchanges among scholars of differing points of view, as well as among the graduate students who are engaged in the experiments that Piaget carefully supervises. Now in his eighties, Piaget no longer rides his bicycle to the university, but he continues to dominate the Center with his sharp intellect and droll humor.

Dr. David Elkind, a psychologist who spent a year in 1965 working with Piaget at the Center, described his schedule at that time:

Piaget's is a superbly disciplined life. He arises early each morning, sometimes as early as 4 A.M., and writes four or more publishable pages on square sheets of white paper in a small, even hand. Later in the morning he may teach classes and attend meetings. His afternoons include long walks during which he thinks about the problems he is currently confronting. He says, "I always like to think on a problem before reading about it." In the evenings he reads and retires early. Even on his international trips, Piaget keeps to his schedule.[5]

During the summers, according to Elkind, Piaget takes all the materials from the previous year's research at the Center and retreats to a farmhouse in the Alps, where he walks, thinks, and writes prodigiously. In the fall he leaves his secret hideaway and returns to the world of research and public responsibilities. With a beret over his snowy hair, a pipe in his mouth, and a twinkle in his eye, he has been for years a familiar figure around the streets of Geneva. And as more and more research bears out his theories, his ideas are becoming familiar around the world.

Fortunately, Piaget has lived long enough to see even those who once scorned his work acknowledge his genius. He has received many academic prizes and honors, including the 1969 Distinguished Scientific Contribution Award from the American Psychological Association, which he was the first European ever to receive. He has at least thirty honorary doctorate degrees from universities in many countries, beginning with Harvard in 1936. On the occasion of his 70th birthday, Dr. Robert Oppenheimer of the Institute for Advanced Study in Princeton, New Jersey, wrote to Piaget:

It is clear to me that in its scope and its conceptions [your work] is both a product of our times and the source of great changes now coming into being in the way we think of nature, and of ourselves as parts of nature and as knowers of it.[6]

2. A Biological Theory of Knowledge

It is interesting to note that Piaget, toward the end of a long career, has come full circle regarding the topics on which he writes. Beginning with the study of biology, he moved into developmental psychology and formulated his theory of stages of cognitive development which he studied in the many areas this book reviews. But in the past decade, Piaget has published *Biology and Knowledge* and *Behavior and Evolution*—books that go back to his original ideas and stress the continuity of development in all living things.

As a matter of fact, Piaget never really left biology, even when he was so occupied with cognitive topics.[1] For example, he has had a lifelong interest in the plant *sedum*, varieties of which are common in many rock gardens. From all over the world Piaget has collected specimens which he then grows in different environments. He transplanted one lush Mediterranean variety to a site over a mile high in the Savoy Alps to see how it adapted to the extreme cold. The plants reacted by putting out much smaller, thicker leaves, to reduce their area of exposure while increasing chlorophyll production and photosynthetic power. While many of these plants reverted to type when transplanted back to Piaget's garden in Geneva, some retained their small size over thousands of descendants.

Similarly, for many years Piaget has studied the snail *Limnaea stagnalis,* which in tranquil waters has an elongated shell. But when moved to the shores of the large Swiss lakes where the waves beat upon the rocks, Piaget reported that the young snail changes in shape. Clamping its sticky foot solidly to the supporting rock, the snail tightens the muscle that attaches it to its shell each time a wave dashes over it. This constant contracting tends to shorten the growing shell until it becomes globular in shape, rather than elongated. In time, the snail's adaptation to the turbulent waters tends to become hereditary in these specimens. Piaget has moved some of them back to his aquarium and to a small, quiet pond, and has watched their descendants for many generations, during which they have retained their globular shape.

For Piaget, these are examples of how organisms may adapt genetically to novel surroundings, a problem to which he has given much thought. While he certainly does not subscribe to Lamarck's discredited theory of the inheritance of acquired characteristics, he feels that living organisms are active and self-regulating in their choices of ways to adapt. Here Piaget differs also from Darwin, who sees organisms as essentially passive, dependent on chance mutation and natural selection for survival. For Piaget, adaptation is, on the contrary, a dynamic, on-going process in which the hereditary structure of the organism interacts with the external environment in such a way as to reconstitute itself for better survival.

When he turned from biology to the study of knowledge, Piaget began to see the continuity between biological intelligence, as shown even by plants and lower animals, and human knowledge as it develops from infancy onward. Knowledge, he concluded, is an evolving relationship between the child and his environment. Just as Piaget's snails reconstructed their shapes as a way of surviving in a hostile environment, so a child will reconstruct his actions and ideas in relation to new environmental experiences—adapting to adult table manners, for example. During this on-going relationship with the environment, the child exhibits at certain ages characteristic *structures* or organizations of action and thought which Piaget has classified as stages. His exposition of the evolving stages in intellectual development has been particularly illuminating to those who work with children. However, Piaget's greatest contribution may be his brilliant analysis of how human knowledge slowly develops beyond its biologic, inherited origins through a process of self-regulation based on feedback from the environment leading to internal reconstruction. The ability to adapt to new situations through self-regulation is the common link between all living things and the basis of Piaget's biological theory of knowledge.

For Piaget, then, *adaptation* is the essence of intellectual functioning, just as it is the essence of biological functioning. It is one of the two basic tendencies inherent in all species. The other is *organization*, the ability to integrate both physical and psychological structures into coherent systems. Adaptation takes place through organization; the organism discriminates among the myriad stimuli and sensations by which it is bombarded and organizes them into some kind of structure. For the newborn, it may be the complex of sensations that eventually means "Mother": the sound of her voice, the softness of her breast, the smell and taste of her milk, the comforting feel of her warm body. For an older child, organization may mean a system of classification that enables him to sort out and label stamps, coins, or shells, as did the young Piaget. The tendency toward organization is implicit in our biological heritage; it is part and parcel of adaptation and cannot be separated from it.

Adaptation has a dual nature; it consists of twin processes that go on continuously in all living organisms. *Assimilation* is the taking-in process, whether of sensation, nourishment, or experience. It is the process by which one incorporates things, people, ideas, customs, and tastes into one's own activity. For example, a child, listening to people talking around him, learns the inflections, the phrasing, and the meaning of language long before he is able to talk himself. He is assimilating everything he hears, and gradually making it his own.

Assimilation is continuously balanced by *accommodation*, the outgoing, adjusting process of reaching out to the environment. The listening child begins to babble in response to conversation around him and gradually approximates the words he is assimilating.

"Daddy" comes out "dada" and "flower" may be "fwodder," but as the child continues his efforts, he accommodates the sounds he makes to those he hears, and his baby talk becomes understandable speech. Thus he adapts to the language requirements of his environment.

These two processes of assimilation and accommodation, functioning simultaneously at all biological and intellectual levels, make possible both physical and cognitive development. We can watch them operating not only among plants and animals as Piaget did with his specimens, but in infants, where human behavior is less complicated and more clearly observed. The baby who is learning to take his first solid food from a spoon must learn to assimilate it by licking and chewing, rather than by his previous method of sucking. At the same time he must open his mouth and accommodate to the size and position of the spoon rather than the nipple he is used to. In this way he adapts to a new experience.

The same thing happens when the baby receives his first rattle. He tries to assimilate it into his mouth, meanwhile accommodating his mouth to the plaything's size and shape. But this experience produces a cognitive rather than a digestive adaptation. The baby learns that this is a suckable but not a swallowable object and henceforth modifies his understanding of objects-that-go-in-the-mouth to include two subcategories: (1) edible objects and (2) nonedible objects. Later on, after he has heard "No, no!" enough times, he will learn that there are objects that do *not* go in the mouth, as well as those that do. Eventually, to use Piaget's term, the *scheme** of food will be clearly differentiated from other schemes or categories of experience such as toys or Mother's cigarette. Schemes also include action schemes or patterns of behavior. The schemes of looking and grasping combine (or are "reciprocally assimilated" to each other) to form the more comprehensive scheme of prehension.

*The term *scheme* (French, *schème*) is used here for *knowing* activities, as differentiated from *schema* (plural, *schemata*), which Piaget uses to refer to figurative representations or symbols which depend more on perception than on mental operations. This practice is more recent than consistent; moreover, translators' practices vary. (See chap. 6).

Thus, while functioning adaptively, the baby is also developing intellectually. He is organizing his new experiences in various ways—differentiating, integrating, categorizing—so that the first global scheme of objects-that-go-in-the-mouth becomes sophisticated and complex enough to include all the varied members of the category "food." It is also evident that in Piaget's developmental psychology the baby is never a passive, helpless infant as some psychologists have pictured him, reacting only to loud noises and loss of support. He is an active and curious organism, reaching out, experimenting, seeking always to regulate a balance for himself between assimilation and accommodation, between his inner reality and that of the world around him. Just as the body seeks to find a physiological state of equilibrium between exercise and rest, or hunger and overeating, so the child's mind seeks equilibrium between what he understands and what he experiences in his environment.

This concept of *equilibrium* is one of Piaget's earliest theoretical insights; he has been thinking about it for many years. He sees it as the arrival at a relatively "steady state" in a system of constantly changing balances and coordinations between the organism and its surroundings. This system is an open system in which feedback from the environment contributes to a constant process of self-regulated, internal reorganization. During the past decade, Piaget has gained new insights from the work of modern biologists, particularly C. F. Waddington, a British geneticist whom he frequently quotes. Piaget's emphasis now is mainly on the *process* that brings about these progressive *states* of equilibrium: the dynamic, ongoing self-regulating process which he calls *equilibration*. This is, according to Jeanette Gallagher, "the core of Piaget's theory of cognitive development."[2] Its function is to bring about a balanced coordination between assimilation and accommodation, just as a thermostat maintains a constant balance between heat and cold. Piaget conceives of this process as the mechanism for growth and learning in cognitive development. "In a sense," he writes, "development is a progressive equilibration from a lesser to a higher state of equilibrium."[3] The mind seeks to understand and to explain at all levels, but the vague, incoherent explanations of childhood are a far cry from the richness and flexibility of adult thought. It is the search for equilibrium, for answers that satisfy, which spurs the mind on to higher levels of thought.

But once the organism is in equilibrium, what upsets it? What stimulates the child to achieve higher stages of cognitive development? Why and how does he learn? In answering these questions, Piaget recognizes first of all the dynamic factor of *maturation,* or the physiological growth of the hereditary organic structures. However, as we have pointed out, Piaget is an interactionist, not a maturationist such as Gesell; he does not view development solely as a reflection of the internal maturation of the nervous system. Rather, he sees maturation as providing "a condition of possibilities" for responding to the environment, a potential for assimilating and structuring new information from it.[4] A child is not capable of thinking like an adult because he does not yet have the logical structures, the organizations of thought, and the methods of reasoning that would enable him to deal with adult problems. This is why you cannot teach calculus to a five-year-old, says Piaget; he simply doesn't have the structures of thought to assimilate it. But as he grows and matures, his mind becomes increasingly alert and active. He becomes, to use Waddington's phrase, *competent;* he is sensitive to new possibilities and capable of finding new ways of dealing with them. As any parent who has lived through the "Why, Mommy?" stage can attest, the child becomes curious about many things. He explores and experiments until he finds an answer that satisfies him, and he achieves equilibrium, at least for his current stage of development.

The second factor that Piaget calls upon to explain cognitive development is *experience.* By this he means physical and empirical experience such as the child encounters while floating boats, counting objects, flying kites, lifting weights, or otherwise interacting with the environment. From experiences such as these the child constructs two kinds of knowledge. First there is *physical knowledge,* which comes from acting on objects and observing how they react or are transformed. Balls bounce and roll, glass breaks, ice melts, sugar dissolves in water but sand does not. Second, there is what Piaget calls *logical-mathematical knowledge;* as the child acts on objects, he constructs logical relationships between or among them. These include comparisons such as higher, lower, faster, or bigger; they involve relationships existing *not* in the objects but in the mind of the child who compares them. Mathematical relationships also are not implicit in objects but are constructed by the observing or counting child. A pencil is a physical object, but two pencils exist in a relationship created by the human mind.[5]

Piaget is fond of telling the story of a friend of his, a brilliant mathematician whose career began with an experience in early childhood. One day when he was about five, he was sitting on the ground in his garden playing with pebbles. He arranged them in a row and counted, one, two, three, up to ten. Then he counted them backwards, and once again there were ten pebbles! With increasing excitement he arranged them in a circle and in various other ways, always with the same result. He had made the marvelous discovery that the sum is independent of the order. This is a logical-mathematical relationship that exists quite independently of those particular pebbles, or of any other specific objects. For this boy the transition to arithmetic and then higher mathematics would come without difficulty, his growing interest and understanding building upon this simple but meaningful childhood experience.

This is why Piaget insists that children must be allowed to do their own learning. Thoughts, or mental *operations,* to use his term, arise out of motor actions and sensory experiences that are "interiorized." The child who has had many physical experiences with a concrete object such as a ball can then form a mental image of that object and act upon it in thought as he has in actual experiences in the past. He can picture the act of throwing the ball, and his thought is "interiorized action." But the child who has never handled or thrown a ball is handicapped in his intellectual development. Teachers and parents of young children will recognize here a plea for enriched experience at the sensory-motor level, rather than accelerated learning brought about by what Piaget calls the "pedagogical mania" of adults.

A third factor contributing to cognitive development is what Piaget calls *social transmission*—information learned from other children or transmitted by parents, teachers, or books in the process of education. He believes that when a child hears contradictory or challenging statements, whether at home or in school, his equilibrium is disturbed. He then sets out in search of an answer that will enable him to achieve a new and higher equilibrium. One of Piaget's students has coined the term *cognitive conflict* for these states of disturbed equilibrium. When an organism is thrown into a state of cognitive conflict, it searches for a solution, like the small girl trying to find out whether or not there is a Santa Claus. When she was younger, she believed in Santa Claus, but now she suddenly begins to notice that there is one on every street corner. Or her siblings tell her there is no such person, and she is disturbed and troubled until she finds an explanation that makes sense to her in her new, less naïve state of development. Thus, as the child's mental structures become competent to grapple with new problems, she is stimulated and challenged by her environment to seek new solutions. Her cognitive conflict spurs her on to higher levels of intellectual development; or to put it oversimply, she learns from her mistakes.

The fourth and most important factor in the development of knowledge, according to Piaget, is the *equilibration process,* which coordinates and regulates these other three factors and brings about progressive states of equilibrium. These states are not permanent because, in an open system based on feedback from the environment, new conflicts or questions are always arising. "The process of coping with these conflicts, disturbances, or imbalances is the self-regulatory process of equilibration."[6] It is the essence of adaptive functioning, which for Piaget is constant at all levels of development, even though the states of equilibrium characteristic of each level or stage differ qualitatively from one stage to the next.

The aim of this book is to describe and explain the mental structures characterizing each stage of cognitive development in childhood. As we follow Piaget in his studies of the various stages common to all children, we see why his ideas are having such a profound effect on present-day psychology. He sees the child, not as a miniature adult, but as living in a world that is completely different from ours and sometimes quite incomprehensible to us. He is interested not in individual differences but in the constancy of modes of conceptualization for children of all races and periods of history. All children, he says, go through certain stages of intellectual development in the same order. Bright children may develop more quickly than dull ones, but the progression from stage to stage is approximately the same for every child as he learns to adapt to the world around him. As the evidence comes in from studies of children in many different countries, it generally provides support for Piaget's theory of a constant sequence of stages in intellectual development.

3. The Beginnings of Intelligence

Babies come alive when one reads Piaget. Suddenly that helpless, red-faced infant, alternately squalling or sleeping, becomes a complex, fascinating organism, groping in a bewildering environment not only to survive but to comprehend and control. Piaget watches intently as the baby struggles to focus on a swinging watch or a familiar voice, and systematically records his responses. Each of his many observations is minutely and precisely detailed, numbered, and labeled as to the child's age: e.g., 0;6(12) means no years, 6 months, and 12 days. Reading them, one wonders how Piaget found time to do anything else, he sounds so absorbed in watching his children:

> Observation 77. At 0;6(0) Jacqueline looks at my watch, which is 10 cm. from her eyes. She reveals a lively interest, and her hands flutter as though she were about to grasp; without however discovering the right direction. I place the watch in her right hand without her being able to see how (the arm being outstretched). Then I again put the watch before her eyes. Her hands, apparently excited by the contact just experienced, then proceed to move through space and meet vio-

lently, subsequently to separate. The right hand happens to strike the watch; Jacqueline immediately tries to adjust her hand to the watch and thus manages to grasp it. The experiment is repeated three times: it is always when the hand is perceived at the same time as the watch that the attempts become systematic. The next day, at 0;6(1) I resume the experiment. When the watch is before her eyes, Jacqueline does not attempt to grasp it although she reveals a lively interest in this object. When the watch is near her hand and she happens to touch it, or it is seen at the same time as her hand, then there is searching, and searching directed by the glance. Near the eyes and far from the hands the watch is again simply contemplated. The hands move a little but do not approach each other. I again place the object near her hand: immediate searching, and again success. I put the watch a third time a few centimeters from her eyes and far from her hands: these move in all directions but without approaching each other. In short there are still two worlds for Jacqueline, one kinesthetic and the other visual. It is only when the object is seen next to the hand that the latter is directed toward it and manages to grasp it. That evening, the same experiment with various solid objects. Again and very regularly, when Jacqueline sees the object facing her without perceiving her hands, nothing happens, whereas the simultaneous sight of object and of hand (right or left) sets prehension in motion. Finally it is to be noted that, that day, Jacqueline again watched with great interest her empty hand crossing the visual field: the hand is still not felt to belong to her.[1]

It is on hundreds of careful observations such as this that Piaget bases his theory of the cognitive development of infants. The results of his investigations form an important part of his genetic theory of knowledge. The behavior of babies, says Piaget, like that of all biological organisms, exemplifies the continuously functioning process of adaptation. Intelligence is an integral part of that adaptation. Just as the infant's respiration, digestion, and motor coordination function to adapt him to the environment, so his intelligence functions to make him increasingly the master of his world. But though intelligent functioning is constant and does not change, the structures through which it manifests itself do. The baby, for example, deals with his environment through his senses and motor activity, while the school child deals with it chiefly through his thoughts. Even though he still uses sensations and actions, he organizes them in his mind so that his relationship with the world is primarily mental rather than physical. Thus, in a normally evolving relationship between the child and his environment, there are broad characteristic structures (in this sense, organizations of behavior) that appear so reliably that they have been used to demarcate as stages those periods in which they appear.

Piaget's stage theory has been much misunderstood; critics have tended to attack him because they found fewer or more stages, or disagreed with the specific ages at which he said certain structures would appear. The important point is not that children show certain structures at specific ages, but that stages of development evolve in a broad, continuous sequence. Each stage arises out of the one preceding it by a reorganization of what has gone before, so that it is qualitatively different from the preceding stage. Its characteristic structure is larger and more complex; it could be represented by a spiral in which each level encompasses and reintegrates in a higher form the achievements of earlier levels. "From this point of view," says Piaget, "mental development is a continuous construction comparable to the erection of a vast building that becomes more solid with each addition."[2] Unlike a building, however, intellectual development is flexible, supple, and mobile, seeking always for adjustment resulting in equilibrium.

Piaget describes the succession of stages as constant, even though the chronological ages at which they appear may differ from child to child and from one society to another. He cites the results of Monique Laurendeau and Adrien Pinard, Canadian psychologists who carried out many of Piaget's experiments and found the same stages among French-speaking children in Montreal. But when they redid the study in Martinique, an island in the Caribbean where French is spoken, they found a delay of about four years in achieving the different stages. Piaget explains this as being due to a very relaxed, simple, nonchallenging tropical civilization. He himself found a systematic delay of two years among children in the Swiss countryside, as compared to Genevan city children.

It is true that in his earlier works, Piaget put a great deal of emphasis upon classifying behavior into discrete stages. This may have been due to his boyhood zoological training and classificatory zeal; or it may have represented an earnest effort at clarification of the steps involved in development. It does seem too good to be true that all sensory-motor behavior, whether in reference to objects, space, time, or causality, should fit neatly into six stages of development. However, whether the development of babies actually occurs in just these stages, or whether they represent mental structures imposed by Piaget in the process of organizing his wealth of observations, is not relevant here. The behaviors that he observed do provide milestones in cognitive development, just as do the first tooth and the first steps in physical development. Piaget would certainly agree that development is a continuous, ongoing process that manifests itself through gradually increasing complexity, differentiation, and enrichment from one stage to the next.

Piaget's use of the term *stages* is confusing, since it differs from earlier to later works. The detailed development of infants followed here is taken from *The Origins of Intelligence in Children,* which is based on Piaget's observations in the 1930s of his own three children. In later publications[3] he uses different classificatory schemes, but all the developments described below are included in his discussion of the first two years of childhood. He calls this the *sensory-motor* period, extending from birth to one and a half or two years. This is followed by three more advanced periods which will be discussed in chapter 4. However, these periods of development are often referred to as stages, in which case the stages that follow below must be thought of as substages occurring during the larger stage or period of development.

Piaget calls this earliest period of cognitive development the sensory-motor period because the infant's earliest manifestations of intelligence appear in his sensory perceptions and his motor activities. His eyes follow a moving object; his head turns in response to a noise; he begins to reach for and grasp his toys. These may appear to be small achievements, and many parents do not find tiny babies interesting. Yet Piaget points out that the child in his first two years effects "a miniature Copernican revolution."[4] He is at first helpless, unaware of the world around him, conscious only of his core self—the center of his own small universe. As he grows and reaches outward, both mentally and physically, he becomes gradually aware of other people, of his physical surroundings, of objects that exist independently of him. By the time he is two, he is aware of himself as part of a larger family, a larger world. He is no longer the center of his own small world, but takes his place in a larger universe which he experiences as external to himself. This is no small achievement.

At birth, says Piaget, the infant is "locked in egocentrism." By this he means not that the baby is self-centered in the usual sense of the word, but that he is unaware of anything beyond himself. He knows nothing of the world apart from his immediate consciousness and therefore cannot at first distinguish himself from it or make any sense out of the variety of stimuli he receives from it. In Piaget's terms, he has no previous body of knowledge into which to assimilate all these new experiences. He comes into the world equipped with a few neonatal reflexes, such as sucking and grasping, which are part of his biological inheritance. Beyond these, his behavior consists of gross motor movements, at first uncoordinated and purposeless. His feet kick, his hands wave, his eyes often do not focus. But sometime during the first month the baby's fist accidentally finds its way into his mouth. By reflex action he begins to suck on it and apparently finds this activity satisfying. At any rate, the baby repeats this action over and over again until he learns to bring his fist to his mouth at will. After that, not only his fist but everything else he grasps will find its way into his mouth. "For him," says Piaget, "the world is essentially a thing to be sucked."[5]

This development marks the transition from the first stage of simple *hereditary reflexes* to the second stage of learned or *acquired adaptations* (one to four months). The baby has put together two separate actions—fist waving and sucking—to form a new behavior pattern or scheme of bringing the fist to the mouth to be sucked. Piaget's observations make it clear that the infant is not just lying in his crib waiting for things to happen to him. He is alert, curious, intent on extending his repertoire of behaviors. The sucking routine is probably well established by now, and the baby has more freedom to look. He gazes intently at his mother's face, taking in every detail. Sometimes he will stop sucking to smile at her—a reflex behavior that has all kinds of social and psychological ramifications. Not only look-ing, but listening increases. The infant turns his head in the direction of sounds he hears. He begins to coo and make noises, sometimes imitating the sounds his parents make to him. His motor activity increases; he lies on his back, kicking his heels and watching the little fists flying past his face. But only very slowly does he come to know that they are attached to him and he can control them. Then, says Piaget, "it is no longer the mouth that seeks the hand, but the hand which reaches for the mouth."[6]

By the third stage (four to eight months), the baby has pretty much familiarized himself with his own body, and his attention turns from himself to events in his environment. He may accidentally hit or bump something, producing a new and interesting noise or move-ment. Always in search of novelty, the baby will move around again, seeking to repeat the experience. This is what Piaget calls a *circular reaction*, in which each action produces a reaction, which again activates the original action. The baby practices over and over, until he can produce the new experience at will. Piaget calls these repeated activities "procedures to make interesting spectacles last." They are the first step in the baby's learning to accommodate to the external world.

> Observation 95. Lucienne, at 0;4(27) is lying in her bassinet. I hang a doll over her feet which immediately sets in motion the scheme of [shaking]. . . . But her feet reach the doll right away and give it a violent movement which Lucienne surveys with delight. Afterward she looks at her motionless foot for a second, then recommences. There is no visual control of the foot, for the movements are the same when Lucienne only looks at the doll or when I place the doll over her head. On the other hand, the tactile control of the foot is apparent: after the first shakes, Lucienne makes slow foot movements as though to grasp and explore. For instance, when she tries to kick the doll and misses her aim, she begins again very slowly until she succeeds (with-out seeing her feet). In the same way I cover Lucienne's face or distract her attention for a moment in another direction; she neverthe-less continues to hit the doll and control its movements.[7]

Here Lucienne is accommodating her foot movements in order to repeat a response she finds new and interesting. Already she is becoming a curious little explorer who repeats actions that please her until she has mastered them. But she still has difficulty coordinating these efforts because the various schemes such as vision and prehension are not yet fully coordinated. As Piaget noted in his observation of Jacqueline at the beginning of this chapter, her eyes and her hands were in different spheres, and she could not use them together. The fourth stage (eight to twelve months) is characterized by the emergence of *intentional behavior.* The child pushes aside an obstacle that prevents him from reaching something he wants. He may use his parent's hand to get something he can see but cannot reach himself.

At 0;7(10) Laurent tries to grasp a new box in front of which I place my hand (at a distance of 10 cm.). He sets the obstacle aside, but not intentionally; he simply tries to reach the box by sliding next to my hand and, when he touches it, tries to take no notice of it. . . . Finally, at 0;7(13) Laurent reacts quite differently almost from the beginning of the experiment. I present a box of matches above my hand, but behind it, so that he cannot reach it without setting the obstacle aside. But Laurent, after trying to take no notice of it, suddenly tries to hit my hand as though to remove or lower it; I let him do it to me and he grasps the box. I recommence to bar his passage, but using as a screen a sufficiently supple cushion to keep the impress of the child's gestures. Laurent tries to reach the box, and, bothered by the obstacle, he at once strikes it, definitely lowering it until the way is clear.[8]

Here the baby is clearly going after an object he wants, as long as he can see it. If the desired object is hidden, however, he acts as though it no longer existed. Piaget explains that the baby has not yet developed a sense of the permanence of objects; he does not know that objects exist in the environment even when he does not see them. This is a manifestation of what Piaget means by egocentrism; the baby is aware only of his immediate experience. If that experience does not include his own perception of the object, then he has no idea that the object is there and has a permanent existence of its own. It is only gradually, after several more months of experience with objects that swing or drop or roll out of sight, that the child looks for them, indicating that he now knows they are there. In this stage babies also begin to anticipate events and respond to cues such as the sound of a mother's voice even when she is still out of sight. Games such as "peekaboo" or "hide-and-seek" now become a source of unfailing delight because of the reappearance of the hidden but expected object. Such activities develop anticipation and help to establish in the child the notion of *object permanence,* a major achievement of the sensory-motor period. This realization of the permanence of objects is essential for later learning; it reduces the child's egocentrism by enabling him to differentiate between himself and external reality which exists independently of him.

The fifth stage (twelve to eighteen months) is marked by the emergence of what Piaget calls *directed groping.* The child begins to experiment in order to see what will happen. No longer does he simply repeat movements in order to produce a desired result. Now he begins to vary his movements as if to observe how the results will differ. Piaget describes his little son Laurent breaking off one piece of bread at a time and dropping it on the floor, watching with great interest to see where it would fall. The average parent would probably take the bread away in annoyance, but Piaget waited quietly, noting the child's absorbed attention. Like a serious young Galileo, the little boy dropped the bread from various positions and watched it land in different places on the floor. Piaget considers this behavior experimental; it differs from that of the preceding stage in that it is not a stereotyped repetition of behavior but introduces experimental variations as if to see what will happen.

Another development of this stage is that the child learns to use new means to achieve an end. He discovers that he can pull objects to him by a string or a stick, or tilt them to get them through the bars of his playpen. In other words, his trial-and-error behavior is directed toward a goal; the child is functioning intelligently.

Observation 155. At 1;0(26) in Jacqueline's presence I place my watch on the floor, beyond her field of prehension. I put the chain in a straight line in Jacqueline's direction but place a cushion on the part which is nearest the child. Jacqueline at first tries to grasp the watch directly. Not succeeding, she looks at the chain. She notes that the latter is under the cushion. Then Jacqueline removes the latter at one stroke and pulls the chain while looking at the watch. The movement is adapted and quick. As soon as the watch is within reach, Jacqueline lets go of the chain in order to grasp the object directly. There is, consequently, no interest in the chain itself; it is the watch that is wanted.[9]

In the sixth and last stage of sensory-motor behavior (eighteen to twenty-four months) the child begins to do his groping mentally rather than physically. As Piaget puts it, the child's physical or motor action is "interiorized"; the child represents to himself in images or symbols how he would do something without actually doing it, until he reaches a satisfactory solution. Piaget calls this *the invention of new means* and says that it develops along with *symbolic representa-*

Figure 1

tion. The child at this stage is making the transition from physical to mental operations and can represent actions in a symbolic way without actually performing them.

Piaget loves to describe how he played with Lucienne when she was sixteen months old by hiding his watch chain in a matchbox. First he left the matchbox open wide enough so that the little girl could get her fingers in and pull out the chain. Then Piaget, keeping his movements out of the child's sight, closed the box except for a small slit, too narrow for Lucienne's eager fingers. A pause followed, says Piaget, during which Lucienne showed that she tried to think out the situation and represent to herself what she must do. She looked at the slit with great attention; she opened her mouth slightly, then wider and wider, mimicking with her mouth what she wished to do with the matchbox. Then she unhesitatingly grasped the box, put her index finger into the slit, and pulled it open wide enough to take out the chain. Piaget says that since Lucienne could not yet think out the situation clearly, she represented it symbolically by her motor imitation of the desired act. By opening her mouth she represented to herself how she could open the box. Lucienne was on the verge of thought!

Thus, in six easy stages Piaget shows us how the infant develops from a biological organism into a social one. He traces the growth of cognition from the first primitive reflex to the complex and varied combinations of behavior soon to be telescoped in thought. Always there is the upward spiraling of development. The various behavior patterns are repeated over and over until they are mastered; then, propelled by the hierarchic movement of growth, they occur again in new and more complicated forms. In two years or less the child has completed the Copernican revolution that Piaget described. He has constructed, first of all, the notion of object permanence, the realization that objects and people have a permanent existence that is independent of his perception of them. He has also developed a primitive notion of *causality,* for like Lucienne kicking her doll, he has discovered that certain actions of his produce certain results. In his experimenting with objects he has acquired rudimentary concepts of *space* and *time;* he can locate his toys and knows that daily events have a certain sequence. (The morning feeding is followed by bath time, outdoor play, nap time, and so forth.) All of these discoveries have helped to increase his awareness of himself as separate from other people, thereby decreasing his egocentrism.

In other words, the baby in his first two years has assimilated a good deal of practical knowledge about the world. His rapidly growing body has accommodated to many changes. By imitating people and events around him, he has constructed mental images of his external experiences. These enable him to represent more than the reality immediately present to his senses, and to anticipate coming events. In so doing, the baby has reached the level of development achieved by the highest animals. A mature chimpanzee can reach for bananas with a stick or indicate with gestures what it is he desires. A dog can fetch his leash as a symbolic indication that he wants to go for a walk. But the child is now ready to surpass the achievements of any animal. In two years he has come a long way.

4. An Overview of Development

It is time to pause briefly and take stock of where we have been and where we are going in our study of cognitive development. Piaget has emphasized the continuity of adaptive growth in all living things. In mankind's cognitive development he sees a continuation of that process. The baby adapts to the world around him chiefly by means of actions; Piaget calls this "practical intelligence." It enables him to interact with the people and things in his life through his self-regulated gestures, cries, and movements. Piaget calls this period, from birth to eighteen months or two years, the *sensory-motor* period.

As he approaches two, the toddler is forming imitations or representations of what he sees or experiences, which are "interiorized" as mental images. These form the basis for memory, and later, for thought. Thoughts are, simplistically put, actions that take place in the mind rather than on the physical plane; Piaget's term for them is *operations*. But this term *operations* implies logical necessity; to the knower it is logical and self-evident that 2 plus 2 equals 4. Operations are also reversible; 4 minus 2 reverses back to the original 2. Furthermore, operations are dissociated from specific content. The symbol 2 represents two of anything, but not any particular thing. The term *operational* applies to thought that has these characteristics.

Obviously, the two-year-old toddler is not yet capable of such logical, operational thinking. There is a period of about five years before him during which he goes through the process of learning to deal with the world on a symbolic level. His symbols include mental images, drawings, dreams, make-believe symbols, gestures, and language. All of these can be substituted for the sensory-motor activities of infancy. Instead of grasping, the child can ask for things. Instead of seeing his mother he can picture her in his mind, and can thus get along without her immediate presence for longer periods of time. Piaget feels that the "make-believe" play of this period is very important, because through it the child is assimilating symbolically the activities, roles, and ideas of the world around him. Jacqueline drank out of a shell as if it were a glass; Lucienne gave her doll an orange peel to eat and called it macaroni. In so doing, the little girls were using symbols for dishes and food, and through their make-believe were assimilating and consolidating as part of their experience the customs and manners observed in their environment. At the same time, this assimilation was being balanced by accommodation, which Piaget describes as being the primary function of imitation. By imitating the speech, the behavior, the activities of adults, children learn to adjust to new situations in their world.

The cognitive functioning of the young child will be discussed in greater detail in chapters to come; the point here is that it is characterized chiefly by symbolic representation, even though it still includes sensory-motor activity. The thinking of the preschool child is still egocentric, tied to his limited experience. His beginning concepts are fuzzy and confused. Slowly he works his way toward more nearly logical ideas about the world, ideas that Piaget calls *semi-logical.* This period, from about two to six and a half or seven, is called the *preoperational* period because the child has not yet achieved true operations as described above.

The school child, during his sixth or seventh year, is able to formulate true operations, which he sees as self-evident and logically necessary. Working with concrete exemplars, he can now operate in thought, classifying them or their representations (pictures, words) into different kinds of groupings. He can serialize, extend, subdivide, differentiate, or combine existing structures into new relationships. He can perform the four mathematical operations of addition and its reverse, subtraction; and multiplication and its reverse, division. But his thought is still limited by his own concrete experiences; he is not yet capable of dealing with pure abstractions in the form of inferences and hypotheses. Therefore Piaget calls this period from seven to about eleven or twelve the period of *concrete operations.* He attempted to discover all the properties of thought operations or groupings observed in the grade-school child during this period, to express them in the language of logic and mathematics. His work on this level is much more difficult to read and understand than his books on young children. However, his description of the properties of children's thought during the school years has been extremely important in stimulating research and discussion and has influenced many areas of curriculum planning.

Piaget is fond of pointing out that thought processes in the operational period are speeded up like a movie film, as compared to the slow-motion succession of slides in a projector that seems to take place during preoperational functioning. Operations or thoughts, freed from the bondage of physical performance, can move forward with amazing rapidity. Thought can project itself ahead in time and space, or reverse itself like a movie being rewound. The achievement of *reversibility* is a tremendously important development, making logical operations possible and affecting the whole quality of thought.

Looking at cognitive development from this level, it is possible to see the outlines of Piaget's "spiral of knowing."[1] The limited "practical intelligence" of the baby is internalized in images and leads to the symbolic thought of the young child, which makes possible memory and language. All these developments are integrated and reorganized in the higher, much more complex structures of logical thought. They, in turn, become part of the hierarchy of abstract thought which we will describe next. Thus each level of cognitive functioning builds on lower levels and contributes to higher levels in the ever-widening and encompassing spiral of knowing.

The last period of cognitive development described by Piaget appears in early adolescence. The youngster now begins to "operate on operations," which means he can think about thought and ideas as well as about concrete things. *Formal operations* are "operations to the second power"; they concern the general laws behind the array of particular instances, such as the Mendelian laws, which manifest themselves in the bewildering variety of genetic mutations. At this stage the adolescent can consider hypotheses and figure out what should follow if they are true. He can follow the *form* of reasoning while ignoring its content, which is why the operations of this period are called *formal.* He can deal with purely hypothetical concepts such as five-dimensional space, or with mathematical models such as matrices. Thus we see how, at each level of cognitive development, the achievements of the former period are incorporated and restructured as the basis for a more advanced, more complex, characteristically different form of functioning.

People whose thinking is at the highest level of formal operations are those who work out the structures of atoms, design computers, or plan the explorations of outer space. The object of their thought is the product of previous thought and may have no exemplification in reality. Einstein's theory of relativity was the product of high-level formal operations, as was the work of astronomers who deduced that there must be another planet in our system and subsequently discovered Pluto. While not all individuals in the formal operational stage reach this highest level of hypothetical thought, the stage in general is characterized by "inferential thinking" as compared to "describer thinking" in the period of concrete operations.

The characteristics of all these periods will be discussed in more detail in the following chapters. The purpose of this summary and review is to give the reader a sense of the scope and direction of Piaget's cognitive theory.

5. Conservation and Identity

Conservation is the ability to realize that certain attributes of an object are constant, even though that object is transformed in appearance. Through Piaget's conservation experiments, which are probably his most famous, he demonstrates the stages of cognition as it develops from early childhood through adolescence. Before taking up the stages separately, let us follow their progression as illustrated by some of these experiments.

Piaget takes two balls of soft clay, making sure that the child agrees they are equal. He rolls one out into a fat sausage and asks whether the amount of clay is still the same. The child younger than about seven years of age thinks that the sausage contains more clay because it is longer. His perception is immediate, egocentric, and limited to the present. He centers his attention on a single, striking feature of the clay—its extended length—and cannot take into account the fact that while the sausage is longer, it is also thinner. If the clay is rolled back into a ball, the child will once more agree that the two balls are equal. But if one of the balls is again rolled into a sausage, the child will again insist that it holds more clay. He does not yet comprehend that matter is conserved regardless of changes in form. Piaget says he has not acquired *reversibility*, the ability to follow a series of size transformations and then reverse direction and think back to when the same piece of clay was a round ball. This would require that the underlying constancy of matter be preserved in thought, and the young child is not yet capable of operating in thought independently of what he sees before him. He cannot get away from the compelling characteristic of the stimulus—its length—and see that the length is compensated for by the lesser thickness, and that therefore the amount of clay in the sausage is the same as in the ball.

Here again the word *operations* is used to refer to actions in thought, or mental operations as opposed to physical actions. A child who cannot escape from the compelling aspects of the immediate concrete stimulus and think about what it looked like previously is said to be in the preoperational or prethought period. This is roughly the preschool period as well. Piaget demonstrates, through his conservation experiments, the various changes that occur in the child's thinking as he matures.

We have already seen how the preoperational child responds to the immediate appearance of two equal amounts of clay when one is rolled into a sausage shape. This process is called *centering*. The child centers on the dramatic difference in appearance of the two equal quantities of clay. But toward the end of the preoperational period the child enters a transitional stage in which he becomes more flexible and mobile in his thinking. He may notice that the sausage is not nearly as thick as the round ball of clay, in which case he will say it contains less clay than the ball. Or he may hesitate between length and width and begin to see that the sausage is also very skinny to compensate for its length. The child is in a state of disequilibrium, pulled back and forth between various aspects of the stimulus. Piaget would say he is *decentering*—he is noticing other aspects of the clay that conflict with his original impression. If the sausage is made very short and fat, he may at first say there is no difference between it and the ball, but as it is rolled out thinner and thinner he succumbs to the perceptual illusion of the increased length and says it contains more clay than the ball. Eventually he will realize that the dimensions are related, that when the sausage is shorter it is also thicker. When he can consistently and with certainty see that all changes in length are compensated for by inverse changes in width, the child is regulating conflicting perceptions on the basis of logic. He has achieved a new equilibrium and has moved into the period of concrete operations. He may even wonder why you are asking him such stupid and obvious questions! He has achieved understanding of the permanence of attributes in changing objects, just as he earlier achieved understanding of the permanence of objects in changing settings during the sensory-motor period.

The child who has fully constructed the notion of conservation can give you the classic arguments that mark the emergence of full-fledged operations. He will tell you that the sausage is the same in quantity as the original ball of clay because (1) it can be returned to its original shape (reversibility); (2) what it gains in length it loses in width (compensation); (3) it is still "the same stuff"—nothing has been added or taken away (identity). This identity argument is a very early forerunner of conservation, which we will discuss in detail a little later in this chapter.

Piaget goes on to show that concepts of conservation are not all constructed at the same time. First the child achieves an understanding of the conservation of *substance*. He will agree that the amount of clay in each piece is the same regardless of shape. But he still does not realize that the two pieces weigh the same or have the same volume. Repeated experiments have shown that the concept of conservation of *weight* during changes in form comes later, and that the conservation of *volume*, as measured by the displacement of water, is not constructed until age eleven or twelve. Again we see here the upward spiraling of cognitive development, repeated in more complex forms at different levels. Many investigators, most notably Norwegian psychologist Jan Smedslund,[1] have repeated Piaget's experiments with approximately the same results. These three concepts of conservation—first substance, then weight, then volume—seem to appear in that sequence despite experimental efforts to accelerate or change their appearance by means of reinforcement.

Piaget uses the evidence of these experiments as arguments for the development of cognitive structures through maturation. Experience with handling, measuring, pouring, and so forth is obviously of basic importance in the development of such structures. But no amount of experience or experimenting, says Piaget, can give a child the notion of the amount of substance.

> This conservation of substance is simply a logical necessity. The child now understands that when there is a transformation you come back to the point of departure and once again have the ball. He knows that something is conserved but he doesn't know what. It is not yet the weight, it is not yet the volume; it is simply a logical form . . . a logical necessity. There, it seems to me, is an example of progress in knowledge, a logical necessity for something to be conserved even though no experience can have led to this notion.[2]

This understanding of the necessity of the conservation of substance has not been achieved by most children until about the age of seven, according to Piaget. Many societies, of course, have agreed on this as the traditional "age of reason." Piaget feels, on the basis of his experiments, that until a child is about seven he is not capable of grasping the notion of conservation because he does not have the logical structures, the mental organization for dealing with them. In this he disagrees with some Americans, notably psychologist Jerome Bruner of Harvard, who believes that any subject can be taught at any age if it is presented in an appropriate form. Piaget chuckles quietly over the urgency of educators in this country who are always trying to speed up the stages of cognitive development. He has been asked so often whether this could be done that he calls it "the American question." He does, however, admit that the child who has a good mental inheritance and an environment that encourages creative experimentation may develop logical structures at an earlier age. In this sense, as Elkind points out, "Piaget's is both a nature *and* a nurture theory."[3]

There are many other kinds of experiments described by Piaget to show how fundamental the concept of conservation is. One might measure one cup of orange juice into a tall, thin glass and another cup into a shallow glass bowl and note the different cognitive levels of response. Most children younger than seven will say the glass holds more because the level of juice in it is higher, although some children may choose the bowl because it is wider. Then there will be a period of confusion and disequilibrium, and finally, when the concept of conservation has been constructed, the children will realize that both receptacles hold the same amount of juice. It is interesting to try these experiments with children and listen to their comments, although it should be noted that the children must be tested separately or they will influence each other's thinking. A student of mine once reported that her little brother refused to drink his milk one day because it didn't come up to the top of the glass. His mother, who had no more milk in the house, did her best to persuade him to drink what he had, with no success. Then my student, mindful of her studies of Piaget, simply poured the milk into a smaller glass so that it came to the top. "*That's* what I wanted," said her little brother, "a full glass of milk!" He drank it happily, with no more complaints.

Figure 2

Other Piagetian experiments demonstrate the development of the conservation of *number*. One might have a child count out the same number of beads twice, dropping them first into a tall, narrow jar and then into a shallow container. Even though he himself put the same number of beads into each container, the young child will respond to the perceptual illusion created by the shape of the tall jar. The conservation of number is also illustrated by presenting two equal rows of buttons, and then spreading out one row or arranging it in two rows instead of one. The preoperational child will say that the double row or the spread-out row contains more buttons. If, instead of being spread out, the buttons in one of the original rows are pushed close together, the child will say that the shorter row contains fewer buttons. The child who is just entering the concrete operational phase will count the buttons each time and then say the number is the same. The child of ten or eleven will count only once and then assert the constancy of the original number so long as no buttons are added or taken away.

Figure 3

Another experiment demonstrating the conservation of *length* uses two identical sticks. When they are laid parallel to each other, the child will state that they are of equal length. But when one is moved ahead of the other, the preoperational child will maintain it is longer. "It's bigger because you pushed it," one of Piaget's children told him. "That [unmoved] one is smaller because it doesn't touch there," said a five-year-old, pointing to the protruding end of the stick that had been moved ahead, but a seven-year-old responded eagerly, "They're still the same, they can't grow. . . . They're always the same length and they'll always stay the same."[4]

Figure 4

The results are similar when two lines of equal length are drawn on a blackboard. The one that extends farthest to the left is usually seen as longer (fig. 4a). Piaget found that the preoperational child is very much concerned with boundaries. If things begin or end at the same place they are seen as equal; if the extremity of one line goes beyond that of another line of the same length, it is seen as longer. If an undulating line is drawn that, stretched out, would have the same boundaries as a straight line, it is seen as shorter than the standard (fig. 4b). Conversely, the undulating line may actually be much longer than the straight line, yet if they share the same boundaries, as in figure 4c, they are seen as of equal length. But the child who has constructed for himself the notion of conservation will point out that "If you count the ups and downs, the wavy line is much longer."

These are some of the many ingenious ways in which Piaget demonstrates the development of conservation. Once a child has firmly constructed the logical structure, the mental understanding of the problem, he cannot be fooled by the external physical appearance of objects. Piaget quotes one little boy who said, "Once you know, you know for always."[5]

Let us now examine briefly the notion of *identity*, which is a very early precursor of the concept of conservation. Its history begins in infancy, but it has to be expanded and restructured before it can be coordinated with other factors (reversibility, compensation) as part of a total operational system.

The first primitive sense of identity is a qualitative one, arising out of the infant's gradual discovery of what is himself and what is his mother. Every time the baby experiences his mother as a separate being who is sometimes available to him and sometimes not, his egocentrism is slowly diminished. Along with the growing realization of his own identity as separate from his mother's comes the gradual awareness of the permanence of objects and people in a world that exists independently of him. This is an extended process that takes the better part of two years, because appearances may change and cause the child confusion. A three-year-old may not recognize his grandmother in a new outfit or a familiar object in a new setting. Piaget describes how Jacqueline, at 2;7, seeing Lucienne in a new bathing suit and cap, asked, "What's the baby's name?" When her mother explained that it was a new bathing suit, Jacqueline pointed right at Lucienne's face and said, "But what's the name of *that?*" As soon as Lucienne had changed her clothes, Jacqueline exclaimed, "It's Lucienne again!" as if Lucienne "had changed her identity in changing her clothes."[6]

This qualitative sense of identity can be studied in several ways. If you ask a four- or five-year-old to draw a picture of himself as a baby and as he is now, he will recognize the difference in size and appearance but will say, "It's still me." Similarly, if he is pouring water into tall and shallow glasses, he will insist that the amount of water is

Figure 5

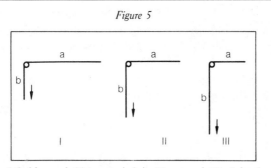

From Inhelder and Chipman (eds.), *Piaget and His School*, p.92.

different, but that it is still "the same water." Even when he begins to notice that the height and the width of the water co-vary, and to regulate the disparity between them, he still has not constructed the logical relation of compensation (higher × thinner = the same amount).

As the child's interactions with objects continue, however, he begins to construct a *semi-logical* notion of identity based on sensory-motor experience and what Piaget calls "articulated intuitions." This means he has achieved a sort of "one-way logic" which is on the way to being, but is not yet, fully operational. As an example, pull a piece of string around a nail so that the two segments *a* and *b* are at right angles. The four or five-year-old can see that as *a* gets shorter, *b* gets longer. He can also tell you that "it's the same string." This is all true, but it is not the whole truth; it is only a partial approximation of it. Nevertheless, by the time this child is seven or eight he will probably have constructed an operational understanding of the conservation of length based upon the knowledge that the string can slide in *both* directions (reversibility) with *a* getting longer as *b* gets shorter (compensation). He also knows that the length of the entire string remains *a* + *b* regardless of the relative lengths of the segments, because nothing has been added or taken away. This is a new and logical concept of identity based on quantity.[7]

Identity is thus no longer a vague qualitative notion; it has been transformed into a quantitative and operational concept leading to conservation. The identity operation can be expressed mathematically as "$+ 0 - 0 = 0$." In conjunction with the other operations required, it forms a total system underlying the concept of conservation, a system that is compelling because of its logical necessity and self-evidence.

6. The Preoperational Child

The genius of Piaget is never more apparent than in his analysis of the little child's way of thinking. He is the rare psychologist who really listens to children and tries to understand not only what they are saying but why they are saying it. When Piaget wanted to understand the "why" questions of the children at the Maison des Petits in Geneva, he recorded all the questions asked by a little boy of six: "Why are there waves only at the edge of the lake?" "Why do butterflies die so soon?" "Why are you going away?" "Why can you see lightning better at night?"[1]

Then Piaget put these questions to six hundred other children, mostly boys from four to nine. Among other things, he discovered that they believed everything has a reason and a purpose. When a little boy asked why there were two mountains above Geneva, the answer he wanted was that the big one was for big people to climb, and the little one was for children. When he asked why a marble was rolling down a hill, he was not satisfied with an explanation about an inclined plane; he wanted to know whether the marble "knows you are down there."

In other words, in the preoperational period the child with his needs and purposes is still the "raison d'être" of the universe; everything is made for man and children according to an established and wise plan with the human being at its center. We have seen how the baby, during the sensory-motor period, gives up his egocentric point of view on the physical level as he becomes aware of the permanence of objects and people around him. On the mental level, however, it is a long time before he relinquishes his egocentrism. New experiences, new words, new problems are all assimilated into his very limited fund of information. Therefore he can interpret them only in terms of his own experiences, his own needs and desires. During the long period of infancy he has been cared for and had his needs anticipated as if by magic. Is it any wonder that the young child's thoughts are colored by magic and egocentrism?

The child's assumption that the world was created for him clearly reveals this egocentrism. It permeates his thinking in many other ways as well—ways that Piaget uncovered by his flexible, open-ended method of questioning his young subjects. His findings are recorded in his five early books (see Appendix B), which are his most charming and the easiest to read. In them a picture emerges of how the world appears to children that is quite different from how it appears to us, or how we usually assume (if we think about it at all) that it appears to them. Piaget's descriptions of children at play or in conversation are delightful as well as penetrating. One pictures the young psychologist, down on his knees in the dirt playing marbles with a little Swiss boy, in order to study the morality implicit in the rules of the game.

"You must show me how to play," he says. "When I was little I used to play a lot, but now I've quite forgotten how to. I'd like to play again. Let's play together. You teach me the rules and I'll play with you."[2]

Then come the questions. Have people always played as they do today? Where do rules come from? Who makes them up? Could you make up your own private rules? What does it mean to play "fair"? And so on, through the problems of punishment to the development of the idea of justice. It is his sensitivity to the child's point of view, his willingness to accept rather than instruct the child, that makes Piaget's approach so fascinating and at the same time so revolutionary. As he remarks plaintively, "It is so hard not to talk too much when questioning a child, especially for a pedagogue."[3]

Piaget's results, first published in the early 1920s, shocked and astounded many readers. Dr. Wayne Dennis, a well-known American psychologist, was unconvinced. He proceeded to put some of Piaget's questions to his own little daughter of almost three.[4] To his surprise, the child showed many of the characteristics of preoperational thought described by Piaget. Today, over fifty years and many follow-up studies later, Piaget's ideas have pretty much been corroborated. Consequently, they have had a tremendous impact on our understanding of children and our ways of approaching them.

The egocentrism of the young child leads him to assume that everyone thinks as he does, and that the whole world shares his feelings and desires. This sense of oneness with the world leads naturally to the child's assumption of magic omnipotence; it is an extension of his power as an infant to get adults to pick him up and care for him. Not only is the world created for him; he can control it. The sun and the moon must follow him when he goes for a walk, or he can make the rain come by dancing around in circles. Witness the following observation of Piaget's daughters. (In these later observations, Piaget used the initials J. and L. for the girls and T. for Laurent.)

When J. was 5;6(11) I overheard a conversation between her and L. in bed. L. was afraid of the dark and J. was reassuring her. L. then asked: "Where does the dark come from?—*From water, because when it's daylight, the night goes into the lake.*" But at 5;6(22) I heard J. alone in the garden saying: *"I'm making the daylight come up, I'm making it come up* (making a gesture of raising something from the ground). *Now I'm making it go away* (gesture of pushing something away) *and now the night's coming. I make the night come up when I go to the edge of the lake: the man* (walking outside the garden) *still has a bit on his coat. I'm making the light come up."* After this, she amused herself the rest of the day in *"making light"* with a stick (making the gesture of pulling it towards her and throwing it away).[5]

Here there is obvious similarity to the magic rituals of primitive tribes. Such rituals are recorded in the rhymes of childhood, such as "Rain, rain, go away," or "Step on a crack, you'll break your mother's back." The implication is that the child by his behavior or incantations can control the forces of nature. Vestiges of such childish magic are familiar to many of us who snap our fingers to make the red light change or carry an umbrella "to make sure it won't rain."

Another manifestation of the child's egocentrism is his inability to put himself in the position of another person. This is apparent on both physical and intellectual levels. The child who has learned his own right and left sides cannot identify the same positions on a person facing him. He cannot describe how a view or a topological display appears to a person looking at it from another angle. Piaget realized this when he took his son Laurent for an automobile ride and discovered that the boy did not recognize the familiar mountain that rises behind Geneva. Seen from his own garden he knew it well; seen from a new perspective it looked different, so Laurent assumed that it was the mountain, not his point of view, that was strange.

In the same way a child has difficulty understanding another person's intellectual or emotional point of view. Elkind has suggested that it is the child's egocentrism, and not his moral perversity, which makes him continue to pester his mother when she has told him she has a headache and wants to be left alone.[6] Any parent who has tried to sleep when a youngster is playing cowboys at dawn knows the futility of expecting the "Bang-bang!" to stop, no matter how reasonable (to the parent) the request. Nevertheless, there is considerable evidence that on an emotional level preschool children respond to each other with empathy sooner than Piaget appears to have observed.[7]

Another characteristic of egocentric thought is known as *animism.* The child believes that the world of nature is alive, conscious, and endowed with purpose like himself. This arises because the child, being unconscious of himself, confuses himself with the universe. The sun follows the child to "show him the way"; the clouds move by themselves and chart their course. This dynamic view of the world, activated by energy and life, is like the primitive cosmologies of tribes such as the Hopi Indians, who believe every tree and every spring is inhabited by a living spirit.

"The sun sometimes watches us," says Fran (9), *"when we're looking nice he looks at us.*—Do you look nice?—*Yes, on Sundays, when I'm dressed like a man."*

"The moon looks at us and watches over us," says Ga (8½), *"when I walk, it walks; when I stand still it stands still. It copies like a parrot.* —Why?—*It wants to do whatever I do.*—Why?—*Because it's inquisitive."*[8]

Piaget observed four stages in the development of animism. Up to four or five years old, the child believes anything may be endowed with purpose and conscious activity. A ball may refuse to be thrown straight, or a "naughty" chair may be responsible for bumping him. Then a transition stage evolves in which the child experiences cognitive conflict and may reverse or contradict himself. Only objects that move, such as floating clouds or a moving car, are alive. Their movements may be determined by physical compulsion or moral necessity; for example, the clouds "know they must move because they bring rain." In the third stage, only objects that move spontaneously are alive; cars or bicycles, which move only when driven by an outside agent, are not. The last stage, in which only plants and animals are considered alive, does not come until about eleven or twelve.

Roger Russell and Wayne Dennis[9] standardized Piaget's questions on animism by making up a list of twenty objects. The first five objects, including some chipped and broken ones, were actually shown to each child. These psychologists found that children, even in the earliest stage, would not attribute life to a broken button or a chipped dish. The instructions for this interview follow, along with answers obtained from a five-year-old girl by one of my students.

Instructions: We are going to play a game. I am going to ask you some questions and we will see how many you can answer. You know what it means to be alive? A cat is alive, isn't it? Tell me something else that's alive. Why? How do you know it's (not) alive? (Repeat this after each object on the list.) Show child the first five objects if possible.

1. Stone—Alive, because it moves.
2. Pencil—Alive, because it writes.
3. Button (broken)—If it's broken, it's no use. It's dead.
4. Watch—It's alive if it tells time, but it's dead if it can't tell time.
5. Dish (chipped)—It's just as dead as a broken button.
6. Candle—Only if it is lit. (What would happen if the light went out, and then came on again?) It would die, then it would come back to life.
7. Bicycle—Alive, because it runs.
8. Chair—Alive, because people sit on it.
9. River—Alive when people go in it.
10. Clouds—Alive, because they're moving all the time.
11. Tree—Alive, because it's waving and growing.
12. Sun—It's always alive, because God helps it.
13. Wind—Alive, because it blows. But when it does not blow, it's not dead; it's just asleep.
14. Automobile—Alive, because it runs.
15. Bird—Alive, because it flies. When they are shot, birds are dead.
16. Fire—Alive, because it goes.
17. Dog—Alive, because it walks.
18. Grass—Alive, because it grows.
19. Bug—Yes, alive, because it runs.
20. Flower—Alive, because people water it a lot.

To this little girl, an object's functioning is very important. Chairs and rivers are alive only when being used by people, another illustration of the egocentric attitude discussed earlier. She is obviously approaching the transitional stage, however, because some objects (watch, candle) are alive only when they are moving.

Closely related to animism is *artificialism,* the tendency of the child to believe that human beings created natural phenomena. Piaget's little daughter, seeing the clouds of smoke rising from her father's pipe, assumed that Papa was responsible for the clouds in the sky and the mists around the mountaintops of Switzerland. Piaget's first awareness of this belief came from listening to children's questions that suggested it. "Who made the sun?" "Who is it puts the stars in the sky at night?" "What makes the moon shine?" Putting the same questions back to the children, he learned that the sun and the moon were made by men, from a flame or a match— or by God, who closely resembled a man. "God lit [the sun] with wood and coal." "Some men made it into a big ball . . . then afterwards they told it to go up in the air." "People took little stones and made them into little stars." The waning moon disappears because "it is hidden in heaven by God." Children in Geneva believe that the lake there was dug by men after the city had already been built. Such thinking is not so different from the anthropocentric view of the world expressed in the Old Testament, in which God created heaven and earth and set the moon and stars in the sky.

Further expressing his egocentrism, the young child regards his own perspective as immediately objective and absolute. To him all things are equally real—words, pictures, dreams, or feelings. Piaget calls this attitude *realism*—the child ignores the fact that his is only one point of view, and thinks that what is real for him must exist objectively. Names, for example, are real and exist as part of the thing named. The young child cannot conceive that he could have been given another name. One is reminded of the beliefs of primitive people in the magic of names and the power they give to one who knows them, exemplified in the story of Rumpelstiltskin.

As the child grows older he begins to realize that names are not an intrinsic part of the object named, but come from somewhere. In transitional stages he will say that the name of the sun is in the sky, or floating in the air, rather than that it is in the sun (i.e., part of it). Or, as in the following example, he may say the moon was given its name by God.

Stei (5½): "Have you a name?—*Yes, André.*—And that?—*A box.*—And that?—*A pen,* etc.—What are names for?—*They are what you can see when you look at things* (Stei thus believes that one has only to look at a thing to 'see' its name)—Why have you got a name?—*So as to know what I'm called.*—Then what are names for?—*To know what things are called.*—How did the sun get its name in the beginning?—*I don't know.*—What do you think?—*Because the sun made the name, the sun gave it in the beginning and so the sun is called sun.*—And how did you get your name?—*We have to be christened.*—Who christened you?—*The clergyman.*—And did you take your name?—*The clergyman makes it for us.*—How did the moon get its name?—*The moon? The moon is called the moon.*—How did it start being called moon?—*God called it that in the beginning.*—How did the clouds start being called clouds?—*God started them by making them.*—But are the clouds' names the same thing as the clouds?—*Yes, the same thing.* "[10]

The writer once questioned a little girl whose parents were Japanese. The child had been born in the United States but had always heard of Japan as a faraway, mythical source of her family's beginnings. When asked where the sun got its name, she replied, "From Japan." This child's older cousin had recently gone back to Japan, so the little girl was asked where her cousin was, and then where her cousin's name was. To the second question she replied, "At the airport"—the last place where she had seen her cousin! Another child, who realized that her name was not a part of her body, said it was "in her pocket." It is not until around six or seven that children realize that names are only verbal labels existing in the minds of the people who use them.

Piaget made an interesting study of realism in children's dreams and found that young children are quite convinced that their dreams are real. At the earliest stage children, when asked where their dreams come from, give them an external origin. Dreams come "from the night," "from the sky," or "from God." Some children believe that it is the people they dream of who cause the dream. This is probably related to the emotional aspect of dreams—they come "because we've done something we ought not to" or because "I saw a man who frightened me in the day and I dreamed of it at night." To the question, "While you dream, where is the dream?" young children answer "in the room," "against the wall," or "in the bed."

Zeng (6): "Where do dreams come from?—*They come from the night.* —How?—*I don't know.*—What do you mean by 'they come from the night'?—*The night makes them.*—Does the dream come by itself?— *No.*—What makes it?—*The night.*—Where is the dream?—*It's made in the room.*—Where does the dream come from?—*From the sky.*— Is the dream made in the sky?—*No.*—Where is it made?—*In the room.*"[11]

Thus the dream is caused ("made") externally and appears externally. It is only when children know that their dreams originate internally and exist internally, although they *appear* to be external, that an awareness of objective reality is achieved. In between exist various degrees of confusion as to how the dream "comes out" as soon as one is asleep, so that its origin is internal but its existence is external. The child in this transition stage confuses *being* with *seeming;* the dream must be outside because "you can't see what is inside the head!" A further source of confusion is that the child remembers seeing himself in the dream but knows he was in bed at the time he dreamed. One little boy of eight drew a picture for Piaget showing himself in his nightshirt, standing in front of the devil, complete with horns, who was about to boil him. Over at the side was the same little boy lying in bed, watching the proceedings![12] This was a very clear example of child realism.

The reasoning of the preoperational child is based not on logic but on contiguity. This is what Piaget calls *syncretic* reasoning. Objects and events that occur together are assumed to have a causal relationship. The road makes the bicycle go; by creating a shadow one can cause the night to come. The thunder makes it rain, and honking the horn makes the car go. My two-year-old grandson once put on glasses to enable him to read a story "because that's how Grammy reads . . . with her glasses." Closely related to this kind of reasoning is the formation of associations between things without any logical connection, simply because, to the child, they seem to "go together." Piaget quotes a little boy who said, "The moon doesn't fall down because there is no sun because it is very high up." These are three separate facts the child has observed about the moon, none of which have any relation to one another. "For the child," says Piaget, "everything is connected to everything else . . ." He cites the following example of Jacqueline's two-year-old reasoning:

> At 2;10(8) J. had a temperature and wanted oranges. It was too early in the season for oranges to be in the shops and we tried to explain to her that they were not yet ripe. "They're still green. We can't eat them. They haven't yet got their lovely yellow color." J. seemed to accept this, but a moment later, as she was drinking her camomile tea, she said: *"Camomile isn't green, it's yellow already. . . . Give me some oranges!"* The reasoning here is clear: if the camomile is already yellow, the oranges can also be yellow—a case of "active" analogy or symbolic participation.[13]

This may sound illogical, but how can one be illogical where no logic yet exists? And how does the young child move from the magical, delightful, distorted world of early childhood into a world of logic and objective reality? Piaget shows how thought develops during the period between two and seven years, through the medium of *symbolic functioning.* We have seen how the baby in the sensory-motor period has already begun to construct mental representations that are based on internal imitations of external activities. Consider the nursing infant carefully scrutinizing his mother's face. By the time he is six or eight months old, he has a mental image of his mother that also includes the sound of her voice, the softness of her body, the smell and taste and feel of her, which is different from all others. This internal mental image of her enables the baby to recognize her in different contexts (after a haircut or in an evening dress). By the end of the sensory-motor period, the baby can recreate internally this image of his mother even when she is not present. He may be said to "remember" and "think about" her, even though these are as yet very primitive thought processes. Piaget calls such mental images *deferred imitations* because they are copies or imitations of past events that are reconstructed at a later time.

The mental image of the mother may also become attached to some substitute object, such as her familiar bathrobe, or a security blanket that is associated with her softness, warmth, and nurturance.

These objects then become symbols of the mother that help the child to summon up her image even when she is absent. In the same way, external activities may become internalized and represented symbolically, just as Lucienne symbolized with her mouth the opening of the matchbox. Thus mental images and symbols arise from deferred imitation and form the basis for the further development of thought. In the child of about two we see the appearance of the symbolic function in several forms. The baby has already showed signs of imitation by mimicking sounds and gestures (saying "Mama," waving "bye-bye") and by recognizing the pictures in his storybooks. The two-year-old is heard to cry out in his sleep because of dreams, which are "pictures in his head." He tries to draw his own pictures and reproduces in make-believe play the activities he has experienced or observed. Most important of all, he begins to develop language, which is a socially understood symbol system in contrast to the private, idiosyncratic symbols of make-believe play. When a child pushes a block across the floor, it could be a car or a train or a steam shovel or a fire engine. But when the child says, "Choo-choo train," he is using a symbol that can be understood by all.

These symbolic functions of language, imitation, and make-believe play will be examined in more detail in later chapters. For the present, let us turn back to the subject of *conservation,* which was discussed in chapter 5. Along with the development of the symbolic functions, the construction of the notion of conservation is a major task of the preoperational period. Conservation, as we have pointed out, refers to the ability to recognize that certain aspects of an object or person remain constant despite changing conditions or transformations. We have already described a number of Piaget's experiments that show how the very young child bases his judgments on the changing perceptual attributes of objects, instead of recognizing that their basic matter or substance is unchanged. He focuses his attention on the separate states or *configurations* of an array (clay ball versus sausage, long row of buttons versus short row, etc.) rather than on the transformations by which one state is changed into another. In other words, the thinking of the early preoperational child is rigid, immobile, and very concrete. Like slides clicking into a slide projector, his mental images move slowly from one static configuration to the next, with no reversibility or flexibility. Piaget calls this aspect of the child's thought *figurative* because it is focused on the perceptual aspects, on the configurations of an object rather than on its transformations. By contrast, the *operative* aspect of thought is dynamic; it relates to transformations and is centered on actions, whether external (sensory-motor) or internal (operations). These different aspects of thought exist side by side, but never in isolation, because some operative aspects are present in all knowing. In the very young child, however, the figurative aspect is predominant, as we saw in the conservation experiments in which the static appearance of the clay sausage or the extended row of buttons take precedence over the dynamic transformations that make up the operative aspects of knowledge (see chap. 5). It is the long process of developing primarily operative thinking that takes place during the preoperational period.

Piaget divides the period of preoperational thought into two stages. The first, which corresponds roughly to the years from two to four, is called the *preconceptual* stage. A preconcept represents the child's first fuzzy attempt at generalization; it falls somewhere between a mental image and a true concept. A preconcept reveals the child's confusion between a class of objects and its members. One man is Daddy, so all men are called daddies. When Piaget asked Jacqueline what a daddy was, she replied, "It's a man. He has lots of Luciennes and lots of Jacquelines." In other words, Lucienne became the exemplar of a class of little girls, while Jacqueline represented the class of big girls. Here Jacqueline was having trouble with the same part-whole relationship that Piaget had found was puzzling to the children of Paris in regard to Burt's question about the bouquet of flowers (see chap. 1). The bouquet (whole) included some yellow buttercups (part) and some flowers that were not yellow (part). It is the same inclusion relationship of parts to the whole, of Jacqueline to the entire class of big girls, that is not yet understood. In the following excerpt, Jacqueline distinguishes between bees and bumblebees, but doesn't differentiate between insects and animals. Moreover, one slug is just like the next to her, so she thinks it's the same one, rather than another representative of the same species.

J. at 2;6(3): *"That's not a bee, it's a bumblebee. Is it an animal?"* But also at about 2;6 she used the term *the slug* for the slugs we went to see every morning along a certain road. At 2;7(2) she cried: *"There it is!"* on seeing one, and when we saw another ten yards further on she said: *"There's the slug again."* I answered: "But isn't it another one?" J. then went back to see the first one. "Is it the same one?—*Yes.*—Another slug?—*Yes.*—Another or the same?" The question obviously had no meaning for J.

At 3;3(0) J. was playing with a red insect, which disappeared. A quarter of an hour later when we were out for a walk we tried to look at a lizard, which darted away. Ten minutes afterwards we found another red insect. *"It's the red animal again.*—Do you think so?—*Where's the lizard then?"*[14]

This same kind of fuzzy, inaccurate thinking appears in the following example, in which Jacqueline confuses her grandmother's house, named "Le Crêt," with "all the houses" that make up the town of Lausanne, north of Geneva on Lake Lemain.

J. at 3;2(23) could not understand that Lausanne was "all the houses together" because for her it was her grandmother's house "Le Crêt" that was *"the Lausanne house."* For instance, talking about a lizard climbing up the wall she said: *"It's climbing up the Lausanne house."* The next day I wanted to see if my explanation had been understood. "What is Lausanne? *It's all these houses* (pointing to all the houses around). *All these houses are Le Crêt.* What's Le Crêt? *It's granny's house, it's Lausanne."* "All these houses" thus constituted a complex object depending on one of its elements which was seen as representing the whole.[15]

In the later half of the preoperational period, however, the child's mind begins to grasp intuitively and uncertainly the relationships of groups and species to each other, and to reason from the part to the whole. Jacqueline at 6;7 was looking for "fuzz-balls" with her father. "They're all called mushrooms, aren't they?" she asked. The following conversation occurred the next day:

At 6;7(9): *"The crows are afraid of us. They are flying away.*—Yes.—*But the blackbirds aren't afraid.*—No.—*They're the same family, blackbirds and crows, so why are they afraid if they're the same family?"*[16]

Here Jacqueline was reasoning intuitively that what was true of one species of birds should be true of another, regardless of other characteristics. Since both flocks of birds were black, both should have been afraid—a *prelogical* conclusion, to use Piaget's term for this stage. Piaget also calls this stage (from about four to seven) *intuitive* because it lacks the stable, reversible character of true operational thinking. Reasoning is still symbolic, based on subjective intuition rather than on objective logic. Piaget quotes Lucienne at 4:10 remarking, "I haven't had my nap, so it isn't afternoon." To her, afternoons were identified irreversibly with naps. No nap meant therefore that it couldn't be afternoon. She was trying to reverse her thinking but was unable to do so correctly because to Lucienne afternoons were a private symbol rather than a socialized concept.

We have seen this kind of intuitive reaching for the truth in the various stages of indecision and disequilibrium we have observed, whether in the child's understanding of rules or dreams or in his grasp of conservation experiments. Always we have noted a transitional period, in which the child is not sure whether the clay sausage is the same size as the ball or not, whether rules come from God or are decided by men, whether names are an integral part of one's identity or given by one's parents. Sometimes the child is right for the wrong reason, and sometimes he is wrong for the right reason—because he is on the right track toward logical reasoning, even though his understanding is still incomplete, still only semi-logical.

We will give more examples of these later stages of prelogical thinking in the following chapter as we describe the child's struggle to free himself from the predominance of perceptual factors and move toward a more stable equilibrium based on self-evident reasoning and logic. In the meantime, says Piaget, ". . . thought at this stage continues to be imaged and intuitive, and the equilibrium between assimilation and accommodation is not yet permanent. It is this intuitive thought, semi-reversible but without rigorous compositions, that constitutes the transition from preconcepts to concepts. . . ."[17]

7. Concrete Operations

As the child approaches seven, the traditional age of reason, we begin to see the fruit of all his years of experimenting with objects, with images and symbols, and finally with thoughts. He is moving into the period of *concrete operations,* a period characterized by the ability to reason logically, to organize his thoughts into coherent, total structures, and to arrange them in hierarchic or sequential relationships. We have seen evidence of this in the conservation experiments, for which Piaget used his new "method of critical exploration." In contrast to the work described in the preceding chapter, which was based largely on verbal questioning, Piaget and his colleagues presented concrete objects for the child to manipulate. They watched, and they also asked questions, seeking to find out why the child acted as he did, and how sure he was of his response.

Anyone who tries these experiments with children knows that most four-year-olds are in a very stable state of equilibrium. It is very obvious to them that there is more clay in the long sausage or more juice in the tall, thin glass. But five- and six-year-olds may not be so sure, particularly if they note that the sausage can be rolled back into a ball, or that the same amount of juice takes different forms in different glasses. This, then, is a stage in which disequilibrium predominates. The child begins to give the right answers tentatively, based on intuition but not on logical conviction. Finally, however, he is able to regulate all the factors involved. He notices both the length *and* the width of the sausage, and how one compensates for the other. He also notices that it can be rolled back into a ball again, and that whatever shape it takes, it's still "the same stuff." When he is asked, "Why do you say it's the same? How do you know?" he will give one or more of the above arguments, or perhaps just stare at the adult who is asking such stupid and self-evident questions!

Such a child, says Piaget, has formed a total, coordinated, reversible structure of thought that is well organized and stably equilibrated. This is the hallmark of a true concrete operation. It is constructed by the child in the course of his activities and observations of concrete objects. Nobody taught him the notion of conservation (nor can it be taught except in a very limited way), so where did it come from? It came from the child, says Piaget, from the interaction of his developing mind with the objects in his environment.

In chapter 2 we discussed briefly the four factors that influence intellectual development; here we see them at work. The seven-year-old child has reached a level of neurological maturation such that his brain is capable of coordinating two or three dimensions of an object (width × height, etc.) at the same time. He is also capable of remembering past activities, which makes reversibility possible. The organizing, integrating capacity of the human brain, part of his heredity that has been evident since birth, is now functioning at a more mature and efficient level. We do not know very much about the neurological structure of the brain, but here we can witness it in action. We notice that the child's thinking is much faster, more flexible, able to range into the past and to anticipate the future. It runs, as Piaget is fond of saying, like a movie film as compared with the slow projection of individual slides during the preoperational years.

Not only mental maturity but the stimulation of the child's environment have helped him to construct the notion of conservation. Since infancy he has been exposed to bottles that are filled and emptied, to sand pies that change in size and shape, to numbers of cookies or spoons or toys that grow or decrease as they are added to or subtracted from. He has also been stimulated by what Piaget calls *social transmission:* his parents have read him stories in which three bears always had an equivalent number of chairs, beds, or bowls of porridge. They have asked him to justify his illogical statements ("The sausage is bigger"), or answered his questions about where the water goes when the level in the bathtub goes down. All of these factors, operating together, have given the child the raw materials; he is now able to organize and coordinate them into a total structure of thought that is in true and stable equilibrium. Thus, says Piaget, is the concept of conservation constructed.

In order to describe the intellectual structures that develop in the school-age child, Piaget turned to the language of logic and mathematics. In mathematics, a *group* is a set of elements whose relations with each other have the properties of combinativity, associativity, identity, and reversibility. These are terms familiar to those who have been exposed to the "new math" in school.

Combinativity (or *composition*) means that any two groups may be combined into one inclusive group: $2 + 2 = 4$, boys and girls are children, $A + A' = B, B + B' = C$.

Associativity refers to the fact that the sum of a series is independent of its order. Two rows of three buttons or three rows of two buttons both make a total of six buttons. (Piaget's anecdote in chapter 2 about the little boy arranging pebbles in his garden illustrates this principle.)

Identity requires that one of the elements of a group be such that combining it with any other element leaves that element unchanged. In addition, the identity element is 0; adding 0 to any number leaves it unchanged. In multiplication, 1 is the identity element; multiplying any number by 1 leaves it unchanged (See chap. 5).

Reversibility means that each element in the set has an opposite that, combined with it, reverses the operation to its starting point. There are two kinds of reversibility: one produces a negation of the previous operation (i.e., $2 + 2 = 4$, so $4 - 2 = 2$), whereas the other simply produces its reciprocal, or opposite (i.e., if A is less than B, B must be greater than A).

At the stage of concrete operations, Piaget observed, most structures of thought do not satisfy these requirements for a mathematical group. In fact, he described only two such groups, one involving addition and the other multiplication, which he found in the child's arithmetical operations. However, he did note a number of organized structures of thought which, though they do not possess mathematical properties, are reversible and logically organized in the sense that every element is related to every other one. Piaget called these structures *logical groupings* (translated from the French *groupements*). They include the logic of classes and the logic of relations. The *logic of classes* refers to operations of class inclusion, which require that a child be able to manipulate part-whole relationships within a set of categories. Classes may be added to form a larger class; i.e., dogs plus cats are animals, $A + A' = B$. They may also be multiplied; multi-

Figure 6

	A_1	A_2
B_1	A_1B_1	A_2B_1
B_2	A_1B_2	A_2B_2

plication in logic simply requires that every element be combined with every other. Multiplying objects or properties on the basis of two criteria would produce the familiar double-entry tables known as matrices (see fig. 6). For example, if we multiply to get all possible combinatory classes of dogs (A_1) and cats (A_2), brown ones (B_1) and black ones (B_2), we would come out with brown dogs, brown cats, black dogs and black cats $(A_1B_1, A_1B_2, B_2A_1, B_2A_2)$.

The *logic of relations* refers to serial ordering operations by which children can arrange things in increasing or decreasing order. If A is greater than B $(A > B)$, and B is greater than C $(B > C)$, then A is greater than C $(A > C)$. Such relationships are described as asymmetric because there is no indication that the relationship between them is consistent; we do not know by how much A is greater than B. Relationships can be asymmetric or symmetric, as in family relationships in which if X is the brother of Y, and Y is the cousin of Z, then X is the cousin of Z. In either case they can be added and multiplied; again, multiplication may be on the basis of two relationships, or of more. Piaget's explanation of the eight possible logical groupings is very long, very detailed, and very difficult to follow except for the trained mathematician or logician. Those who share his passion for orderly classification and algebraic formulation are referred to Flavell[1] or Baldwin,[2] as well as to Inhelder and Piaget's books[3] on the growth of logical thinking. Suffice it to say that the eighth grouping, called "Co-univocal multiplication of relations," contains equations such as this:

$$(A \xleftrightarrow{a'} \downarrow^b B) \times (B \xleftrightarrow{o'} \downarrow^a C) = A \xleftrightarrow{a'} \downarrow^c C$$

To the initiated, this represents a relationship such as the following: If A is first cousin to the grandfather of B, and B is the brother of the father of C, it follows that A is first cousin to the great-grandfather of C.[4]

Rather than attempt to discuss each of these logical groupings, we will consider only certain ones for which Piaget devised experiments, and which can clearly be shown to exist in the organization of children's thought.

One important grouping is called the *additive composition of classes*. It describes the organization among a set of nested classes in which each one is included in the next larger one, like a set of mixing bowls. This kind of grouping applies to many relationships. Boys and girls are children; children and adults are people; people and fur-bearing animals are mammals. This grouping is expressed algebraically as $A + A' = B$, $B + B' = C$, $C + C' = D$, and so on. The relationships can be reversed: $B - A' = A$, or children, excluding girls, are boys. To demonstrate children's grasp of this sort of hierarchical classification, Piaget gave them objects that could be sorted into classes on the basis of different characteristics. This sort of experiment is the backbone of all psychological research on concept formation; in fact, there is an intelligence test based on exactly this kind of object sorting (Hanfmann-Kasinin Concept Formation Test).

In one experiment in this series, Piaget and his co-worker Inhelder presented their subjects with a variety of geometric figures, some made of wood and some of plastic. Moreover, objects of the same shape came in different colors: there were red and blue squares as well as circles. The children were asked to put together the objects that

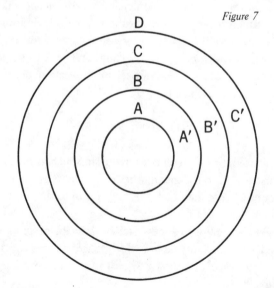

Figure 7

were alike. They might group them on the basis of shape, or color, or material, or even angularity as opposed to roundness.

The results showed that the youngest children tended to form what Piaget called *graphic collections*. The objects were sorted on some basis of similarity, but the bases tended to change as a child proceeded. For example, he might make a row of four squares, the last two of which were red. Then, as if the redness took precedence over the shape, he might add red circles or red triangles. Some children made simple designs, others more complex mosaics; in other words, the sorting was based not on logical classes but on perceptual attributes.

Jos (3;1) first places six semi-circles (two blue, two yellow, one red and one blue) in a line. Then she puts a yellow triangle on a blue square, and then a red square between two blue triangles with all three touching. She goes on to make a row of almost all the squares and triangles (touching one another still, but the shapes and colors taken haphazard). She now places a triangle and three squares in a line, and while doing so she decides that it is a house: she continues by adding a square below the three others. The last response therefore belongs to the category of "complex objects" [see fig. 8].[5]

After a period of arranging on the basis of one or another property, such as color, the most highly developed classification emerged among the children of seven or eight. This included subdivisions

Figure 8

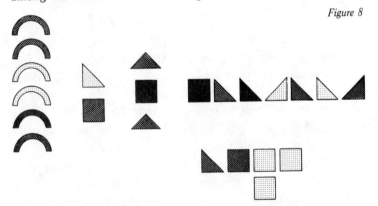

From Inhelder and Piaget, *The Early Growth of Logic in the Child*, p.21.

based on the same criteria: for example, all squares in one group and all triangles in another, and both of these separated from the curvilinear group containing circles, half-circles and rings.

> Rob (8;2), given the materials . . . starts with four classes: *(a)* the circles, semi-circles, and sectors, *(b)* the triangles, *(c)* the squares, and *(d)* the rings. Then he unites *(b)* and *(c,)* saying, *"all the squares and triangles"* (i.e. rectilinear shapes, but he keeps them separate in one box), and [then he puts together] *(a)* and *(d,)* saying, *"all the rounds"* (= curvilinear forms), which are also subdivided according to variety.[6]

A similar way of testing children's understanding of the relationship of nested classes was to lay before each child a row of counters that included red and blue squares and blue circles but no red circles. The child was then asked, "Are all the squares red?" "Are all the circles blue?" To the latter question, a four- or five-year-old would typically answer, "No, because there is a blue square." In other words, he was responding to the blueness rather than the circleness and answering the question as if it had been, "Are all the blue ones circles?" Some children also seemed not to understand the terms "all" and "some"; "all" to them meant a lot rather than only two or three. One five-year-old, who was shown three red squares, two blue squares, and two blue circles, was asked if all the circles were blue. He replied, "No, there are only two," as if "all" had to include a larger number.

This is the familiar part-whole relationship that Piaget first studied on a verbal level in Paris; he called it the *inclusion of classes.* On a nonverbal level he devised a task in which he presented children with a box containing twenty wooden beads. A few were painted white; the rest were brown. The child was asked whether the box contained more wooden beads or more brown beads. Little children would answer, "More brown ones." Piaget pointed out that the young child could not think about the whole (wooden beads) and its parts (brown and white beads) at the same time. He was still functioning on a perceptual level and had succumbed to the visual impression that there were more brown beads. The difficulty of overcoming this pervasive error is illustrated by the following excerpt:

Bis (6;8): "Are there more wooden beads or more brown beads?— *More brown ones, because there are two white ones.*—Are the white ones made of wood?—*Yes.*—And the brown ones?—*Yes.*—Then are there more brown ones or more wooden ones?—*More brown ones.*— What color would a necklace made of the wooden beads be?—*Brown and white* (thus showing that Bis clearly understood the problem).— And what color would a necklace made with the brown beads be?— *Brown.*—Then which would be longer, the one made with the wooden beads or the one made with the brown beads?—*The one with the brown beads.*—Draw the necklaces for me. (Bis drew a series of black rings for the necklace of brown beads, and a series of black rings plus two white rings for the necklace of wooden beads.)—Good. Now which will be longer, the one with the brown beads or the one with the wooden beads?—*The one with the brown beads.*" Thus, in spite of having clearly understood, and having correctly drawn the data of the problem, Bis was unable to solve it by including the class of brown beads in the class of wooden beads![7]

This stage was followed by an intermediate stage in which the intuitive discovery of the correct answer came through trial and error. Finally the child constructed the operational coordination between the parts and the whole in his thinking and could comprehend that the whole was greater than its parts. (Brown beads + white beads = wooden beads.)

Bol (6;6): *"The wooden necklace will be longer than the brown one.* —Why?—*Because there are more.*—But why are there more?—*Because there are the white ones as well."*[8]

Inhelder and Piaget also devised experiments to point up the difficulties that children have with special kinds of classes. For example, it was much harder to form a hierarchical classification if one class contained only one member. Even more difficult was the null class, the class with no objects in it. When children were asked to sort a series of picture cards that included some blanks, even some ten- and eleven-year-olds did not realize that the blank cards formed a class of their own. This brings to mind the problems children have in dealing with the concept of zero in arithmetic. It is only when it is presented to them in a very concrete way as a place-holder that primary children can understand zero. Many teachers utilize the empty seat in a row of children, or the empty desk being held for an absent child, to help youngsters understand this place-holding concept.

Another kind of grouping described by Piaget illustrates *seriation,* or the coordination of relationships. This grouping is one in which objects can be arranged in order of size or weight or height or any other property, such that if A is less than B and B is less than C, it follows that A is less than C $(A < B, B < C,$ therefore $A < C)$. The reverse of this, of course, is the "greater than" relationship, in which objects are arranged in ascending order, with A greater than B, and so on. This reversal, as we have pointed out, is not a negation, as in $B - A' = A$, but is rather a reciprocal relationship; if A is less than B, then B must be greater than A.

As one way of testing the child's ability to seriate or to arrange things in a logical series, Piaget would show a child two sticks, one of which was a little longer than the other $(A > B)$. Then, hiding the longer stick A, he would show him stick B and a still shorter stick C $(B > C)$. With A still hidden, he would ask whether A was longer than C. A little child could not tell without actually seeing A and C together, but an older child, operating logically, would give the correct answer. (This experiment was successful only if the difference between the sticks was not so dramatic that it could be solved by visual perception rather than by logic.)

This kind of serial relationship must logically precede the numerical operation of counting. In the above experiment there is no way of knowing whether A is longer than B to the same extent that B is longer than C. If the latter were so, then it would be possible to move from this grouping to a numbered system of integers, because the difference between A and B would be the same as the difference

Figure 9

between B and C; if $A - B = B - C$, the difference between them is interchangeable. This ability to transpose differences between items in a series is known as *transitivity;* it is a logical operation that underlies the construction of number.

A classic seriation task based on such a symmetric relationship involves asking a child to put in order a graded set of ten sticks, each differing by 1 centimeter in length from the one before or after it in the series (see fig. 9). To do this successfully, the child has to coordinate both ends of the sticks, keeping the baseline straight while the tops of the sticks increase in height. Younger children may place only two or three sticks in serial order, or arrange the tops of the sticks in stepwise progression, while the irregularly protruding bottom ends escape their notice. The children who are aware of the ordinal relationships between the members of the series are those who can construct it correctly.

One more type of grouping which will be discussed here is the *multiplication of relations.* This is a bit simpler than the system of family relationships previously referred to, because it deals with objects arranged with respect to only two attributes at a time, instead of several. For example, if glasses were arranged in a horizontal series by heights, and in a vertical series by widths, the result would be a matrix in which height increases across the top of the matrix and width increases down the side (see fig. 10). This kind of multiplication of asymmetrical relations (increasing heights multiplied by increasing widths) is what the child must deal with to understand the kinds of questions that were asked in the conservation experiments. Piaget used such a matrix with certain cells empty and asked his subjects to select what would fit in a particular cell, in terms of both horizontal and vertical dimensions. Jerome Bruner[9] has also published the results of a very similar experiment, using a three-by-three matrix of glasses. He not only asked his subjects to replace a few glasses; he took out all the glasses and asked them to reproduce the matrix. Then he put the shortest, widest glass in the corner where the tallest, thinnest one had been, and asked them to transpose the whole matrix. As might be expected, only the oldest children in his population of three to seven years could do this successfully. Bruner found the younger children very dependent on the perceptual features of the task. They could remember where the glasses had been before and replace them in accordance with a visually perceived pattern. But only the seven-year-olds could grasp the logical organization inherent in the array of glasses and express it, like one little girl who said, "It gets fatter going one way and taller going the other."

Piaget himself studied this multiplicative relationship by asking children to put two sequences in one-to-one relationship. One such problem, on a verbal level, that younger subjects found very difficult is quoted by Flavell:

Figure 10

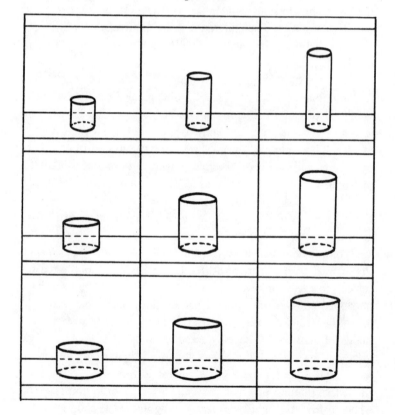

There are only three knives in a store. Two of these knives have two blades; they cost eight francs and ten francs. Two of these knives have a corkscrew; they cost ten francs and twelve francs. I choose the one which has two blades and a corkscrew; how much does it cost?[10]

A much easier experiment used a double series of objects to be manipulated. It involved having each child arrange a series of dolls and then a series of canes according to size, so that each cane was placed with the doll of equivalent size. Piaget found that this kind of pairing could be accomplished readily by the child of about seven. He would usually select the biggest (or the smallest) doll, and then the biggest of those that were left, and so on until he had the dolls in serial order by size. Then he would do the same with the canes, pairing each cane with its corresponding doll in the series. However, as we shall see in the discussion of time concepts (see chap. 17), when it came to pairing such a double series in inverse order, so that as one series decreased the other increased, there was much more difficulty involved.

These, then, are some of the logical groupings that Piaget observed in the thinking of the concrete operational child. His experiments show that from about seven years on a child is capable of many kinds of classification and seriation. Not all aspects of an operation necessarily develop at the same time. Seriation problems on a manipulative level, we have just shown, are much easier than on a verbal level. In discussing conservation, we mentioned the lag in the development of conservation of weight and of volume, which appear a year or so apart and later than the conservation of substance. But on a concrete level the child has the ability to construct relationships among the objects he sees around him. What he still does not have is the ability to think of all possible kinds of relationships, whether actual or hypothetical. In discussing the period of formal operations we shall describe the development of this kind of inferential thinking.

8. Formal Operations

Piaget uses the term *hypothetico-deductive thinking* to describe the mental operations of adolescents and adults, a term he himself characterizes as "barbarous but clear." We have already described such operations based on the *form* of a proposition as *formal,* in contrast to the concrete operations of the preadolescent, which are based on existing reality. By hypothetico-deductive thinking, Piaget means thinking based upon a hypothesis that leads to certain logical deductions. Such a hypothesis may exist only in form (e.g., what would happen if no one ever died?), or it may have conclusions that can be verified in concrete reality. It was the working out of such hypotheses that made possible the successful landing of men on the moon. The feats of scientists who have exploded hydrogen bombs and harnessed atomic energy are examples of the results of such thinking. No one has ever seen atoms or quarks; yet the dramatic developments of nuclear theory are becoming part of our daily reality.

For his books on logical thinking, Piaget joined forces with Professor Bärbel Inhelder, an experimental child psychologist at the University of Geneva. She was doing research on how children and adolescents come to understand the laws of natural science at the same time that Piaget was working out his logical formulations for the structure of adolescent thought. They compared notes and realized "the striking convergence between the empirical and the analytic results."[1] Piaget's logical analysis provided the appropriate structural model for Inhelder's data on adolescent reasoning. This was the beginning of a long and scientifically fruitful relationship.

These authors have already shown us that the child of seven to eleven is capable of dealing with the logic of classes and relations. He understands the relationships of classes within classes; he can put objects and events in serial order. This has been called "describer-thinking," dealing with concrete facts in a real and visible world. But the adolescent is capable of inferential thinking, or what Piaget calls "second-order operations." By this he means thinking about thoughts rather than about things that exist. Not only can he deduce from hypotheses ("if . . . then . . ." propositions), but he can take account of all possible combinations of factors or relationships, organizing them into a combinatorial system. He can study one variable while holding all others constant, thus carrying out complicated, multifactor experiments. To describe the integrated structures of formal operations, Piaget turned to the propositional logic of groups and lattices. We have discussed briefly the characteristics of arithmetic groups, as opposed to groupings (see chap. 7). But an even more sophisticated "four-group" was borrowed from the Bourbaki school of mathematicians by Piaget to express the flexibility of adolescent thought. This is a group of four transformations, known as the *INRC group*. The letters stand for *I*dentity, *N*egation (or inverse), *R*eciprocal, and *C*orrelative transformations. They are best illustrated by describing an actual experiment.

To study the operational scheme of equilibrium (referring here to physical balance), a scale was set up, provided with varying weights which could be placed at different points along the crossbar. The scale was first set up with equal weights on each arm, but so placed that the scale was out of equilibrium. The subjects were asked to make the arms balance. The youngest children did so by pressing down on one arm—an extension of their own sensory-motor experience with weight as something that pushes down heavily. When asked to make the scale balance without the help of his hand, one four-and-a-half-year-old replied, "You can't!" Another put two weights on one arm, but nothing on the other, and wondered why the scale didn't balance!

Five- and six-year-olds began to experiment with adding weights to each side; but the idea of reversibility, of subtracting weight to reach a balance, did not emerge until around seven. Older children groped around by trial and error, without real understanding. Finally, in preadolescence, the youngsters could formulate a relationship stated something like this: "The heavier it is, the closer to the middle."

> Sam (13;8) discovers immediately that the horizontal distance is inversely related to weight. "How do you explain that? *You need more force to raise weights placed at the extremes than when it's closer to the center . . . because it has to cover a greater distance.* How do you know? *If one weight on the balance is three times the other, you put it a third of the way out because the distance* (upward) *it goes is three times less.* But once you referred to the distance (horizontal gesture) and once

Figure 11

From Inhelder and Piaget, *Growth of Logical Thinking*, p.165.

to the path covered? *Oh, that depends on whether you have to calculate it or whether you really understand it. If you want to calculate, it's best to consider it horizontally; if you want to understand it, vertically is better. For the light one* (at the extremity) *it changes more quickly, for the heavy one less quickly.* "[2]

Here we see how the INRC group structure expresses the proportional scheme. If a weight is placed on one of the arms, thus destroying the equilibrium of the scale, the balance can be restored by simply taking off the weight (negation). Or an equal weight can be added at an equal distance on the other arm (reciprocal). Third, a heavier weight can be added at a distance closer to the center, or a lighter one farther away (correlation). Last, all the weights can be removed, returning the scale to its original equilibrium (identity).

This is a very much simplified explanation of a mathematical expression that includes all possible relationships of the weights and the distances to each other. Those who understand the language of symbolic logic are referred to chapter 11 of Inhelder and Piaget's *The Growth of Logical Thinking.* Flavell[3] and Baldwin[4] also give shortened explanations of the logic of groups and lattices.

The lattice, in mathematics, is a more sophisticated structure than the double-entry matrix that we discussed as characteristic of concrete operations. Instead of considering just black dogs, black cats, brown dogs, and brown cats, as in our earlier example, it would also include such combinations as black and brown dogs and black cats, or brown dogs and cats but no black ones. The lattice is a mathematical model that is composed of the sixteen possible combinations of four binary propositions, ranging from none of them (the null class) to all four of them. Piaget turned to it as a model of the adolescent's hypothetico-deductive thinking, of which the hallmark is the ability to take into account all possible combinations of events.

To give a very simple example of the workings of the lattice structure, let us suppose that a school administrator, faced with the problems of integration, wanted to consider every possible arrangement for grouping boys and girls, both white and black, in the first grade. Operating on the concrete level, he might simply tally up the number of white girls, of black girls, of white boys, and of black boys (four propositions). Then he might assign them to first-grade classes in equal numbers. But if he were operating at the hypothetico-deductive level of thought, he might want to consider all the possible arrangements for any particular classroom. These would include the following:

1. No children at all
2. White boys only
3. White girls only
4. Black boys only
5. Black girls only
6. White boys and white girls
7. Black boys and black girls
8. White boys and black girls
9. Black boys and white girls
10. Girls only, white and black
11. Boys only, white and black
12. White boys and girls, and black boys
13. White boys and girls, and black girls
14. Black boys and girls, and white boys
15. Black boys and girls, and white girls
16. White boys and girls, and black boys and girls

This lattice of sixteen possible combinations, while it may not represent practical solutions, at least gives the harried administrator the satisfaction of knowing that he has considered all the logical possibilities open to him. If none of them seems desirable, he may want to go back and reconsider the first proposition. Or he may find it simpler to resign! In any case, by following the formal reasoning of this logical structure and ignoring the impractical content, our administrator has shown himself capable of operating at the level of pure thought.

Using the lattice as a model, Inhelder and Piaget devised an experiment that showed the adolescent's ability to deal with all possible combinations in a systematic fashion. They set up four similar flasks containing colorless, odorless liquids that looked alike but were quite different in chemical composition. One contained water, another dilute sulfuric acid, a third oxygenated water, and the last thiosulfate. There was also a bottle of potassium iodide equipped with a medicine dropper (top row, fig. 12). Since oxygenated water oxidizes potassium iodide in an acid medium, a mixture of oxygenated water, sulfuric acid, and potassium iodide will produce a yellow fluid. Inhelder and Piaget presented their subjects with two glasses, one containing water and the other a mixture of sulfuric acid and oxygenated water. To each glass they added a few drops of potassium iodide (bottom row, fig. 12). The liquid in one glass, of course, turned yellow; in the other it remained clear. Had the thiosulfate been added to the first glass it would have bleached out the color. The youngsters were then asked to make the yellow "syrup" by combining the substances in any way they chose.

The preoperational children combined two elements at a time without any systematic procedure or any proof of the results. Their

Figure 12

The four similar flasks in the top row contain colorless, chemically different liquids: (1) dilute sulphuric acid, (2) water, (3) oxygenated water, (4) thiosulphate. The small flask (g) contains potassium oxide. The two glasses below are presented to the child; one contains 1 + 3, the other 2. The liquid in the first glass turns yellow when the experimenter adds several drops of g; the liquid in the second glass remains colorless when several drops of g are added to it.

hypotheses were guesswork: "Maybe it's because the water changes," or "Maybe the color melted." The children at the concrete level began by combining potassium iodide (g) with liquid from each of the four flasks, but it did not occur to them to go beyond pairs of combinations until the experimenter suggested it.

Ren (7;1) tries 4 × g, then 2 × g, 1 × g, and 3 × g: "*I think I did everything. . . . I tried them all.* What else could you have done? *I don't know.*" We give him the glasses again: he repeats 1 × g, etc. "You took each bottle separately. What else could you have done? *Take two bottles at the same time*" (he tries 1 × 4 × g, then 2 × 3 × g, thus failing to cross over between the two sets [of bottles], for example 1 × 2, 1 × 3, 2 × 4, and 3 × 4). When we suggest that he add others, he puts 1 × g in the glass already containing 2 × 3 which results in the appearance of the color: "Try to make the color again. *Do I put in two or three?*" (he tries with 2 × 4 × g, then adds 3, then tries it with 1 × 4 × 2 × g). *No, I don't remember any more,*" etc.[5]

Here it is interesting to see that Ren came upon the correct combination only through luck and experimental prodding. Once he hit upon it, he couldn't remember how he achieved it!

Gradually, however, the older children began to construct two-by-two or three-by-three combinations. Sometimes, after adding g to the contents of each flask separately, a youngster would put the combinations together and thus get the yellow color fortuitously or discover how to bleach it out.

Kis (9;6) begins with (3 × g) + (1 × g) + (2 × g) + (4 × g), after which he spontaneously mixes the contents of the four glasses in another glass; but there are no further results. "*O.K., we start over again.*" This time he mixes 4 × g first, then 1 × g: "*No result.*" Then he adds 2 × g, looks and finally puts in 3 × g. "*Another try* (1 × g, then 2 × g, then 3 × g). *Ah!* (yellow appeared, but he adds 4 × g). *Oh! so that! So that's* [4] *what takes away the color. 3 gives the best color.* Can you make the color with fewer bottles? *No.* Try" (he undertakes several 2-by-2 combinations, but at random).[6]

Finally, around twelve or thirteen, the youngsters began to work in a systematic way, taking into consideration all possible n-by-n combinations.

Cha (13;0): *"You have to try with all the bottles. I'll begin with the one at the end* (from 1 to 4 with *g*). *It doesn't work any more. Maybe you have to mix them* (he tries 1 × 2 × *g*, then 1 × 3 × *g*). *It turned yellow. But are there other solutions? I'll try* (1 × 4 × *g;* 2 × 3 × *g;* 2 × 4 × *g;* 3 × 4 × *g;* with the two preceding combinations this gives the six two-by-two combinations systematically). *It doesn't work. It only works with* (1 × 3 × *g*). *Yes, and what about 2 and 4? 2 and 4 don't make any color together. They are negative. Perhaps you could add 4 in 1 × 3 × g to see if it would cancel out the color* (he does this). *Liquid 4 cancels it all. You'd have to see if 2 has the same influence* (he tries it). *No, so 2 and 4 are not alike, for 4 acts on 1 × 3 and 2 does not. What is there in 2 and 4? In 4 certainly water. No, the opposite, in 2 certainly water since it doesn't act on the liquids; that makes things clearer. And if I were to tell you that 4 is water? If this liquid 4 is water, when you put it with 1 × 3 it wouldn't completely prevent the yellow from forming. It isn't water; it's something harmful."*[7]

Here we see a complete difference in attitude, shown in the logical approach to the problem and the understanding that the color results from the combinations of elements. The final phase occurs when a youngster establishes that the color is due to a combination of 1 × 3 × *g*, and then experiments with 2 and 4 to verify which one will bleach out the color. Here, "the combinatorial system becomes an instrument of conclusive deduction."[8]

The development of logical thinking demonstrated in this experiment is a good example of what Piaget means when he says that organization is inherent in intellectual functioning and imposes its structure on thought. He then raises the question of what brings about these progressive restructurings of thought which we have observed at the various developmental levels. The children's responses, at least at the formal level, bear such similarity to the approaches to problem solving taught in school that it might be thought that adolescent structures of thought were imposed by education.

Piaget rejects this argument flatly. "Society does not act on growing individuals simply by external pressure, and the individual is not, in relation to the social any more than to the physical environment, a simple *tabula rasa* on which social constraint imprints ready-made knowledge. For, if the social milieu is really to influence individual brains, they have to be in a state of readiness to assimilate its contributions."[9]

Here Piaget reiterates his position that formal structures are neither innate and "inscribed in advance" on the nervous system nor created by a society that imposes them on the individual from outside. Rather, they are forms of equilibrium that are constructed during the interchange between adolescents and other people, and between them and the physical world in which they develop. Mature cerebral structures are a necessary part of this interchange—necessary, but not sufficient. For "between the nervous system and society there is individual activity—i.e., the sum of the experience of an individual in learning to adapt to both physical and social worlds."[10]

We have seen this "individual activity" develop from the simple coordinations of reflexes at the sensory-motor level to the logical, systematic consideration of all hypothetical possibilities at the level of formal thought. Probably the most fascinating thing about reading Piaget is that he makes us aware of the rhythm inherent in the process of growth, beginning with the repetition of the infant's circular reactions and continuing through the entire cycle of development. The physical tasks the child faces at the sensory-motor level (e.g., learning to walk) are repeated at the symbolic level of the preoperational child (e.g., learning to talk). The young child can act upon concrete objects; the schoolchild can act upon them in thought; the adolescent is freed from the bonds of physical reality to soar into the realm of hypothetical possibilities. The process of equilibration is repeated at each level of development, in many different areas (i.e., conservation first of substance, then of weight, and finally of volume). There is a period of puzzling, of searching for new and better adjustments, of striving to achieve a balance between past experience and present uncertainties. When equilibrium is established in one area, the restless organism begins to explore in another. This is the common characteristic of all living beings, as Piaget sees them. At every biological and intellectual level there is an urge toward adaptation, understanding, and mastery, based on continuous feedback from the environment. Far from being "empty organisms" reacting passively to stimulus and shock, human beings are active explorers, adjusting to the world as they find it, but also modifying the world to meet their needs.

It becomes clear as we look back that for all his emphasis on discrete stages, Piaget views development as continuous and consistent. Each stage evolves out of the one before it and contributes to the following one, as in a spiral. Some children mature faster than others, but the sequence is unchanging. Moreover, development is horizontal as well as vertical. The structures of thought at each level are richer, more complex, more inclusive. Piaget's life has been a never-ending search for these underlying *structures d'ensemble*, or structures of the whole, which exemplify the organizing and integrating properties of cognitive development.

Development is continuous for Piaget not only within the individual but throughout all evolutionary levels. From the biological to the social to the intellectual level, the unity of nature is preserved in his theory. The functioning of the lowliest mollusk is based on the same fundamental processes as that of an Einstein. We will see these processes of self-regulation and equilibration repeated over and over again as we turn now to the consideration of the child's adaptive development in a number of specific areas.

9. Imitation and Play

We turn now to a more detailed consideration of imitation and make-believe play because of their importance in the formation of symbols during the period of preoperational thought. Piaget did his best to discern six stages in the development of imitation and of play to parallel the six stages of sensory-motor development already outlined (see chap. 3). The first three stages do not emerge very clearly, but the last three seem to be delineated by fairly characteristic behavior. We must remember, however, that Piaget made his observations over half a century ago, largely on his own three children. Modern research by Bower,[1] Uzgiris,[2] and others has shown that even newborns will open their mouths, stick out their tongues, or flutter their eyelashes in imitation of an adult model. Uzgiris, working with twelve infants, found imitative behavior undergoing "an epigenesis closely paralleling the course outlined by Piaget."[3]

Piaget, too, found evidence of imitative behavior in the very earliest days of a baby's life. He cites the case of his son Laurent, who like many babies began to cry when he heard the wailing of other infants around him in the hospital. The night after he was born, Laurent was awakened by the crying of babies near him and began to cry in chorus with them. This happened several times in the next few days. When Papa Piaget imitated Laurent's whimpering, the baby began to cry in earnest, whereas he made no response when his father whistled or made other kinds of cries.

Piaget attributes this oft-observed phenomenon to a vocal reflex, set off by the crying of the other babies. This would explain why Laurent did not respond to whistle or other noises, but only to crying, which in his state of infantile egocentrism he could not distinguish from his own. While scarcely a conscious imitation, this behavior corresponds to that of the first stage in the development of intelligence, which is characterized by neonatal reflexes, with no awareness of a distinction between self and outer reality.

In the next few months of life Piaget observed *vocal contagion* in all three of his babies, which he has defined as "merely stimulation of the child's voice by another's voice, without exact imitation of the sounds he hears."[4] He describes how he listened to Lucienne's spontaneous sounds at one month old, and how, by systematically imitating them, he was able to get Lucienne to make these sounds in response to his initial sounds. This occurred when she was about three months old.

According to Piaget, vocal contagion develops easily into phonic imitation. The baby responds in some way to the sound of another's voice, then in a vaguely imitative way, and finally, at about six months, in a precise and systematic way. He illustrates this development clearly in the case of Jacqueline, who at six months of age invented a new sound by putting her tongue between her teeth. The sound came out something like *pfs*. Her mother imitated the sound, and Jacqueline, laughing delightedly, repeated it. This went on for three weeks, by which time either father or mother could say *pfs* and Jacqueline would imitate them.

Piaget traces the same developments in the field of vision. He describes how Lucienne, at almost two months, would watch him when he moved his head quickly from left to right, and then reproduce the movement. By two and a half months she could differentiate between sideways and up-and-down movements of her father's head and imitate them accurately. When Piaget went on to more complex motor actions, however, he discovered that a model is imitated only if it can be assimilated to a sensory-motor behavior pattern that has already been formed. For example, Jacqueline, who at six months could reach out and close her fingers around toys, would not imitate her father opening and closing his hand until two months later. Then he observed her alternately opening and closing her fingers, while watching with great attention, as if this were a new and isolated bit of behavior for her. From observations such as this, Piaget concluded that a child can learn to imitate new patterns of motor behavior if they are practiced where he can clearly see them.

This brings up the question of how so many babies can learn to wave "bye-bye" if it is to them a meaningless act that they cannot see themselves perform. Piaget admits that young babies can be trained to do "all kinds of tricks," but he calls this *pseudo-imitation*, not true imitation, requiring constant practice and encouragement by the adult model. Without an enthusiastic example to stimulate such behavior, it is soon forgotten. However, when Daddy waves and smiles every morning when he leaves, or Mommy opens wide her mouth to coax the baby to eat, the child learns early to imitate their behavior and respond to their warm approval.

By eight or nine months of age the baby has reached Stage 4 of his sensory-motor development and is ready to learn more complex coordinations of previous behavior patterns. At this time he will imitate movements already familiar but not visible to him, if he has an adult model. He also begins to imitate sounds and gestures that are new to him, with greater flexibility and responsiveness. For example, Lucienne at ten months tried to imitate her father hitting his stomach and lifting a ball. Just under two months later she would imitate him when he hid objects under a handkerchief. Previously she had hidden her feet under a blanket and had played at looking for hidden objects with her father, but had never before hidden the objects herself.

Piaget explains this interest in new behaviors as a sign of the child's developing intelligence. Up until now the child has been interested only in activities that appeared to be a continuation of his own, beginning with the imitation of crying that he could not distinguish from his own, to the attempts to prolong interesting activities by repetitive imitation. Now he is responding in new and more complex ways, stimulated by "models closely enough related to his own activity to provoke the tendency to reproduce, and yet at the same time distinct from his existing schemes."[5]

The next stage of imitation parallels the fifth stage of sensory-motor development. The child, now about one to one and a half years old, begins to imitate new models, varying familiar patterns in different ways, as if to observe different results. This is heard in the child's babbling, where he may go from "da-da" to "ba-ba" to "pa-pa," experimenting with new combinations of sound in an effort to imitate adult phonemes. Or it may appear in motor behavior, such as when Jacqueline imitated her papa drawing lines on a piece of paper. She managed a few strokes with her right hand, and then transferred the pencil to her left. In the process she turned it around, so that when she tried to draw with the wrong end, nothing happened. To encourage her, Piaget went through the motions of making marks with his finger, whereupon Jacqueline promptly imitated him with *her* finger.

The last stage of imitation described by Piaget is a very interesting one characterized by *deferred imitation*. Piaget gives several examples in which his children observed something one day and later imitated it, thus indicating the presence of a mental image of past events.

At 1;4(3) J. had a visit from a little boy of 1;6, whom she used to see from time to time, and who, in the course of the afternoon got into a terrible temper. He screamed as he tried to get out of a play-pen and pushed it backwards, stamping his feet. J. stood watching him in amazement, never having witnessed such a scene before. The next day, she herself screamed in her play-pen and tried to move it, stamping her foot lightly several times in succession. The imitation of the whole scene was most striking. Had it been immediate, it would naturally not have involved representation, but coming as it did after an interval of more than twelve hours, it must have involved some representative or pre-representative element.

At 1;4(17), after a visit from the same boy, she again gave a clear imitation of him, but in another position. She was standing up, and drew herself up with her head and shoulders thrown back, and laughed loudly (like the model).[6]

This incident is reminiscent of Lucienne during the sixth sensory-motor stage, imitating with her mouth how to open a matchbox. The children at this stage give evidence of having mental images or concrete symbols of past events or invisible objects. They are emerging from the sensory-motor phase into the long preoperational period in which their activities deal not just with objects, but also with mental representations of them.

Arising out of these stages in imitation, and often inseparable from them, are the beginning stages of play, which Piaget distinguishes chiefly by *functional pleasure,* expressed in smiles and laughter, which accompany the activity. In imitation the child seems to be making a serious effort to accommodate himself to new objects and activities. In play, he is assimilating objects and activities to his own satisfaction. "Just for fun" he builds castles out of sand, or pretends to fly like Superman. Such activity "is no longer an effort to learn, it is only a happy display of known actions."[7]

Even Piaget, with all his passion for classification, has difficulty in distinguishing the early stages of play from sensory-motor behavior in general. He mentions "the pleasure of feeding time" at the reflex level of the first stage; and at the second and third stages can only refer to the "ever-increasing enjoyment" shown by his babies as adaptive behaviors become easier and more familiar. At the fourth stage he describes how Laurent, who is learning to push aside his father's hand in order to reach a toy, becomes more interested in the contest with his father than in the toy. He pushes aside his father's hand and bursts into laughter, forgetting all about the toy he had been trying to reach! Thus his interest is transferred from the goal of his action to the action itself, and what had been intelligent adaptation has momentarily become play.

During the fifth stage the child characteristically varies familiar behavior patterns in order to observe different results. Piaget says, "It often happens that, by chance, the child combines unrelated gestures without really trying to experiment, and subsequently repeats these gestures as a ritual, and makes a motor game of them."[8] He describes

Jacqueline, who at a year old was holding her hair with her right hand during her bath. Her hand, being wet, slipped and struck the water with a splash. This produced an enjoyable new experience which Jacqueline immediately repeated. She varied the height and the position of her hand on her hair, but during succeeding days this behavior pattern was repeated with the regularity of a ritual. Once Jacqueline struck the water as soon as she was put in the bath, but suddenly she stopped and put her hands up to her hair, thus renewing her familiar game.

· These behaviors are curious, says Piaget, in that they are not adapted to external circumstances. Such childish rituals are based not on a feeling of compulsion (as older children avoid cracks in the sidewalk, or hit each banister as they pass) but on the pleasure of self-entertainment. Insofar as it goes beyond the necessity for adaptation, such play is seen to be "the function of assimilation."

In the sixth stage, Piaget describes the emergence of *ludic symbolism,* the term he uses to define the "make-believe" games of children in which a stick becomes a gun or a corncob represents a baby doll. The immediate stimulus, the stick or the corncob, is for the child the ludic (playful, jesting, as in "ludicrous") symbol for the gun or doll baby of which he or she is thinking. Thus the child's make-believe play stimulates the development of thought about the nonexistent objects that are represented by these symbols. Jacqueline, at 1:3, saw a fringed cloth whose edges reminded her of her pillow. She lay down and pretended to go to sleep, laughing all the time. Five months later she pretended to eat a piece of paper, saying, "Very nice." Lucienne, at about the same age, pretended to drink out of a box, and then held it to the mouths of all who were present. This symbolic use of the box had been preceded by playing at drinking out of empty glasses, with all the accompanying noises of lips and throat.

Thus, as early as the beginning of the child's second year, Piaget discerns the "make-believe" games "characteristic of the ludic symbol as opposed to simple motor games."[9] They are also differentiated from imitation in that the function of imitation is to copy or accommodate to the objects of reality, while the function of ludic or symbolic play is to distort the objects of reality to suit the child's fancy.

Imitation (based on accommodation to reality) and play (based on assimilating reality to private, egocentric thinking) therefore represent the extremes of the two functions that must work together to achieve equilibrium.

By the end of the sensory-motor period (two years), evidences of both imitation and symbolic play are clearly discernible in Piaget's observations. Both are moving away from dependence on concrete objects in the direction of mental representation, or thought. But in the case of imitation the mental representation is a copy of reality or an image of the object thought of. In the case of ludic play, the object is a symbol that suggests something else existing in the mind of the child. The connection may be obvious or it may be quite remote, depending on how egocentric the child's thinking is. An acorn is an obvious substitute for a dish, but when Jacqueline (at 1;11) slid a shell along a box, only her explanation, "Cat on a wall," made it clear what this symbolized for her. However, the important point is that in either play or imitation the child by the age of two is functioning at the beginning level of thought rather than at the level of sensory-motor activity.

Piaget then goes on to study the evolution of children's play, searching for explanations of it and of why it disappears in later years. He concludes that there are three main categories of play: practice games, symbolic games, and games with rules. Practice games appear first and are an outgrowth of the imitative activities described during the sensory-motor period: pitching pebbles, jumping rope, stringing beads, piling up blocks. Such games may lead simply to improved motor performance or to destructive performance (e.g., knocking over blocks). They may produce new and pleasing results by chance, or by intention, as in the case of many educational games. They may develop into symbolic games, such as building a castle out of sand, or constructive games or even games with rules, such as hopscotch or marbles. Constructive games like building or weaving are regarded by Piaget not really as games, but as a bridge between play and work, merging imperceptibly into the practical skills required in adult life. But games with rules are essentially social, leading to increased adaptation. Piaget feels that since they persist even among adults, they

may provide the explanation of what happens to children's play—
that it dies out in later years in favor of socialized games.

Most of Piaget's interest, however, centers upon symbolic games,
which "imply representation of an absent object" and are both imitative and imaginative. Insofar as these games symbolize for the child
his own feelings, interests, and activities, they help him to express
himself creatively and to develop a rich and satisfying fantasy life.
While Piaget agrees with Freud that children may use make-believe
play to express forbidden feelings or unfulfilled wishes, his thinking
about the cognitive aspects of such play goes much further. As has
been suggested, he feels that ludic symbolism is a necessary step on
the way to developing adapted intelligence. When children have
completed the long development from sensory-motor activity to operational thought, these symbolic games gradually disappear in favor of
daydreaming or games with rules.

Between the ages of two (end of the sensory-motor period) and
four, symbolic play is at its peak. Piaget, as usual, carefully classified
into types and subtypes all the developments he observed in his
children's play. Type I includes the projection of the earliest symbolic
schemes onto new objects. Jacqueline moved from pretending she
was asleep to making her dog and her bear go to sleep. Lucienne
pretended to telephone, then made her doll telephone, and finally
used all kinds of things, such as a leaf, instead of a real receiver. In
the following months the children began to use their bodies to represent other people or things (Type II). Jacqueline at two moved her
finger along the table and said, "Finger walking . . . horse trotting."
Lucienne was the postman, or her godmother, or "Thérèse with her
velvet hat."

> At 4;3, L., standing at my side, quite still, imitated the sound of bells.
> I asked her to stop, but she went on. I then put my hand over her
> mouth. She pushed me away, angrily, but still keeping very straight
> and said: *"Don't. I'm a church"* (the belfry).[10]

In the Type I games, says Piaget, the child is trying to "use freely
his individual powers, to reproduce his own actions for the pleasure
of seeing himself do them, and showing them off to others, in a word

to express himself, to assimilate without being hampered by the need to accommodate at the same time."[11] But he soon moves on to Type II games, reproducing other people's looks and actions, or making his toys reproduce his own. In Type III we find the transposition of whole scenes instead of isolated bits, and long, complicated episodes of playacting sometimes sustained over periods of time. At around two and a half Jacqueline pretended to prepare a bath for Lucienne, using an empty box for the bath and a blade of grass as a thermometer. She plunged the thermometer into the bath, and finding it too hot, she waited a moment and tested it again. "That's all right, thank goodness!" she said, and then pretended to undress Lucienne, garment by garment, without actually touching her.

About a month later Jacqueline pretended to be walking a baby to sleep, talking to it as she held it in her arms. A week later, as she played the same game, she stopped talking when anyone came near. From a distance Piaget could hear her saying things like, "Now we're going for a walk." Already Jacqueline's make-believe play was becoming a secret inner experience.

Imaginary companions often appear at this stage of children's symbolic play. Jacqueline at four had a dwarf, followed by a Negress named Marécage. Piaget feels that children create these characters to "provide a sympathetic audience or a mirror for the ego."[12] They become playmates, inseparable companions, and sometimes even take on the moral authority of the parents to make the children behave. Children may refer to them quite openly or whisper to them in secret. What happens to them eventually? Piaget feels that just as Jacqueline stopped talking out loud and interiorized her make-believe play, so these imaginary characters may become in time interiorized in fantasy and daydreams.

Piaget also includes *compensatory play* in his discussion of Type III games. This involves doing in make-believe what is forbidden in reality. He describes Jacqueline at 2;4 going through the motions of pouring water with an empty cup after she had been forbidden to play in the real washtub. At 2;7 she wanted to carry Lucienne, who was then a newborn baby. When her mother told her she could not carry the baby yet, Jacqueline folded her arms and announced that she had the baby—there were two babies. Then she rocked and talked to the imaginary baby, and even said she *was* the baby when she was scolded for screaming with temper, thus excusing her behavior. By the time she was four, Jacqueline had a well-developed imagination, and whenever she was restricted in any way, she could make up a "compensatory" tale in which the direction of her desires was clear. When she was angry at her father she announced that Marécage (her imaginary friend) "has a horrid father. He calls her in when she's playing. Her mother chose badly." When she was told to take a nap, Jacqueline said, "Marécage never lies down in the afternoon; she plays all the time." Clearly, she was working out in her make-believe play what was forbidden in reality.

Closely allied to compensatory play is play in which emotion is acted out in gradual degrees, so that it becomes bearable. Freud calls this lessening of emotion through imaginary rehearsal "catharsis"; it has been frequently noted in the play of children who must deal with death or illness or hospitalization, to mention some of the traumas of childhood. Piaget gives the example of Lucienne, who at two was afraid of tractors and planes. "Dolly told me she would like to ride on a machine like that," she said. At three, she remarked that when one of her dolls was a baby, "they gave him a little steam-roller and a tiny tractor."[13] The obvious implication here is that through her dolls Lucienne gained in experience with machines and gradually overcame her fear of them.

Play therapists are familiar with this type of play in which children typically act out unpleasant scenes or actions. In reliving them by transposing them symbolically, they reduce some of the unpleasantness and make the situations more tolerable. This is the usual explanation of why children enjoy horror movies on TV. They know the scene is not real, that they can turn it off at will, so they are able to cope with the horror and master their own fear in slow degrees. In the following observation Jacqueline shows how a child acts and learns to live with the unpleasant realities of life.

At 3;11(21) J. was impressed by the sight of a dead duck which had been plucked and put on the kitchen table. The next day I found J.

lying motionless on the sofa in my study, her arms pressed against her body and her legs bent: "What are you doing, J? Have you a pain? Are you ill? *No, I'm the dead duck.*"

At 4;6, I knocked against J.'s hands with a rake and made her cry. I said how sorry I was, and blamed my clumsiness. At first she didn't believe me, and went on being angry as though I had done it deliberately. Then she suddenly said, half appeased: *"You're Jacqueline and I'm daddy. There!* (she hit my fingers). *Now say: 'You've hurt me.'* (I said it.) *I'm sorry, darling. I didn't do it on purpose. You know how clumsy I am,"* etc. In short, she merely reversed the parts and repeated my exact words.[14]

In these forms of play, as Piaget points out, the child increases his awareness through new experiences or takes his revenge on reality for unpleasant ones. He may even anticipate the results of his actions and construct in his imagination the consequences that would ensue if he disobeyed instructions or got into trouble. Thus the function of symbolic play is clearly seen in the "make-believe" games of children from two to four. It is "to assimilate reality to the ego, while freeing the ego from the demands of accommodation."[15] This is the age at which the child's fantasy play is the most far-fetched and his view of reality the most distorted.

During the second half of the preoperational period, from about four to six, symbolic games begin to lose their importance. It is not that they decline so much as that they come closer and closer to reality as the child accommodates to a greater and greater extent to the world around him. Piaget notes that after the age of four symbolic games become much more orderly, as opposed to the incoherence of earlier games. The child is improving in language skills, and also emerging from the egocentric world of his own needs to the world of reality. He notices how events follow each other in time and space, and his stories become much more precise and coherent.

Another characteristic of play at this age is that it reproduces an increasingly precise imitation of reality. There is "increasing attention to exact detail in the material constructions which accompany these games: houses, cots, tables, kitchens, drawings and models."[16] This is the time when little girls delight in dollhouses complete to the tiniest pots and pans, and boys like realistic forts and guns. Their play becomes increasingly a replica of reality, not only on the level of the setting and properties, but also on the level of what happens in their games. From about five and a half onward, Jacqueline constructed an entire village, which she called Ventichon. She, and later Lucienne, spent hours acting out real-life scenes in the lives of its inhabitants —weddings, family visits, dinner parties, and so on. The little girls began to play "permanent parts as mothers of families with numerous children, grandparents, cousins, visitors etc., the husbands being rather in the background. 'Mrs. Odar' and 'Mrs. Anonzo,' etc. thus became the starting point of new cycles, analogous to those of the preceding stages, but much closer to reality, always true to life and with scenery and buildings which became more and more elaborate."[17]

A third characteristic that Piaget notes is that after the age of four or five symbolic play becomes increasingly social. *Collective symbolism* is his term for play in which children take different parts and act them out with an awareness of each other, as in the cases of Mrs. Odar and Mrs. Anonzo above. This is in contrast to the symbolic play of younger children, which tends to be carried on alone, even when the child is in the company of others. As in parallel play, in which the preschool child plays beside another child without playing *with* him, so early symbolic play is usually carried on individually, using dolls or a much younger child who passively carries out his role, without really understanding or taking part in it. ("You can be the baby and sleep in the carriage," four-year-old girls will say to a much younger child.) But Piaget traces the way in which this sort of imaginary parallel play evolves into group play with each child taking a different role and reacting to the others involved. The following delightful observation shows clearly how Jacqueline at four was ready for a collective, socialized game, while Lucienne, who was only two, was not.

At 4;7 (12) J. did her utmost to stage a scene with a car ride. L., who was 2;2(18), was in process of constructing a bed, and said "Brr" to show that she was taking part in the movement of the car, but did not stop her own game. What followed was for L. a confused medley of the two games, while J. perseveringly arranged the parts. J. came off victorious, and made L. the wife of a doll, *"You're the wife of this husband. Yes,"* and herself another lady: (J.) *"We're two ladies in a car.* (L.) *Are you in a car, madam?* (J.) *Yes, and I'm throwing your husband and your child through the window* (she threw the doll away)." But L. went and got it and forgot the game.[18]

We have seen how, during the intuitive period, the use of symbolic play declines in favor of imitation of real-life activities. This is so because the child is reaching a better balance between assimilation and accommodation, and is more interested in the real world than in his private fantasies. By the age of seven or eight, says Piaget, "there is a real reintegration of play and of imitation in intelligence." Adapted thought increases while symbolic play declines. This age marks the emergence of concrete operations; it also coincides with increased interest in school, and in socialized activities and games with rules. The symbolic games lessen as socialization progresses until by eleven or twelve (period of formal operations) they disappear or are transformed into daydreams (internal) or dramatics (external).

Symbolic play seems to end with childhood; we have seen how the ludic symbols imitate reality ever more closely. As the child accommodates better to the outer world, he has less occasion to assimilate reality to his personal inner needs, thereby distorting it. Accommodation and assimilation, which are increasingly differentiated in the early preoperational period, gradually converge in the years after five until they are once more in equilibrium. Piaget traces this transition from symbolic games to spontaneous creative activity in the play of his son Laurent, who like his sisters created an imaginary village. At about seven, he began to make maps of the country where this village was and to imagine all sorts of people who lived there and the adventures they had. After the age of eight the imaginary characters disappeared, but the careful, detailed maps grew into cartographic models. During an illness that year Laurent worked out descriptions of the climate in different zones of his country, which he called Siwimbal. At nine his interest advanced to real maps of all parts of Europe. Finally, when he was about ten, Laurent's symbolic play appeared on another plane. His maps were quite correct and objective, but the boy now became fascinated with the study of history and reconstructed the costumes, furniture, and architecture of various periods. He dressed tiny toy animals in the costumes of the Middle Ages, the Renaissance, or the eighteenth century. He and a school friend went carefully through the literature on each period so that they could make their reproductions exactly. Here symbolic play began to merge with intellectual and artistic creativity. As Piaget says, "One needs to have seen a little monkey in a wig, a three-cornered hat, silk breeches and lace ruffles, in an eighteenth century setting made of cardboard, in order to understand the pleasure that two eleven-year-old boys can find in spending their leisure time in evoking the spirit of the past."[19] In this description we see clearly how the ludic symbol has developed into "an image whose purpose is no longer assimilation to the ego but adaptation to reality."[20] Laurent's imaginative activities no longer represent private fantasy but socialized study. The long period of childhood is at an end.

Piaget concludes his analysis of children's games with a summary of how games evolve. Practice games grow out of sensory-motor activity and range from mere repetition to chance variations to purposive combinations. If the child begins to arrange blocks according to size and shape, for example, he is passing from mere games to construction, the intermediate step between play and adapted work. If, on the other hand, the child uses blocks to make an imaginary train, his activity is more symbolic than constructive. Symbolic games decline after the age of four, while games with rules increase in interest for children and persist even into adult years. This is because the child, with the help of language, is becoming increasingly socialized, and adapting to the world of reality rather than to the distortions of his own fantasy. These distortions are caused by his original egocentrism, which is only slowly modified, and by his emotional need to work out forbidden feelings. Such feelings may be unconscious or quite openly expressed; in either case, they find outlet in the child's fantasy play and thus help him to adapt to the socializing demands of adult authority. Play, therefore, allows the ego "to assimilate the whole of reality, i.e. to integrate it in order to re-live it, to dominate it, or to compensate for it."[21]

In his theory of play, Piaget goes far beyond the thinking of other authorities of his time. For him play is not just a pre-exercise of the activities a child will need in adult life or an expression of instinctive behavior. Nor is it, as Freud has stated, merely the expression of unfulfilled wishes or subconscious feelings. Symbolic play, says Piaget, "derives essentially from the structure of the child's thought . . . [it is] merely egocentric thought in its pure state."[22] Its sole aim is the free and uninhibited satisfaction of the ego at a period in the child's life when he most needs it. Although Piaget does not say so, he would probably agree that between the ages of two and four the child is subjected to more parental demands than at any other time in his life. Constantly he hears, "No, no," "Don't touch," "Stay out of the street," "Don't get dirty," "Time for bed." He must be toilet-trained, learn to talk correctly, adapt to a time schedule, and acquire proper table manners. His daily life is polarized around his efforts to adapt to reality and thus please his parents (accommodative imitation) and his efforts to escape from these demands and satisfy his own ego (assimilative symbolic play). As the accommodation to reality becomes easier, the polarity between these two processes decreases. Gradually they converge in increasingly well-adapted functioning, until the child's play becomes almost indistinguishable from his daily reality.

As to the question of whether children believe in their symbolic play, Piaget feels that it depends on the age of the child. While children very early make the distinction between pretense and reality, he says, they refuse to allow the world of adults or of ordinary reality to interfere with the enjoyment of their private reality. It is only after the age of seven that play really becomes make-believe. "The two- to four-year-old child does not consider whether his ludic symbols are real or not. He is aware in a sense that they are not so for others, and makes no serious effort to persuade the adult that they are. But for him it is a question which does not arise, because symbolic play is a direct satisfaction of the ego and has its own kind of belief which is a subjective reality."[23]

One last question remains to be answered. What happens to fantasy, the lovely private world of make-believe, when childhood is left behind? Piaget suggests briefly that some of it is "interiorized" in daydreams and much of it goes to enrich developing intellectual interests, as in Laurent's study of historical periods. He also states, "Creative imagination . . . does not diminish with age, but . . . is gradually reintegrated in intelligence, which is thereby correspondingly broadened."[24]

In this statement Piaget seems to ally himself with cognitive psychologists and those who in recent years have become increasingly concerned with developing creativity in children. The research of Drs. Dorothy and Jerome L. Singer of Yale supports their belief that fantasy is a creative, constructive skill associated with self-control and the ability to delay gratification and work for long-range goals. They cite studies in Russia and Israel, as well as in the United States, which show that parents and teachers can make effective models for encouraging spontaneous make-believe play among nursery school children. "While the capacity for fantasy or pretending is inherent in all reasonably normal human beings," they write, "the degree to which it is used by children depends to a large extent on whether parents or other adults have fostered it."[25] The Singers and other cognitive psychologists are thus beginning to substantiate their belief that make-believe play, the ability to engage in fantasy or daydreaming, is a highly desirable skill closely allied to originality, flexibility, and creative imagination. Teachers and parents, it appears, would do well to follow Piaget's example and encourage ludic play among their children, particularly in the preschool years.

10. Language

We come now to a consideration of language and its role in cognitive development. Although infants respond very early to being talked to, their own language does not usually appear until during the second year, along with other symbolic functions: make-believe play, deferred imitation, and mental images, all of which have their roots in imitation. However, Piaget points out that language is an arbitrary sign system; its signs or words have public meanings that are shared and understood by society. This is in contrast to symbols, which are private and personal, often understood only by the individual child. Symbols may bear some resemblance to that which they signify; for example, an acorn easily suggests a cup. But most words have no resemblance to what they represent, so their meanings must be slowly assimilated by the child through a variety of experiences. The majority of the funny stories about children's sayings are due to the egocentrism and limited experience that are reflected in the meanings that children give to words. For instance, the small boy who refused to go in a car pool because he didn't know how to swim was exhibiting his concrete response to the word "pool." Dr. Ruth Formanek, a psychologist, tells of a little girl who was asked what "marriage" meant and replied, "Marriage means your name is Rappaport."[1] Here again the child's understanding of the word "marriage" was apparently limited to a single experience.

In spite of the egocentrism of early language, many social scientists have noted that with the acquisition of language the powers of thought increase tremendously in range and rapidity. They tend to attribute this to the development of language, but Piaget sturdily disagrees with this position. Language, he insists, does not constitute the source of logical thinking but is, on the contrary, structured by thought. He points out studies by Furth and by Oléron which have shown that deaf children, who had no language, acquired logical operations only a year or two later than normal children. On the other hand, a study by Hatwell showed that blind children who had normal language but were severely limited in sensory-motor experience, exhibited a delay of up to four years or more in the construction of logical operations, as compared to normal children.[2]

Furthermore, Sinclair at the University of Geneva has demonstrated that, of a group of children who could successfully perform conservation tasks, only 70 percent correctly used comparative terms in justifying their responses (e.g., more than, less than, longer but thinner, etc.). By contrast, 90 percent of the children who were nonconservers did not verbally compare or coordinate two dimensions but used absolute terms such as, "One is big and one is little." These results suggest that logical operations develop ahead of the language that describes them; conversely, the language of comparatives does not precede the appearance of logical operations. Teaching nonconservers the verbal terms for comparing two dimensions was very difficult in the absence of logical operations; only about 10 percent of the subjects demonstrated conservation after they had been taught the coordinated terms "long and thin" or "short and fat." As Piaget points out repeatedly, it is very difficult to "teach" a child logical operations; he must construct them for himself through his own actions. Then, and only then, can he assimilate the full meaning of the language that describes these actions or transformations.[3]

In another Genevan experiment, children from three to eight were shown a graded series of ten sticks and asked to reconstruct the series from memory and then to describe it verbally (see p. 65). Interestingly, the words used to describe the sticks followed the operational level at which the series was constructed. The children who could not yet construct a series used absolutes: "This one is short, this one too, this is a long one." Children who were beginning to understand the relationships in a series might say, "Tiny, very short, a bit short, middling long, long, very long." But children who had clearly assimilated the series and could reconstruct it in either direction used only comparatives: "Short, longer, longer," or "Long, shorter, shorter." This study indicates that children could not clearly express their ideas in language until those ideas or logical operations were themselves firmly entrenched. Piaget's argument is that language serves mainly to communicate what is already understood.

On the basis of research such as this, as well as his own observations, Piaget maintains that language development is structured by, and dependent upon, cognitive development.* It is no accident, he feels, that the first words of a toddler emerging from the period of sensory-motor activity are often onomatopoetic, imitating the object or activity described. "Mama" (or "maman" in French) arises naturally out of the sound of contented lip-smacking *(mmmm)*. Dogs are "bow-wows" and cows are "moo-moos." Piaget shows how these early verbal signs become generalized to larger *verbal schemes.*

> At 1;1(0) J. used the conventional onomatopoeic sound *tch tch* to indicate a train passing her window, and repeated it each time a train passed, probably after the suggestion had first been made to her. But she afterwards said *tch tch* in two quite distinct types of situation. On the one hand, she used it indiscriminately for any vehicles she saw out of another window, cars, carriages and even a man walking, at 1;1(4). At about 1;1(6) and on the following days any noise from the street,

---

*This is in contrast to the position of the psycholinguist Noam Chomsky, who hypothesizes that the grammatical structures of language are innate and universal.

as well as trains produced *tch tch*. But on the other hand, when I played bo-peep, appearing and disappearing without speaking, J. at 1;1(4) also said *tch tch*, probably by analogy with the sudden appearance and disappearance of the trains.[4]

Here the sound *tch tch* at first represents a sensory-motor experience, the sound and motion of a passing train. Then other kinds of experience are assimilated to the same verbal sign, so that it assumes a broader meaning that includes any noise, any movement, and any appearing and disappearing. These meanings are private and egocentric; they are related to each other only in Jacqueline's experience and are not shared by the rest of society.

Soon the child begins to put two or three words together to express desires ("No more") or to recount events ("Baby cry" or "Mummy gone"). It is clear to any observant parent that the child at this time understands much more language than he can produce. His early vocabulary consists chiefly of nouns and verbs, subjects and objects, and the interactions between them. This distinction between self (subject) and nonself (object), or between agent and action, reflects the major achievements of the sensory-motor period from which the child is emerging. "Baby cry," for example, or "Car go" expresses the awareness of objects other than the self, and of the actions that they initiate as separate from the acting agents.

At about this time the appearance of the ever-recurring question "Whaddat?" indicates the child's need to learn the names of things, to "get a handle" on them. As Jacqueline at three said to her father, "I like it when you tell me the names." She was beginning to conceptualize, to put things into some kind of ordered relationship, as we saw in studying the development of the preconcept (see p. 52–53). Interestingly, the child's grammar at this early stage is often more logical than correct. He may refer to "foots," forming the plural in the regular way; irregular verbs are often transformed into a regular form (e.g., "I goed home," "Mommy singed to me").

Piaget, however, is less interested in the structure of language than he is in its function. His very first book, published in 1923, was a study of the functions of language, of what needs they serve in the young child. Even then, before he had constructed his stage theory of development, he was classifying children's language into *egocentric* and *socialized speech*. He collected his data by following young children around in school and unobtrusively taking down every word they said for a specified period of time. Then he analysed the data into eight fundamental categories of speech, which we will briefly review.

The preoperational child, as we have described, lives in a world that is an extension of himself. His thinking is magical, animistic, and prelogical; he assumes that his speech is understood by others because *he* knows what he is trying to say. Most adults are familiar with the recital that goes ". . . and then he came and did it, and she said . . ." with never a clue as to the identity of he, she, or it. The child does not express himself from the point of view of his hearer, probably because he thinks the latter magically knows what he is saying, and also because he is unable to take the perspective of the other person. Often he talks to himself, not knowing whether anyone is listening to him, and not caring whether they respond to him. This is the essence of egocentric speech: the child talks only about himself, to whomever is around, with the apparent illusion that he is being heard and understood. "He feels no desire to influence his hearer, nor to tell him anything," as Piaget dryly remarks, "not unlike a certain type of drawing room conversation where everyone talks about himself and no one listens."[5]

The following are the three categories of egocentric speech:

Repetition—in which the child echoes words and phrases, just for the pleasure of talking, of mastering new sounds such as "rubbish" or "cockatoo." "This is the remnant of baby prattle," says Piaget, "obviously devoid of any social character." A decade later he would probably have characterized it as imitation, and compared it to the repetitive circular reflexes of the infant seeking to master his bodily actions.

Monologue—in which the child talks to himself, as if he were thinking aloud or giving a running commentary on his actions. "I want to do that drawing there . . . I want to draw something, I do. I shall need a big piece of paper to do that. . . . Now I want to do something else."[6]

Collective monologue—in which children talk *beside* rather than *to* each other, just as they play side by side in parallel play but not *with* each other. The presence of another child seems to serve as a stimulus to the conversation, although neither child listens or responds to the other.

It is interesting that in this first book Piaget kept careful statistics and even computed a "coefficient of egocentrism" for each of his subjects. (Later his work was criticized, particularly by American psychologists, for its lack of statistical measures.) Based on his analysis of the conversations of children that he had recorded, Piaget determined that about 45 percent of the conversation of children between seven and eight years was egocentric in content. He noticed that these children seemed to talk to each other a great deal more than to adults, but that for the most part they were only talking to themselves. His conclusion was that children's egocentric speech "serves to accompany and reinforce individual activity . . . before it can be used to socialize thought."[7]

As these same children approached the age of eight, they became more interested in true communication with their peers, and socialized speech increased rapidly. Later on, Piaget would doubtless have said that socialized speech appeared as children become capable of concrete operations. He classified socialized speech under the following five categories:

Adapted information—in which the child attempts to make his hearer listen to him, and to influence him by telling him something. In so doing, he takes his listener's perspective into account and tries to communicate something. For example, while two boys are building with blocks, one says, "We could do that with parallels, too." The other replies, "I want to put the parallels on." A seven-year-old says, "My daddy is a tiger." "No," says her literal-minded friend, "he can't be. I've seen him." Here the children are communicating and responding to stated facts; however, Piaget was impressed by the absence of any kind of causal explanations. He found that questions about causality, as we shall see, seemed to be confined to conversations between children and adults or older children.

Criticism or derision—which are self-evident and familiar to all caregivers from Piaget's time to ours. Cries of "That's not fair!" or "Pooh, that's no good," are as old as the derisive chants of childhood:

> You liar, you liar,
> Your pants are on fire,
> Your tongue is as long
> As a telephone wire.[8]

Commands, requests, threats—which are also easily recognized, and which range from mild entreaties such as, "Would you mind helping?" to affect-laden comments such as, "You wait and see what a slap I'll give you!" Often the commands are part of a make-believe play situation: "Tickets, please. You can't come in without paying."

Questions and answers—which Piaget places in separate categories. Since answers are largely adapted information—statements of fact—or responses to queries, commands, and requests, they will not be discussed further.

Questions are a very important and interesting part of socialized speech. From the earliest question of "Whaddat?" the child moves to "Why?" questions, which seem to reach a crescendo between three and four. Their variety can be astonishing:

> "Why haven't little goats any milk?"
> "Why don't ladies have beards?"
> "Why does a crane have wheels?"
> "Why are your tears salty?"

We have already mentioned that Piaget recorded the questions of a six-year old and then asked them of other children. Their answers taught him a great deal about children's egocentric thinking (see chap. 6), for the answers children gave were couched in terms of their own emotional needs or *precausal* thinking (things that happen together cause each other). In fact, Piaget soon learned to duck such questions by asking, "What do *you* think?" thus seizing the chance to assess the child's level of intellectual functioning before framing an answer. He found that Jacqueline, at five, thought that clouds were made of cement, but later on (having obviously received a scientific explanation from her papa) she said they were made of "water, evaporated water." Thus, a child often asks a question for which he already has an answer, which he apparently wants confirmed or corrected by an adult; this may account for the lack of causal explanations in children's conversations with their peers. The answers given to children, says Piaget, should be framed in terms of what they are ready to assimilate and understand. He gives the example of a three-year-old who asked, "Why do trees have leaves?" At that age, he may have expected an anthropomorphic explanation ("Because God put them there") or one that served his needs ("So people might sit in the shade"). Later on he would look for a purposive answer: "To breathe with" or "To cover them." As he approached the concrete operational period, he would want an answer based on biological reasoning or logical classification: "Because all plants have leaves," or "Because trees are members of the vegetable family." Such answers stimulate children to think further, and help to correct their preoperational ideas of cause and effect. This is what Piaget calls *social transmission;* learning from other people and, eventually, from books.

As the "Why?" questions diminish, the "How?" questions increase. Children want to understand how things work, how long it is till Christmas, and most of all, how babies are born. Birth and death are topics of compelling interest to children and may come in many disguised forms. Parents who are asked a lot of questions about the origins of things—the sun, the moon, plums and cherries (from seeds) —should suspect a deeper question, as did Piaget when Jacqueline asked, "Are stones born in the lake?" Children who receive evasive answers soon lose faith in adults; it is better to be honest if one does not know the answer and admit it, saying, "Let's look it up." Scepticism is not unhealthy in this day and age, and occurs almost inevitably somewhere in the first years of school. As one of Piaget's little boys remarked, "Then Daddy can't know everything, nor me, neither?"

Piaget never seriously continued his study of language, although in later papers he has elaborated his basic position that language develops in the service of cognition but is not the source of it. He does not deny its importance as a means of communication and socialization, the source of history, culture, and moral values. But he feels that language is most appropriate for expressing the hypothetico-deductive propositions of the formal operational period, ". . . for these operations are no longer related to the objects themselves as concrete operations but to statements and hypotheses verbally expressed."[9]

Piaget's interest in the study of language has now been taken up mainly by Hermine Sinclair, one of the professors at the University of Geneva, who is conducting and publishing research in developmental psycholinguistics. Thus the work of Piaget, begun so long ago as a preliminary study, continues in the research of Inhelder, Sinclair, Voyat, Chipman, and many others who make up what is now called "the Genevan school." And Piaget's insights, which offered "a completely new version of the child's mind," according to Claparède's introduction to this first book, are now becoming familiar to parents and teachers around the world.

11. Perception

We turn now to what Piaget calls the *figurative* aspects of knowledge —perception, imagery, and memory—which focus more on the *configurations* of objects, on their static appearance rather than on their transformations. This does not mean that *operative* aspects are not also present, focusing on the dynamic, changing action of objects during transformations. But since about 1940 Piaget has been interested in perception and how it differs from knowing, as well as how it contributes to it. His many researches have been summed up in an imposing volume entitled *The Mechanisms of Perception,* from which the experiments described below were drawn.

Perception is a subject that has interested scientists and philosophers as far back as Descartes. There have been many schools of thought, from the eighteenth-century associationists, such as Hume and Locke, to the modern "transactionalists," for whom perception involves a transaction between the perceiver and the setting in which the stimulus is perceived. Basically the major controversy is between nativism and empiricism. The nativist school believes that perception

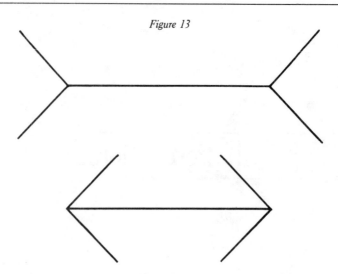

Figure 13

is innate and immediately given. We see things as they look to us because that's the way they are. The empiricists argue that we learn through sensory experience to see things and that we see them as we expect or wish them to be. To counter the nativist position, they cite optical illusions such as the familiar Müller-Lyer illusion, in which two lines are of equal length but appear to be unequal. Ames, in a famous experiment to show how experience affects our perception, constructed what looks like a rectangular window moving back and forth (see fig. 14).[1] Actually it is a trapezoid with one end much longer than the other, which makes it look the way a rectangle looks in perspective. Moreover, the whole "window" is rotating, but since the front end *(A)* is longer, it always appears nearer than the back end *(B)*, and thus is seen as moving back and forth closer to the observer than *B*. Experiments such as this draw attention to the fact that we see what we expect to see—what we have experienced before and therefore are familiar with.

Piaget accounted for the innate-versus-acquired problem by distinguishing between *perception,* which is the quick, immediate view of the stimulus one gets at first glance, and *perceptual activity,* which involves experience, judgment, and correction of distorted first im-

Figure 14

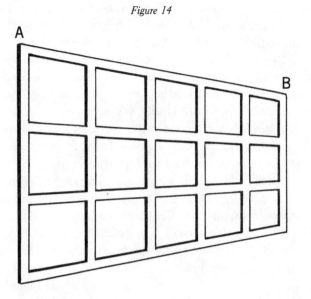

pressions. Both are involved in the perceptual act, which consists of a series of encounters. Piaget's theory of encounters is based on a probability model. If one were to look at a picture with 100 details (encounterable elements) in it, he might perceive half of them at the first brief encounter, leaving 50 elements unnoticed. On the second encounter, he would focus on half of the remaining elements, leaving 25 unnoticed. On the third encounter, he would perceive half of the 25, or 12½, and so on, until all encounterable elements had been observed. Thus the rate of encounters per microinterval would be represented by a curve that levels off by gradually decreasing amounts: 50 of the elements sampled on the first encounter, 75 (50 + 25) on the second, 87½ (75 + 12½) on the third, and so forth.

Piaget does not define exactly what an encounter is (perhaps a micro-movement of the eyes),[2] but he advances this theory because it explains several kinds of phenomena. For one thing, it accounts for error in perception. A lot of details may be overlooked in a hasty first encounter; the eye tends to fixate or *center,* to use Piaget's term, on only the most compelling elements. This leads to a distorted perception, which must then be gradually corrected by *decentering*. During subsequent encounters the eye has time to fixate different parts of the stimulus and visually explore all its elements. Mistaken first impressions are corrected as the multiple encounters are compared and integrated; thus distortion is replaced by accuracy of perception.

Decentering assumes a very important position in Piaget's theory, both perceptually and intellectually. We have seen in the conservation experiments how centering on the length of the clay and not the width brought about errors in judgment. In the study of number we will see how children construct a staircase by centering only on the tops of graded sticks or cards, without regard for keeping a consistent baseline (see p. 147). Decentration provides correction and regulation, leading to equilibrium. Centration leads to errors.

The reason for this, according to Piaget, is that objects seen in space are not all equally well perceived. Suppose the stimulus is a line; if it is encountered only briefly (e.g., flashed on a screen for a fraction of a second), it is seen as shorter than a line of the same length presented in full exposure. If the line appears directly before the eyes, it stimulates the center of the retina and appears longer than one which is on the periphery of the visual field. The duration of the exposure time, the clarity of the lighting in which the line is seen, its distance from the eyes, and the degree of attention with which the observer focuses upon it—all of these factors contribute to a tendency to overestimate or underestimate. A line seen at the center of the visual field, fully exposed in clear light, by an attentive observer is perceived as longer than it really is. Piaget calls this *elementary error I:* overestimation owing to centration.

Another related error to which centration leads is the "error of the standard" *(elementary error II)*. This arises when a subject is asked to compare objects, one of which is left in place (the standard) while the others are presented one at a time. "The standard is systematically overestimated," Piaget explains, "just because it plays a privileged role in the comparison."[3] The subject keeps returning to the standard to make his judgments, thereby centering it much more often.

An experiment conducted with Marc Lambercier, an associate of

Piaget's, demonstrated these findings clearly. The subjects, including both children and adults, were asked to make a comparison between a standard vertical rod and a number of other rods, ranging from shorter to longer than the standard. They were asked, "Is this one [the variable] shorter or longer than this one [the standard], or is it equal to it?" When the two rods were close together (i.e., in the center of the retina), the standard was underestimated. But as the distance between them was increased, the standard was consistently overestimated. Piaget's explanation for this is that "the subject, being forced constantly to return to the standard in order to make his comparison at greater distances of separation, centered it more frequently, or for a longer time, or more attentively, etc., and by this very fact came to overestimate it. At smaller distances, on the other hand (smaller for children than for adults), the subject, having both the standard and the variable constantly in view at the same time, and being familiar with the standard which he did not in any case have to lose sight of, preferentially centered the variable and thus over-estimated it."[4] He found support for his hypothesis in the results of two variations in the experimental procedure. If the standard and the variable were both removed at the same time, and the standard was then replaced without the subject's knowing that it was the same standard, he was less likely to overestimate it. Also, if the instructions were reworded so that the variable became the standard of comparison, and the subject was asked to compare the previous standard with the variable, it often happened that the variable then became the one that was overestimated!

Piaget became very much interested in this question of the relationship between comparison figures and set himself to work out the following problem: why, if A is less than B, is B perceived as larger when accompanied by A than when perceived alone? He expressed this as $B(A) > B$; or B in relation to A is greater than B by itself. In his characteristically rigorous way, Piaget then proceeded to study at least a dozen well-known visual illusions and to express his findings in a mathematical formula that would predict the size of the error that could be expected in relation to the changing values of elements in the perceptible situation: the length of lines, the distance between stimuli, the age of the subjects, etc. In the case of the Müller-Lyer illusion, the error of estimation of length was found to vary predictably with the length of the barbs on the ends of the equal lines, and the size of the angles formed by the barbs with those lines. Piaget called his formulation *the law of relative centrations;* it represents, as Flavell says, "the high-water mark of quantification in Piaget's theoretical system."[5] The contrast between the precise, carefully controlled, statistically reported experiments in perception and Piaget's unstandardized clinical approach to his early studies of intelligence is nowhere more clearly evident. However, since the explanation of these experiments is highly technical and requires a specialized background in the field of perception, we will turn from them to a consideration of the relationship between perception and intelligence.

Piaget feels that perception and intelligence evolve independently of each other; that intelligence is continually developing, whereas perception shows no such development but rather is "enriched" by the emerging structures of intelligence. To illustrate this, he describes an experiment which points up the difference between perception and conception.[6] As part of the investigation of a constant error arising in the comparison of the length of two parallel lines, two lines of equal length were presented, one set to the left of the other, as in figure 15. The subjects were children of five, eight, and eleven, as well as adults. It was found that five-year-old children were less subject to perceptual illusion than their elders. They tended to judge the displaced line as being only slightly longer, whereas eight-year-olds made the maximum error in judgment. The error was less for eleven-year-olds and even less than that for adults; but the five-year-olds performed considerably better than adults. Piaget explains that

Figure 15

the younger children have not yet learned to structure their perceptual space in terms of the natural coordinate axes; this Euclidean notion of space does not develop until the age of concrete operations (see chap. 16). Older children, used to thinking in terms of verticals and horizontals, overestimate the line that is displaced horizontally.

In contrast to this perceptual task, Piaget describes a conservation experiment in which two rods of equal length were presented first, with the subjects agreeing that they were equal.[7] When one rod was projected ahead of the other, however, the younger children reported that it was longer because it "reached farther." The transitional children wavered back and forth between the uneven appearance of the lines and their demonstrated equality. But by the age of seven, the subjects were certain that the lines were equal in length, not because they looked the same, but because they *were* the same.

The juxtaposition of these two experiments points up very clearly the difference between perception and conception (or operations). Perception depends upon immediate experience and is subject to error. Conception depends on thought, which can go back in time to the point at which the two rods were seen to be equal and form a judgment strong enough to overcome the perceptual illusion.

While perception is less stable and dependable than the structures of intelligence, Piaget believes that through perceptual activity children do learn to correct distortions and compensate for illusions. The child of two can recognize his toys from any perspective, even though he may not *conceptually* realize that things look different from different points of view. In fact, during the preoperational years, a child's perceptual activity is better adapted to the real world than is his thinking. We have seen that the young child's thought is magical, illogical, animistic, and based on intuition rather than reality. He believes that the moon follows him around, that clouds move in order to bring the night, and that mountains grow because stones have been planted. In spite of all these misconceptions, the preschooler can find his way around the neighborhood and operate very realistically in a world of constantly changing perceptions. Colors look different against different backgrounds, people look smaller when they are a block away, and objects look different when they are upside down or inside out. Yet the little child soon learns to cope with these changing impressions of constant objects by developing what is called *perceptual constancy.*

This means that we learn to perceive sizes and shapes and colors as they are, even when we see them from angles and perspectives that make them look distorted. Just as the baby learns that objects exist permanently, even when they are out of sight, so the preschooler learns that Daddy is still six feet tall, even when he is a block away and looks smaller. Perceptual constancy sets the stage for conservation, which is really constancy of quantity, number, weight, etc., despite transformations in form. But conservation depends on thought and therefore is of a higher order than perceptual activity of any kind. "Perception is not, therefore, the source of knowledge," writes Piaget, "because knowledge derives from the operative schemes of action as a whole. Perceptions function as connectors which establish constant and local contacts between actions or operations on the one hand, and objects or events on the other."[8]

Thus Piaget makes it quite clear that structurally and functionally, perception is subordinate to intelligence. Perception gives us direct knowledge of the world around us, but it is subject to error. Perception corrects itself through decentration, but it is not reversible, as is thought. Perception transmits messages describing the world as it is seen, but intelligence decodes them. Perception at its best never goes beyond the level of preoperational thought, and as such is immediate, intuitive, and sometimes wrong.

What Piaget is really rejecting here is the position of the Gestalt psychologists, who had dominated the field of perception since the thirties. They argued that the laws of organization, of figure-ground discrimination and perceptual constancy, are innate and immediate, whereas Piaget has shown that they are acquired gradually through sensory-motor experience. He is not alone in this; there are a number of American psychologists,[9] whose research supports a developmental view of perception. The importance of their work, and of Piaget's, is that it helps parents and teachers to understand the learning problems of children. If, as Piaget shows, there are systematic distortions in children's perception such as *the error of the standard,* we begin to understand why young children may have difficulty in copying letters from the board or recognizing the same word in different typefaces. As adults, our perception is so highly developed, through years of perceptual activity, that we forget that a page of print does not look to children as it does to us. Children tend to center on certain words and not see the rest of the sentence, whereas our decentered vision takes in a whole line in one sweep of the eyes. Now, thanks to Piaget, we have a rationale and a sequence of experiences to help us correct children's inadequacies and give them a more mature approach to learning.

Today, school specialists in learning disabilities and many observant classroom teachers have learned to recognize the child "who has not completed the sensory-motor stage in certain areas and who is attempting to build acts of intelligence on a structure that is not yet free of the demands of the sensory-motor period."[10] In such a case, what is needed is more experience at the sensory-motor level in order to develop the necessary perceptual processes. Piaget says that "perception renders indispensable services to sensory-motor activity, but that it is reciprocally enriched by this activity. . . . [For example] the size of an object is variable to the sight but constant to the touch . . . the whole sensory-motor development imposes a coordination between the visual and the tactilo-kinaesthetic sensations."[11]

If a child is not succeeding in the activities generally expected of kindergarten or first-grade children, the teacher well versed in Piagetian theory can take a careful look at him and see at what developmental level he *is* operating. Perhaps he cannot copy letters from the board like other children. She might give him a sheet of paper and ask him to draw a circle or a square. If he does not know how, she might present him with models and ask him to copy them. If he can produce only a lopsided circle or a square with "ears" for corners instead of sharp angles, she goes back to an earlier level of development and gives him experience with handling and copying forms at a gross motor level. She might give him form boards into which he can fit large circles, squares, and triangles after he has felt them and observed their distinctive characteristics. Or she might ask him to go to the board and draw big round circles with chalk until he has the feeling of a circle in his muscles as well as an image in his mind.

Once the child has constructed a kinesthetic and tactile as well as a visual image of a circle, the teacher might begin to help him scale down his reproductions. She might give him plastic templates to trace inside of, or put lines on the board to limit the size of his circles. Eventually her goal would be to have him copying circles from the board on paper at his seat. Then by adding lines in the right relationships to the circle, the child could begin successfully to reproduce letters such as *a, b,* or *p.*

There are many ways in which sensitive teachers can observe and provide for deficiencies in children's perception. Perhaps the child has trouble with auditory discrimination—he can't hear the difference between *cap* and *cat.* This will give him problems in learning to read and spell. The teacher may expose him to high and low tones, different kinds of musical instruments, and all sorts of listening games, which will enrich the child's experience and give him a broader base for the recognition and discrimination of sounds. In other words, teachers are becoming increasingly adept at "prescriptive teaching"—pinpointing a child's areas of weakness and providing perceptual activities especially selected to help him overcome them.

This kind of training also gives many kinds of concrete experience from which a child gradually constructs logical-mathematical relationships. For example, a teacher helping children to build an understanding of *same* and *different* might line up two boys and one girl and ask the class which one was *different.* Or she might choose three boys and have one face the blackboard while two faced the class. She might have children put chairs in a row, but have one chair faced in a *different* direction. She might make a pile of four blocks and ask a child to make one using the *same* number of blocks. There are a thousand and one ways in which a capable teacher can provide experiences from which a child can construct relationships adapted to his particular level of intellectual functioning, beginning with his own body and extending out into the world around him.

This brings us to the problem of timing or, as J. McV. Hunt calls it, the problem of *match.* [12] We must learn to match our teaching to the child's level of competence, whether it be at the preschool level of perceptual and symbolic activity, or at more advanced operational levels. If we teach at a level below the child's stage of development, he is bored because it is too easy for him. If our teaching is over his head, the child is frustrated and confused. But if it is geared to the child's operative level, then it can present him with just enough "cognitive conflict" to stimulate and interest him. Thus learning and educational experiences must be kept in equilibrium with the child's level of development. As F. H. Hooper puts it, he must have "the right kind of experience at the right time."[13] We need a great deal more research in order to know precisely what to teach when, and how best to fit our teaching to the individual child. But we are making progress, and it is indicative of the genius of Piaget that his theories are finding applications in special education as well as among normal children.

12. Imagery and Memory

In contrast to perception, which develops early in infancy, mental images seem to appear toward the middle of the second year, along with symbolic play, deferred imitation, and language. Like all the symbolic functions, mental imagery, according to Piaget, arises out of imitation and consists of internalized reproductions functioning in the absence of the imaged objects. But, as we shall see, this does not mean that images are exact copies of reality. "Images," says Piaget, "are instruments of knowledge and therefore depend on cognitive functions."[1]

In other words, images develop in close relation with intellectual functions. They occupy an intermediate position between perception (which is largely figurative) and intelligence (which depends on operations). Mental images include, therefore, both figurative and operative aspects, but do not have the complete mobility and reversibility of fully developed operations. They act as symbolic instruments of thought, making it possible to reconstruct the past (*reproductive* images) and to anticipate the future effects of actions and transformations (*anticipatory* images).

Since mental images are essentially private, Piaget and Inhelder devised ways of studying them through gestures, drawings, and verbal explanations, applied to a variety of materials. For example, they presented children from four to seven with two cardboard squares, one above the other as in *A* (see fig. 16). The task was to draw the squares as they would look if one square were moved to the right, as in *H*. Only the seven-year-old group could complete this task correctly; 75 percent of them achieved success. The younger children demonstrated, among other problems, a need to stay within the boundaries of one side or the other (see *F* and *G*), a difficulty we have observed in other cases (see pp. 69–71).

After finishing the drawings that anticipated how the squares would look, the children were shown H and asked to draw it. These reproductive drawings showed the same developmental progression toward success as did the anticipatory drawings, with the four-year-olds demonstrating the least accuracy. Nor was this a function of the children's drawing ability; the same pattern of results was observed when the subjects were presented with predrawn figures and asked to select the correct one.

Piaget and Inhelder worked with some thirty collaborators, who came up with many ingenious experiments to study both reproduc-

Figure 16

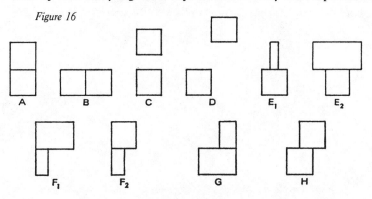

From Piaget and Inhelder, *Mental Imagery in the Child*, p.51.

tive and anticipatory images. They found that images could be *static* or *kinetic* (involving movement) or could include a transformation, as in twisting a straight wire to form an arc. Children might be shown an upright rod and asked to draw the positions through which it fell to land in a horizontal position. Or they had to imagine the track of a toy snail held by a concealed magnet to the inside of a metal circle. They were asked to draw the snail in four positions as it moved around in a circular path. Before the age of seven most children had difficulty picturing the snail's movement and described only static images; "It is on one side and it sticks." By age seven more than half of the children were using kinetic images in describing the snail's path, although one child of 7:3 refused to draw the snail upside down "because here he is standing on his head!"[2]

The results of these experiments, reported in *Mental Imagery in the Child*, will be summarized briefly. The clearest is that, strictly speaking, mental images do not display stages of development such as we have observed in cognitive functions. The second is that there is a parallel between the improving fit of mental images to reality and the operational level of intellectual development. This is particularly true in the case of anticipatory images. The Geneva group did not study hallucinations or auditory images, but only tasks of an operative type; therefore the development of mental imagery, like that of memory, appears to be characterized by progressive improvement in tandem with intellectual development, although to a lesser degree

Figure 17

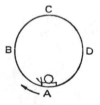

From Inhelder and Piaget, *Mental Imagery in the Child*, p.88.

than in memory, which we will discuss next.

The study of memory has been a subject of interest to psychologists since the days of Ebbinghaus, about one hundred years ago. Traditionally, memory research has depended upon learning lists of nonsense syllables, or words paired with each other so that to the stimulus word "boot" for example, the subject responds "shoe." Piaget approached the study of memory, as might be expected, in quite a different way. While he and Inhelder were studying mental imagery, they serendipitously came across evidence to suggest that a child's memory of a visual configuration showed considerable improvement six months *after* viewing the stimulus. Traditionally, memory traces are expected to fade with time, but here was evidence quite to the contrary! Piaget and Inhelder promptly set to work to devise experiments that would illuminate the relations between memory and intelligence. More specifically, they wanted to find out whether memory images could be retained in the absence of the schemes of thought necessary to support them.

Take, for example, the ability to arrange sticks in a graded series from short to long, which requires the logical operation of seriation (see fig. 9, p. 64). Could preoperational children who had not yet discovered this relationship remember and reconstruct such a series? Piaget and Inhelder presented a series of ten graded sticks to children aged three to eight, asking them to look at the sticks carefully and remember them. A week later the children were asked to draw what they had been shown. Six to eight months later they were asked to repeat their drawings without seeing the model again. After this, the children were given the sticks and asked to construct the series themselves so that their level of intellectual functioning could be determined.

The results, shown in figure 18, were most interesting. While there was some overlap, the drawings fell quite clearly into the stages of organization that might be expected of children at each developmental level. The youngest children, three and four years old, simply drew a row of sticks, as shown in *1*. The children of four and five showed transitional levels of awareness of size differences, as shown in *2a, 2b*, and *2c*. By about five years there were trial-and-error attempts at

Figure 18

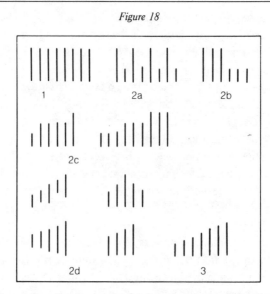

Three types of memory reproduction of a size graded seriation.
From *Piaget and His School* (eds.), Inhelder and Chipman, p.104.

seriation, as shown in *2d*, leading to a correctly drawn series *(3)* by most of the children who were six or seven.

These results seemed, to quote Inhelder, "too good to be true."[3] After an interval of six to eight months, 74 percent of the group as a whole and 90 percent of the children between five and eight had made drawings that showed improvement over their first attempts. While progress was always gradual, there was an observable movement from preoperational, through transitional, to clearly operational levels of performance. Furthermore, incidents of regression were very rare, thus contradicting the traditional theory that forgetting takes place over time.

This study gave important support to the Piagetian contention that memory is not just a passive copy of what is seen or heard, but is structured by the intelligence. Taken by cross sections, the children's drawings corresponded to their developmental levels, so that the youngest subjects drew oversimplified representations rather than copies of what they had seen, while older groups drew increasingly closer approximations of the series of sticks. Looked at longitudinally, the data also gave support to Piaget's theory, in that the drawings of individual children improved over time. In other words, if memory is an integral part of the structure of intelligence, and if that structure progresses over time, then memory must also change and reintegrate at more advanced levels as development proceeds.

In their usual thorough manner, Piaget and Inhelder then devised a whole series of experiments, which is reported in *Memory and Intelligence*. In it they classified memories into three types: *recognition* of familiar objects or persons, which occurs even in babies and animals; *reconstruction*, the intentional reproduction of a particular action, as in imitating it; and *evocation*, the recall of certain events in the past. Their chief interest was in evocative memory and how it is structured and supported by operative schemes. Of particular interest is one experiment in which a conflict was deliberately provoked between two schemes that do not develop synchronously, to see whether the conflict between them would cause a deterioration of memory. It had been shown in previous research that the numerical scheme of one-to-one correspondence develops early in the preoperational period, at a time when spatial correspondence is based on the coincidence of the extremeties or boundaries of an array. Accordingly, Piaget and Inhelder presented forty children from five to nine with two figures, each made from four matchsticks, as in figure 19. This configuration could be assimilated either as a numerical relationship (four matchsticks in each line) or as a spatial relationship (one line longer than the other). From their previous studies, Piaget and Inhelder were well aware that boundaries play a predominant role in the perception of preoperational children. In figure 19, the zigzag line of matchsticks does not extend as far as the straight line, but since the number of matches is the same in each line, the young child might well think that the boundaries *should* coincide.

The memory drawings of the matchsticks made six months later showed clearly the conflict set up by the contradicting tendencies (see fig. 20). The youngest children simply drew a double line of matches

Figure 19

From Inhelder and Chipman (eds.), *Piaget and His School*, p.110.

without any numerical or spatial correspondence (Type 1). A slightly more advanced group (Type 2) drew straight and zigzag lines, but the need to match the boundaries or extremities of the lines predominated over any attempt at numerical correspondence. In the Type 3 group the conflict was resolved by two lines with four matchsticks in each, but those in the zigzag line were spaced out so that the boundaries were forced into coinciding. The Type 4 group approached a similar resolution of the problem, but then extended the straight line so that numerical correspondence was lost, even though the spatial relationship was achieved. In the Type 5 group, sufficient development had apparently taken place so that the conflict between the two schemes was overcome and a faithful reproduction of the original configuration was achieved. This is a most interesting example of how memory is distorted by the assimilatory schemes with which different children respond to the same configuration.

These are only two of the many series of experiments that Piaget and Inhelder describe to support their theory of memory as it is related to the general structure of intelligence. Their data indeed indicate that a child remembers what he has understood rather than what he has perceived. In other words, memory images appear to be dominated by operative schemes; if the schemes evolve further during the time between perception and evocation, then the memory reflects the more advanced level of the schemes in evidence at the time of evocation. Thus Piaget and Inhelder

Figure 20

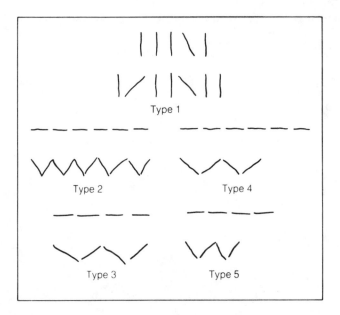

From Inhelder and Chipman (eds.), *Piaget and His School*, p.111.

feel that they have demonstrated the importance of operative structures in all the figurative areas: perception, mental imagery, and now memory.

The publication of this theory has aroused considerable scepticism and stimulated many attempts to repeat and enlarge upon these experiments. While some later studies have supported the Genevan claims, others have not. The evidence has been fully reviewed by Lynn Liben,[4] who has made a considerable contribution to the research herself. She feels, on the basis of her own and others' work, that there is dependable evidence for the existence of long-term memory improvement. However, subsequent studies have raised serious doubts and criticisms about the Piagetian interpretation of this improvement. The existing data bearing on these issues is simply not conclusive; we will have to wait for further evidence before a resolution of these issues can be reached. In the meantime, Piaget's theory provides fresh and interesting material for speculation and observation, as well as for actual involvement in the necessary research.

13. Morality

The essence of morality is respect for a system of rules. Most of these rules are handed down from parent to child, but in the case of children's games, the rules are passed from older children to younger ones. So, to study the development of morality at this simplest social level, Piaget got down on his knees and played marbles with little Swiss boys. He found that even in this elementary game different rules, rituals, and expressions were used in different parts of Switzerland and that most children were aware of these variations. How they adapted themselves to these rules and how they looked upon them were the questions to which Piaget sought answers in an effort to cast light on the development of moral attitudes in children.

In the very earliest stages of play with marbles, Piaget observed only motor manipulation, with no consciousness of rules. He described his three-year-old daughter, Jacqueline, digging a "little nest" in the ground in which she buried the "baby balls." Preschool children of four or five would imitate the rules for playing marbles by drawing a square in the ground but would play in an egocentric way, either by themselves or with others. Their understanding of the rules consisted only of going through the accepted motions, with individual variations as fancy dictated. These were the children who would say, "We've both won!"

Around the ages of seven or eight, however, Piaget noted that the children became increasingly aware of the rules of the game. These were regarded as sacred and unchangeable, invented by daddies, God, or "the gentlemen of the Town Council." Piaget investigated the children's attitudes toward rules by asking questions. How did rules begin? Can they be changed? Have rules always been the same as they are today? Here are the answers of one small boy, Fal, to Piaget's questions:

Fal (5) . . . "Long ago when people were beginning to build the town of Neuchâtel, did little children play at marbles the way you showed me?—*Yes.*—Always that way?—*Yes.*—How did you get to know the rules?—*When I was quite little my brother showed me. My Daddy showed my brother.*—And how did your daddy know?—*My Daddy just knew. No one told him.*—How did he know?—*No one showed him!* —Am I older than your Daddy?—*No, you're young. My Daddy had been born when we came to Neuchâtel. My Daddy was born before me.* —Tell me some people older than your daddy.—*My grand-dad.*—Did he play marbles?—*Yes.*—Then he played before your daddy?—*Yes, but not with rules!* [said with great conviction].—What do you mean by rules?—. . . [Fal does not know this word, which he has just heard from our lips for the first time. But he realizes that it means an essential property of the game of marbles; that is why he asserts so emphatically that his grand-dad did not play with rules so as to show how superior his daddy is to everyone else in the world.]— Was it a long time ago when people played for the first time?—*Oh, yes.*—How did they find out how to play?—*Well, they took some marbles, and then they made a square, and then they put the marbles inside it . . . etc.* [he enumerates the rules that he knows].—Was it little children who found out or grown-up gentlemen?—*Grown-up gentlemen.*—Tell me who was born first, your daddy or your grand-dad?— *My Daddy was born before my granddad.*—Who invented the game of marbles?—*My Daddy did.*—Who is the oldest person in Neuchâtel?—*I dunno.*—Who do you think?—*God.*—Did people know how to play marbles before your daddy?—*Other gentlemen played* [before? at the same time?].—In the same way as your daddy?—*Yes.*—How did they know how to?—*They made it up.*—Where is God?—*In the sky.*—Is he older than your daddy?—*Not so old.*—Could one find a new way of playing?—*I can't play any other way.*—Try . . . [Fal does not move]. Couldn't you put them like this [we place the marbles in a circle without a square]?—*Oh, yes.*—Would it be fair?—*Oh, yes.*—As fair as the square?—*Yes.*—Did your daddy use to play that way or not?—*Oh, yes.*—Could one play still other ways?—*Oh, yes."* We then arrange the marbles in the shape of a T, we put them in a matchbox, etc. Fal says he has never seen this done before, but that it is all quite fair and that you can change things as much as you like. Only his daddy knows all this![1]

This little boy expressed great respect for rules, which he attributed to his father, who was older and wiser than either God or his grandfather. Rules to him were endowed with divine right; when he was shown a new way of playing, he felt that he was merely rediscovering what his father already knew. This represents the attitude that Piaget calls *the morality of constraint.* Rules are first made for children by adults; and children, when they are small and dependent, accept them as final and inviolable. Many of the children questioned by Piaget expressed more resistance than Fal to any change in the rules.

After about ten years of age, however, Piaget noted a complete transformation in children's attitudes toward rules. They became no longer sacred laws laid down by adults, but decisions made by the children who played the games. They depended upon local custom and agreement among the players and could be changed at will, so long as everyone agreed. This attitude toward rules Piaget calls *the morality of cooperation;* it is illustrated by this interview:

Ross (11) belongs to the third stage in regard to the practice of rules. He claims that he often invents new rules with his playmates: *"We make them* [up] *sometimes. We go up to 200. We play about and then hit each other, and then he says to me: 'If you go up to 100 I'll give you a marble.'*—Is this new rule fair like the old ones, or not?—*Perhaps it isn't quite fair, because it isn't very hard to take four marbles that way!*—If everyone does it, will it be a real rule, or not?—*If they do it often, it will become a real rule.*—Did your father play the way you showed me, or differently?—*Oh, I don't know. It may have been a different game. It changes. It still changes quite often.*—Have people been playing for long?—*At least fifty years.*—Did people play marbles in the days of the 'Old Swiss'?—*Oh, I don't think so.*—How did it begin?—*Some boys took some motor balls* (ball bearings) *and then they played. And after that there were marbles in shops.*—Why are there rules in the game of marbles?—*So as not to be always quarrelling you must have rules, and then play properly*—How did these rules begin?—*Some boys came to an agreement amongst themselves and made them.*—Could you invent a new rule?—*Perhaps . . .* [he thinks] *you put three marbles together and you drop another from above on to the middle one.*—Could one play that way?—*Oh, yes.*—Is that a fair rule like the others?—*The chaps might say it wasn't very fair because it's luck. To be a good rule, it has to be skill.*—But if everyone played that way, would it be a fair rule or not?—*Oh, yes, you could play just as well with that rule as with the others.*"[2]

In this example we see a great change in attitude; respect for rules is now based upon mutual consent and cooperation, whereas for the younger boy, Fal, rules were based on unilateral respect and the acceptance of commands received from powerful elders.

From a consideration of these two positions exemplified in children's games, Piaget went on to study the development of moral judgment in children. He did this by presenting pairs of stories illustrating different degrees of responsibility for damage done. For example, in one story a child accidentally knocks over a tray and breaks fifteen cups. In its companion story, a boy climbing up to steal jam out of a cupboard, against his mother's orders, knocks over one cup, which falls on the floor and breaks.

In comparing responses to these pairs of stories, Piaget found that children under the age of ten tended to measure the gravity of the deed in terms of the amount of damage done. Thus the child who broke fifteen cups deserved a greater punishment than the one who broke only one, because by objective standards his was the greater guilt. This view Piaget considers a direct outgrowth of what he calls *moral realism*, which "demands that the letter rather than the spirit of the law shall be observed."[3] Moral realism, he feels, grows out of adult constraint; rules are given to children ready-made and external to subjective feelings. China is expensive and it is forbidden to break cups; regardless of the child's motives, the one who breaks fifteen cups is objectively responsible for much more damage than the child who breaks only one. In this view the child is reflecting the values that have been communicated to him by adults who become angry and scold him for breaking, soiling, or spoiling objects. This attitude is inculcated very early in children and is stronger in some than in others, depending upon how angry the parents become at their children's unintended clumsiness or "accidents" during toilet training. Some children feel they must clean up their plates, hungry or not, or become very concerned about dirtying their clothes. Piaget shows how even mild and loving parents who do not lay down categorical rules somehow communicate this sense of *objective responsibility* to their youngsters. He describes how upset Jacqueline was at the age of two when she was given a diarrhetic, even though she had been warned about its effects: "Her face assumes an expression of distress, her eyes fill with tears, her mouth droops, and she is obviously experiencing the same feelings as if the thing had happened in normal circumstances through her own negligence."[4]

At about ten years of age, however, children gradually lose this sense of objective responsibility and begin to place more emphasis on *subjective* intentions. Then the child who did not mean to break the cups is excused, while the one who was deliberately disobeying or who intentionally spilled ink or stole candy in a store becomes the more guilty one. Piaget argues that the answers children gave to his stories express "two distinct moral attitudes—one that judges actions according to their material consequences, and one that takes only intentions into account. These two attitudes may co-exist at the same age and even in the same child, but broadly speaking, they do not synchronize. Objective responsibility diminishes on the average as the child grows older, and subjective responsibility gains correlatively in importance."[5]

The same developmental process can be seen in children's attitudes toward lying and stealing. The youngest children Piaget questioned did not even know what a lie was. It was "words you mustn't say"; "naughty words"; "when you talk nonsense." In other words, a lie is something parents don't approve of. Piaget found that by about seven children knew that a lie was an untruth. However, they still did not always discriminate between a deliberate lie and an error.

The following is Piaget's account of interviews with two youngsters:

Mab (6): "What is a lie?—*When you talk nonsense.*—You tell me about something that is a lie.—*A boy once said he was a little angel, and it wasn't true.*—Why did he say that?—*For a joke.*—Are we allowed to tell lies?—*No.*—Why not?—*Because it's a sin and God doesn't want us to sin.*—A boy told me that 2 + 2 = 5. Is it true? —*No, it makes 4.*—Was it a lie or did he make a mistake?—*He made a mistake.*—Is making a mistake the same as telling a lie or different? —*The same.*—Look at me. I'm 30. A boy told me I was 60. Was it a lie or did he make a mistake?—*It was a lie.*—Why?—*Because what he said was a sin.*—Which is naughtiest, to make a mistake or to tell a lie?—*Both the same.*"

Chap (7): "What is a lie?—*What isn't true, what they say that they haven't done.*—Guess how old I am.—*Twenty.*—No, I'm thirty. Was it a lie what you told me?—*I didn't do it on purpose.*—I know. But is it a lie all the same, or not?—*Yes, it is all the same, because I didn't say how old you really were.*—Is it a lie?—*Yes, because I didn't speak the truth.*—Ought you to be punished?—*No.*—Was it naughty or not naughty?—*Not so very naughty.*—Why?—*Because I spoke the truth afterwards!*"[6]

Many of the younger children evaluated lies objectively; the bigger the story, the worse the sin. The same held true of stealing: a boy who stole a roll was worse than a girl who stole a ribbon in the companion story, because "rolls cost more"; or "the roll is bigger than the ribbon." A very clear indication of how objective responsibility arises out of constraints exercised by adults is seen in the children's feeling that you mustn't tell lies "because you get punished." Piaget told one story in which two children each broke a cup and lied about their responsibility. One mother believed her child and didn't punish him; the other mother did. "Are both lies that they told equally naughty?" asked Piaget. "No," said some children. "Which is the naughtiest?" "The one who was punished," came the answer. Piaget also reported that a little girl at the Maison des Petits told a lie and was asked by her teacher if that was right. "It doesn't matter," said the child. "My mummy can't see."

Gradually, however, children's attitudes toward lies show progress in the direction of mutual trust and respect. From being wrong because it is "naughty" and the object of punishment, a lie becomes something wrong in itself; the bigger the lie, the worse the wrong. Finally, a lie is seen as wrong because it is in conflict with mutual trust and understanding. The children realize that what is bad about a lie is that "you can't believe in it." As one ten-year-old expressed it, "You can't trust people any more."

According to Piaget, the early stage of moral realism is a "natural and spontaneous product of child thought." It is closely related to the realism in nature that we discussed in chapter 6. If clouds move because they "must hurry" and the sun shines in the day because it is "not allowed" out at night, it is only a short step to the moral realism we have described; children must clean up their plates and brush their teeth and not disobey their parents. The morality is in the external rules, just as the lie is in being caught. Thus the parents are the source of moral realism; and the stricter the parents, the greater the objective responsibility the child feels. And as Piaget says, "The majority of parents are poor psychologists and give their children the most questionable of moral trainings. It is perhaps in this domain that one realizes most keenly how immoral it can be to believe too much in morality, and how much more precious is a little humanity than all the rules in the world."[7]

How then do children develop from a morality based on parental constraint to one based on mutual cooperation? To cast light upon this question, Piaget takes up the development of the idea of justice in punishment. For he notes that "it is often at the expense of the adult and not because of him that the notions of just and unjust find their way into the youthful mind."[8] Children, particularly after they enter school, develop a strong sense of solidarity with their peer group. They stand united against what they consider "unfair," and those who are "tattletales" soon find themselves excommunicated from the group. And this is precisely the age at which "the equalitarian notion of justice begins to assert itself with sufficient strength to overcome the authority of the adult."[9]

Piaget began his study of justice in his usual disarming way. "You know," he said, "it isn't at all easy to know how to punish children so as to be quite fair. Lots of fathers and teachers don't know how to. So I thought I would ask the children themselves, you and your friends. I shall tell you all sorts of silly things that little children have done, and you'll tell me how you think they ought to be punished."[10] Then he told a story of some childish misbehavior, followed by three possible punishments. He asked his listeners how they would have punished the young offender, and analyzed the results.

The earliest concept of justice, Piaget found, was based on retribution. The child who has misbehaved must be punished, and to the younger children the fairest punishment is the most severe. It may be an arbitrary kind of punishment, which bears no relation to the misdeed (being spanked or deprived of some outing) but makes expiation for it. Or the punishment may grow out of the consequences of the misdeed, such as being put to bed when one has pretended to be ill; this Piaget called *punishment by reciprocity.* The older children favored the latter, which would include the ancient Talon Law, "An eye for an eye and a tooth for a tooth." The younger ones, at least in discussing *other* children, favored the most strict or painful expiatory punishment. As one child said, "He ought to be stopped doing what he liked doing best."[11]

Piaget felt that these two attitudes toward punishment corresponded to the two levels of morality. Adult constraints produce expiatory punishment based on the objective degree of damage; but punishment based on equality and mutual cooperation is reciprocal and takes motives and subjective responsibility into consideration. There even comes a time in this latter stage when children feel that punishment is not necessary, that explanation is sufficient "because I can understand much better when people explain things to me," as one boy put it.

In studying children's attitudes toward justice, Piaget came across an interesting phenomenon. He found among young children the notion that justice is immanent in the natural order of things; that knives cut children who have been forbidden to use them or that old bridges give way under children who cross them to steal apples. This would seem to be a residue of the magic omnipotence of early childhood (see chap. 6). As Piaget puts it,

. . . it seems quite natural to the child that a fault should automatically bring about its own punishment. For nature, in the child's eyes, is not a system of blind forces regulated by mechanical laws operating on the principle of chance. Nature is a harmonious whole, obeying laws that are as much moral as physical and that are above all penetrated down to the least detail with an anthropomorphic or even egocentric finalism. It therefore seems quite natural to little children that night should come in order to put us to sleep, and that the act of going to bed is sufficient to set in motion that great black cloud that produces darkness. It seems quite natural to them that their movements should command those of the heavenly bodies (the moon follows us in order to take care of us). In short, there is life and purpose in everything. Why then should not things be the accomplices of grownups in making sure that a punishment is inflicted where the parents' vigilance may have been evaded?[12]

From the age of about eight on, this early belief in *immanent justice* tends to disappear slowly, though occasionally we find traces of it among uneducated people, or those religious individuals who say, "God is punishing you." Children who masturbate often have fantasies that their health or their intelligence may be affected as a result of their forbidden habits. Piaget cites the case of his psychiatrist friend who had a vivid childhood memory of the cover of a basket unexpectedly closing on his hand when he was reaching inside for apples. He was doing no wrong, but he was immediately overcome with a sense of guilt and felt that he was being caught and punished. Piaget feels that "belief in immanent justice originates . . . in a transference to things of feelings acquired under the influence of adult constraint."[13] As the child grows older and sees that "wickedness may go unpunished and virtue remain unrewarded," his belief in immanent justice gradually fades away.

We have already discussed the second stage of *retributive justice,* during which children believe punishment is the necessary retribution for disobeying their elders. As they grow older and form groups in school they learn to put equality of treatment and mutual cooperation above punishment and to be more aware of individual motives and circumstances. These are the youngsters who make allowances for the clumsiness of little children or for those who are doing something wrong for the sake of someone else. Piaget feels that most children by eleven or twelve years of age have progressed to this third or final phase of *distributive justice*. This consists of taking account of varying degrees of responsibility—not only inner motives but factors such as age and experience. Youngsters who have reached this stage will give little children who are just learning a game an extra try or overlook accidental errors.

Piaget closes his study of morality with an interesting sociological analysis of how morality based on cooperation can develop out of a childhood morality based on parental authoritarianism. As we have already seen, children are basically egocentric; their understanding of right and wrong is based on their own distorted perceptions and a reification of their parents' commands. But in the course of all the spontaneous give and take that occurs within families and among playmates, children gradually move outside their egocentrism and come to see another person's point of view. They begin to think of right and wrong in terms of the circumstances of the person involved rather than in terms of retributive justice. Just as the mountain looked different to Laurent when he saw it from another perspective, so moral sanctions appear different in differing circumstances. Adult authority is not sufficient to create in children a true sense of justice. As Piaget points out, this is a situation which is not in equilibrium and therefore cannot be stable. The adult is strong and demanding; the child feels weak and inferior. Unilateral respect leads only to moral constraint. The factor essential to moral development is mutual respect and cooperation—"cooperation between children to begin with, and then between child and adult as the child approaches adolescence, and comes, secretly at least, to consider himself as the adult's equal."[14]

Piaget thus leads us to see that it is the growth of strong moral solidarity among grade school children that brings about equilibrium, an equilibrium based on mutual respect and consideration. Wise parents and teachers have always been aware of this, and by being gentle, considerate, and fair with children, have achieved much happier results than those who ruled by authority. In these days, when discipline is a major problem in our schools, educators and counselors would do well to read *The Moral Judgment of the Child*, especially the last chapter. If young people can come to see that the need for "law and order" is as much theirs as their elders', the generations can learn to work together in mutual respect, cooperation, and harmony.

Piaget did not continue with his studies of moral growth, but his work has been taken up by others, principally Lawrence Kohlberg of Harvard.[15] Kohlberg has extended Piaget's studies into the young adult years and has been able to describe three additional moral stages beyond Piaget's three stages of childhood. These culminate in the construction of universal ethical principles of justice, equality, and respect for the dignity of all human beings. Out of this work has grown a new interest in developmental moral education and "values clarification" in the schools. Students at all age levels have been involved in class groups to discuss moral dilemmas and to make judgments regarding their own discipline. The goals of these discussions have been to encourage the active cooperation of the students and give them the experience of governing themselves. Children, we have found, must construct their own moral standards in the same way that they develop their own logical understandings. "In the moral as well as in the intellectual domain," says Piaget, "we really possess only what we have conquered ourselves."[16]

14. Emotional Development

Piaget says comparatively little about the child's emotional life, and he scatters his observations in paragraphs or short chapters here and there in his books. In comparison with most modern theories of personality, his ideas are limited and inadequate. In his search for the universal structures of intelligence, he has not been interested in individual differences, nor in the impact of personal emotions on mental development. As a result, he has obviously given much less thought to this aspect of personality than he has to cognitive or even perceptual functioning. However, his statements are worth thinking about, and so we present them for consideration.

Piaget does not overlook or deny the importance of feelings—*affects* is the term he uses—but he has focused his interest primarily on the growth of intelligence, which he views as central in the life of each person. He concedes, however, that every intelligent act is accompanied by feelings (of interest, pleasure, effort, etc.) and that these feeling provide the motivation, the energy that sparks intellectual growth. Emotion is what makes intelligence dynamic, directed, ever seeking a better equilibrium; emotion and intelligence are two sides of the same coin. "What common sense calls 'feelings' and 'intelligence,' regarding them as two opposed 'faculties,' are simply behavior relating to persons and behavior affecting ideas or things; but in each of these forms of behavior, the same affective and cognitive aspects of action emerge, aspects which are in fact always associated and in no way represent independent faculties."[1]

For Piaget, then, every action involves a structural or cognitive aspect and an energetic or affective aspect. The two are not causally related, but their development is parallel. "Just as there is no purely cognitive state, there is no purely affective state."[2] Intelligence provides the structure for actions while feelings provide the dynamics. Since the two are interdependent, emotional development requires the same continuing process of adaptation as cognitive development. Emotions have to assimilate new situations from the outer world and accommodate to them to create new "affective schemes," or ways of responding. If a baby finds a person who loves him, he grows affectionate toward that person; if he meets rejection or hostility, he develops aggressive tendencies. But even these emotional responses involve intelligence and reasoning. "Personal schemes, like all others, are both intellectual and affective. We do not love without seeking to understand, and we do not even hate without a subtle use of judgment. Thus when we speak of 'affective schemes' it must be understood that what is meant is merely the affective aspect of schemes which are also intellectual."[3]

In one of his papers, Piaget traces the parallel between emotional and intellectual life throughout childhood and adolescence.[4] He consistently refers to the motivational aspects of behavior (interest, curiosity, will, determination) and the value systems (moral standards, ideals, goals, aspirations) as part of emotional life. So in describing the emotional life of the infant, Piaget includes not only the primary emotional reflexes of love, rage, and fear but also the instinctive strivings of the infant for food, comfort, and mastery. He shows how the growing baby strives to achieve pleasure and avoid pain through his sensory-motor actions, thereby gratifying his own body and his primitive ego, which is not even aware of other people at this point.

The whole development of object permanence (including person permanence), which we have previously discussed, is here very closely related to Freud's concept of "object-choice." As the baby realizes that his mother exists as a separate person and that she is the source of food, warmth, dry diapers, and all his primitive gratifications, he comes to depend more on her and less on himself. He turns from narcissistic self-interest to increased awareness of his mother, and then of others in his external world. His mother becomes his first love-object—or "object-choice," to use psychoanalytic terminology. Awareness of her as a "permanent" person leads him to construct the permanence of objects. Thus through her he learns to differentiate between himself and external reality, not only intellectually as we have already discussed, but emotionally as well. He becomes interested in pleasing her (the dawn of motivation) and aware of her moods, which he reflects. This is the beginning of the child's emotional as well as his intellectual life.

At this point we must discuss Piaget's use of the word "ego." He speaks of the ego as the primitive sense of self, not as selfish but simply unaware of others and their points of view. Egocentrism is not the same as egotism, as we have pointed out before. But in describing the primitive ego of babies, he seems to be referring to what Freud calls the "id"—the lowest level of consciousness, concerned with primary gratification and primitive emotions.[5]

At the preoperational level, Piaget describes an emerging sense of self-in-relation-to-others, which more nearly fits the Freudian definition of "ego." The child at this period, he says, acquires new interests and values, shows emerging moral sentiments, and develops interpersonal emotions beyond the range of his immediate family. His newly developing interests are an outgrowth of the primitive needs of babyhood, extended now to include interest in drawing pictures, in learning new words, and in all the symbolic activities that are part of his intellectual growth at this stage.

The amount of interest and motivation that the child shows is closely connected with his self-image. If the image of himself that he sees reflected back to him in his mother's eyes, in his family's attitudes, in the way he is treated by other children, is warm and positive, he will see himself as a "good" person. The way he behaves, the confidence with which he tackles new problems, the interest he shows in learning new things—all are a function of his self-image. His attitude about himself is reflected in his emotional responses to other people. He may be a happy, loving, outgoing youngster, quick to sympathize with others, willing to share his toys and get along with his playmates. Or he may be anxious, sullen, withdrawn, or hostile, thereby expressing his anger and fear at the way the world has treated him. The child's motivation to learn and to achieve is inevitably affected by his emotional environment.

We have seen in our discussion of the morality of the young child that respect for adults is the source of the earliest moral feelings. Respect, says Piaget, "consists of affection and fear, and fear is the reason for the inequality in such an affective relationship."[6] Thus lies to adults are prohibited, but not lies to one's playmates. This is the morality of constraint, which we have discussed; rules are made by adults and justice is based on the Talon Law. Adults, at this period of a child's life, are extremely important to his emotional and moral development.

This importance slowly declines, however, as youngsters enter the middle years of childhood. As they become intellectually capable of seeing another person's point of view, they also become emotionally empathetic. "Cooperation among individuals coordinates their points of view into a reciprocity which assures both the autonomy of the individual and the cohesion of the group."[7] Mutual respect among youngsters changes their moral feelings: rules depend on cooperation, and justice becomes "distributive." One who lies to his peers or tattles on them now becomes a social outcast. The morality of cooperation, a higher form of equilibrium, has at this stage replaced the morality of submission to authority.

The other hallmark of this stage of emotional development, says Piaget, is the appearance of *will power*. Will is the final outgrowth of childish needs and interests. Piaget compares its function to that of logical operations; it represents a stable equilibrium of organized emotions. When there is a conflict of emotions (the desire for pleasure, for example, as opposed to the demands of duty), will power reinforces "the superior but weaker tendency so as to make it triumph."[8] As such, it is a regulator of energy, reinforcing the superior choice just as logical reasoning reinforces the correct deduction that is in conflict with perceptual appearance. Thus, will power helps one stay on a diet when tempted by chocolate cake, just as logic helps one to know that a ball of clay remains the same, no matter how much larger it looks when flattened out.

In adolescence, Piaget finds the major emotional achievements are the development of personality and of ideals. He more or less dismisses the emotional changes brought on by puberty and says that the fundamental problem of adolescence is that the individual begins to take up adult roles. This means he has to discipline himself to goals and ideals. For Piaget, "personality is the submission of the ego to an ideal which it embodies but which goes beyond it and subordinates it."[9] A strong personality is one that is able to discipline the ego by opposing it. Whereas the ego is self-centered, personality is "the decentered ego."

What Piaget is saying here is that the child has a limited ability to understand and cooperate with others. He relates to his own peers and comprehends concrete experiences such as personal unhappiness he may have suffered. But he is unable to relate to humanity as a whole or to comprehend abstract ideals such as patriotism or social justice. That is why full personality, according to Piaget's definition, does not emerge until adolescence, although it has its roots in the development of will during middle childhood. The child is not capable of constructing theories and analyzing his own thinking. Nor is he much concerned about people outside of his own familiar circle. But the adolescent can think beyond the present and the familiar, to build political ideologies or philosophical systems. He is a dreamer of dreams, a righter of wrongs, a defender of civil liberties and political freedom. He tends to have nothing but contempt for the society that produced him, and sometimes his plans are tinged with megalomania. He may attribute to himself an essential role in the salvation of humanity, or take part in radical movements, as do some students in every generation.

The cure for the adolescent's untempered idealism, says Piaget, is work—"effective enduring work, undertaken in concrete and well-defined situations, cure[s] all dreams."[10] Just as experience reconciles hypothetical possibilities with the practical reality of things, so professional work restores equilibrium and "marks the advent of adulthood." Piaget's words were written in 1940, but his message is relevant today. "One should not be disquieted by the extravagance and disequilibrium of the better part of adolescence. . . . True adaptation to society comes automatically when the adolescent reformer attempts to put his ideas to work."[11]

In recent years there has been a marked increase of interest in Piaget's work among neo-Freudian ego psychologists. While Piaget's theory lacks a theory of personality and emotional development, Freudian theory lacks a strong theory of intellectual development. There have been a number of attempts to reconcile the two theories, thus strengthening them both. The works of Wolff, Gouin-Décarie, Anthony, and Weiner have all made strides in this direction. Most recently, the comprehensive "developmental structuralist" approach of Stanley I. Greenspan is an impressive attempt to integrate both emotional and cognitive development within the same frame of reference.[12] Such an approach makes it possible to understand individual differences, not considered in Piaget's "elegant normative theory,"[13] and to comprehend the whole person rather than his separate facets. Piaget seems to welcome such efforts; as he said in a lecture several years ago before the American Society of Psychoanalysis, "I am convinced that there will be a time when the psychology of the cognitive functions and psychoanalysis will have to blend into a general theory which will improve both by correcting each."[14] It is this higher equilibrium of dynamic and developmental psychologies that is the goal of much current research in the field of emotional development.

15. Numbers

Piaget's theory has had its greatest impact upon the teaching of mathematics and science in the elementary school. Particularly in the area of mathematics, the old rote learning methods have left scars for life. There must be thousands of adults today who say, "I never could do math," or "I hated arithmetic and I never understood algebra." But their children are learning through practical problem solving: How many children in this room are boys? How many are girls? Are there more boys or more girls? How many more are there? How can we find out? When the children have counted fifteen boys and twelve girls, the teacher may ask them to construct a row of Unifex blocks (colorful snap-on plastic cubes) to represent each sex and then figure out how many more boys there are than girls. (The row of fifteen is three blocks longer than the row of twelve.)

There are many other kinds of manipulative materials that help to teach arithmetic. Some teachers utilize dried pumpkin seeds at Halloween; toothpicks, tongue depressors, pipe cleaners, small uncooked pasta and dried beans are also used. Later on, pictorial representations such as graphs are used to express arithmetic relationships symbolically. The children count cars in the school parking lot, for example, and make a graph with a red block for each red car, blue blocks for blue cars, and so forth. Looking at the graph tells them in symbolic form which car color predominates, and by how much, over its competitors. The aim of such representations is to lead children to *think* about math, and to construct the operations that will help them solve technical and practical problems. Once they understand what they are doing, the algorisms of arithmetic can be memorized as convenient shortcuts to solutions already worked out on concrete objects.

In spite of past changes that may have been too radical (such as some concepts introduced in the "new math"), Piaget has been, says an English mathematician, "the major influence on recent attempts to reconsider the nature of the mathematical experiences provided for children in primary schools."[1] He has brought about a greater concern for concept development and for concrete action with manipulative materials. For half a century he has been quietly pointing out that "knowing is action on objects," and that lack of experience with concrete materials leads to inadequate mental operations and inadequate development of the abstractions required for more advanced mathematics. Piaget feels that children in the classroom suffer from "cognitive passivity": they need to take a more active part in discovering facts and constructing relationships. He has shown over and over again how sensory-motor structures gradually become internalized and reintegrated to form intellectual structures, how logical-mathematical relationships such as number are not inherent in the materials but are constructed in the mind of the child (see chap. 2). By actively grouping objects into separate classes or arranging them in serial order, children integrate the one-to-one sequence of numbers into sets that can be grouped in different ways: $6 = 3 + 3$ or $2 + 4$ or $5 + 1$. They come to realize that numbers can be reversed (by subtraction) or combined (by addition) and that they have the group structure characteristic of the logical groups discussed in chapter 7 (combinativity, associativity, identity, and reversibility). Thus, the construction of number goes along with the construction of logic in the child's mental development; number operations grow out of simple overt activities such as counting beads, classifying objects, and seriating by length or height.

Piaget feels that, to a remarkable degree, children develop mathematical concepts independently and spontaneously. Parents may spend hours teaching a child to count, but what they are teaching him is mere rote verbalization. Everyone has had the experience of hearing a little child count "one, two, free, five, seven, ten." He knows the names of the numbers, but not what they mean or why they follow a particular order. Teachers who have worked with kindergarten and first-grade youngsters know how long it takes to construct number relationships, and how slow and difficult is the process of teaching arithmetic before the structure of number is understood. Piaget implies that there is no sense in rushing this process. The young child can deal only with small numbers, which he can understand intuitively. A three-year-old can usually recognize and count numbers up to three, a four-year-old up to four, and five-year-old up to five—these are perceptible figures, says Piaget. But "the indefinite series of numbers, and above all the operations of addition (plus its inverse, subtraction) and multiplication (plus its inverse, division), are, on the average, accessible only after the age of seven."[2] The reason for this, he points out, is that numbers are both cardinal (1, 2, 3, etc.) and ordinal (1st, 2d, 3d, etc.). This means that children must come to understand that a whole number represents not only a collection of equal units (3 = 3 units) but also a position in an ordered series (3 = 3d in a series). It is only after a great deal of concrete experience that the child grasps this dual concept of number and can understand the logic of the indefinite series of numbers. Here Piaget is repeating his arguments for learning by doing. We cannot teach the structure of numbers, he says; we can only create situations in which the child can discover these structures for himself, thus reinventing number relationships.

Before the concept of numbers can develop the child must construct the principle of one-to-one correspondence. He must count each object once, and only once. Next comes the notion of conservation of quantity. Seven pebbles are seven pebbles, no matter how they are arranged. When children realize that quantity is conserved despite changes in appearance, they are ready to accept the fact that the number of objects in a group does not vary, no matter how they are arranged. We have already discussed the experiments with buttons, in which youngsters presented with two equal rows of buttons no longer judged them equal if one row was spread out or pushed close together to change its length (see page 36). We have also seen that the next step was the development of a one-to-one correspondence between the two rows. Finally, the older children realized that the numbers in each row were the same, however spaced. "Once you know, you know for always," as we have quoted before.

Piaget, in his book with Szeminska, *The Child's Conception of Number*, shows how the distinction between cardinal and ordinal numbers grows very gradually out of many experiences of ordering sets of objects in a one-to-one relationship. Such a process is fundamental to the construction of number, since it provides the simplest and most direct measurement of the equivalence of two sets. Piaget had his children match bottles to glasses, by emptying each bottle into a corresponding glass. Then he had them put flowers into vases; only he discovered that some youngsters put more than one flower in a vase! So he switched to eggs and egg cups, and again found the same three stages: the first, in which the sets were not seen as equal; the second, in which there was an intuitive kind of correspondence based on perceptual judgment; and the last, in which the sets were seen as equal in number regardless of changes in grouping.

> Lau (6;2) made 6 glasses correspond to 6 bottles. The glasses were then grouped together: "Are they still the same? *Yes, it's the same number of glasses. You've only put them close together, but it's still the same number.* And now, are there more bottles (grouped) or more glasses (spaced out)? *They're still the same. You've only put the bottles close together.*"[3]

Next Piaget posed a problem in which the child had to pick out a number of objects to match a set supplied by the experimenter. He might be shown a row of five beans, or six identical counters arranged in the form of a hexagon. He would be given a box of beans or counters and told, "Pick out the same number." The younger children would say, "I don't know how many there are," or "I don't know how to do it." The transitional children would take a guess at the number or construct a figure that looked like the model but usually contained more than six counters. A more advanced child would break up the figures and arrange them in a row which he could match up to his counters. One child, shown a collection of eleven counters, took fourteen out of the box, one or two at a time, and matched them up to eleven. Then he put the last three back. Piaget pointed out that this freedom from perception (the collection of eleven looked much like the pile of fourteen) marked the beginning of operational thinking.

Interestingly, Piaget found that counting aloud had little influence on convincing a child of the equivalence of two sets until he already operationally understood equal quantities. "At the point at which correspondence becomes quantifying," he wrote, ". . . counting aloud may no doubt hasten the process of evolution. Our only contention is that the process is not begun by numerals as such."[4]

In these experiments we see that the concept of cardinal numbers grows out of an ordered relationship, one that can be counted. The only way to tell one counter or one bean from another is to put it either before or after the other in time and space. Thus the order of enumeration develops out of the one-to-one correspondence of equivalent sets. But cardinal numbers do not precede ordinal ones, Piaget found. Rather, they develop side by side. When dealing with beans or counters or any other set formed of similar elements, the only thing that distinguishes one element from another is its position. The fourth bean is just like the fifth bean except that it *is* the fourth bean; in fact the beans can be arranged in any order, provided there is an order such that each bean is counted once and only once.

But when the elements of a set differ in respect to some characteristic such as length or width, they can be arranged in a series determined by that characteristic. In such a case, the ordinal position of each element is important; the smallest element must always be at one end of the series and the largest at the other. Piaget studied the development of this notion of ordinal correspondence by providing ten wooden dolls of clearly differing heights, the tallest being twice the height of the shortest. He also provided ten sticks, graded in size but with less difference between them, to be matched to the dolls. He told each subject that the dolls were going for a walk, and asked him to give each doll the walking stick that belonged to it. Once the two series were arranged to correspond in height, Piaget would reverse or disarrange the sticks and then, randomly picking up a doll, would ask which stick belonged to this particular doll. The child had to have a concept of ordination to be able to match the third longest stick, for instance, with the third tallest doll.

The youngest children, as might be expected, arranged the objects every which way, with no systematic correspondence. Sometimes they matched the tallest or shortest units, but not the rest. Then came progressive intuitive attempts at constructing a series on the basis of perception alone. Finally, the youngsters were able to match up the two series immediately, showing an operational understanding of the correspondence of sizes between them. Piaget noted that there were three ways of going about this. The children might line the dolls up first by height, then line up the sticks, and then put each stick with the corresponding doll. Or they might line up just the dolls, and then pick a stick for each doll, beginning with the smallest, and then the smallest of those remaining, etc. The third way involved just visual judgment; the child would pick up the smallest doll, and then the smallest stick, thus proceeding to build the two series simultaneously, without any previous clues! Here the children were constructing a double asymmetrical series of the type discussed under multiplication of relations (see chap. 7), which Piaget represented by the following formula:

$$A < B < C < D$$
$$\downarrow \quad \downarrow \quad \downarrow \quad \downarrow$$
$$A_1 < B_1 < C_1 < D_1$$

When the serial order of the sticks was reversed or disarranged, Piaget found that preschool children were bewildered and chose whatever stick happened to be opposite a given doll. Transitional children tried to discover the correct correspondence by counting, or by perceptually judging the relative sizes. Both of these methods proved inaccurate; when the children counted they consistently made a mistake of one unit. For example, in trying to locate the fifth doll, a child might count the four preceding it and say, "There are four in front." Then he would count the sticks, 1, 2, 3, 4, and announce that the fourth stick belonged with the fifth doll. The most advanced children were those who had no problems in dealing with a double series.

Piaget attributed the lack of coordination in the transitional stage to the fact that ordination was not yet fully operational. Ordination depends on position in a series; when the series was disarranged the child could not reestablish the correct serial correspondence, and thus turned to cardinal correspondence or counting. He was going by the number of the sticks leading to the doll's position, rather than the length of the stick that would correspond to the doll's height.

This confusion between cardinal and ordinal numbers when the series of dolls was disarranged led Piaget to another very interesting experiment. He gave each subject a set of ten sticks of gradually increasing lengths (signified by capital letters A to K; Piaget omits the letter J) and asked him to put them in serial order. When this was done, he gave the child another series of nine sticks (a to i) of lengths that fitted between the sticks of the first series as follows: $A \ a \ B \ b \ C \ c \ D \ d \ E \ e \ F \ f \ G \ g \ H \ h \ I \ i \ K$. These intermediate sticks were given to the child one at a time, in random order, and he was asked to insert each one in its correct place in the first series. When that was done, Piaget asked him to count the whole series. Depending upon how far he could count without hesitation, Piaget now shortened the series of sticks; if the child stumbled at ten, Piaget left only eight sticks in front of him so that he was confronted with a group of sticks only as large as he could cope with.

Then Piaget brought out a little doll and told the child to make the doll climb the stairs (represented by the increasing lengths of the sticks). When the doll was on the fifth stair, for example, Piaget would stop the child and ask how many stairs the doll had already climbed and how many he had left to climb. This experiment demonstrated very cleverly whether the child understood the relation of

Figure 21

A a B b C c D d E e F f G g H h I i K

ordinal to cardinal numbers; the doll on the fifth stair must have already climbed four stairs (ordinal position minus 1), and must have three stairs left to go (total number of stairs minus number of ordinal position). The last step in the experiment was to disarrange the series of sticks and then randomly pick out a stair and ask the same questions—how many came before it and after it?

The results were very enlightening to anyone interested in how children's number concepts develop. The preschool children could not even construct the first series of ten. They could pick out the smallest stick, but "biggest" meant any big stick, independently of its relationship to the other sticks. Another characteristic, which we shall see again in considering the development of time and speed, is that these little children paid attention to only one end of the sticks at a time, so that they constructed a staircase by serializing the tops of the sticks, without regard to the bottoms, or the base line.

Lil (4;0): "Show me the smallest step. (She pointed to the right one.) Now find one that's a tiny bit bigger than that one. (She picked out a big one and put it next to A.) Show me the biggest. (She pointed at random to a big one without attempting to compare it with others.) Now try to put first the smallest, then one a little bit bigger, then another a little bit bigger, and so on. (Lil took I and put it next to A, then E, then H, etc., regardless of order.) We put them like this, look (A, B, C). They make a kind of staircase. Now you go on. (Lil continued with K, F, D, I, G, disregarding the order.) *Like that?*" Having reached this point Lil discovered a procedure, characteristic of this stage, for making a staircase. She took stick B, then stick H, but made the top of B project slightly beyond that of H without paying any attention to the base. She then added K, F, D, I, G, etc., making a series only with the tops. She was then asked to begin again, but with a ruler as base to ensure that the sticks were placed horizontally. She made the series A, C, H, G, E. This was disarranged and the whole staircase constructed and then broken up, and Lil was asked to remake it. She placed the sticks in the order A, B, C, D, H, F, E, G.[5]

Here we have a fine example of what Piaget calls the "global" approach of the preconceptual child. There is no analysis of details or understanding of what the situation calls for—merely a manipulative, sometimes bewildered, attempt to do what the experimenter asks. In the second stage we see what Piaget calls a "perceptual reading of the situation." By trial and error, depending on visual judgment, the child gropes his way toward a correct solution. In the following example we even see "the dawning of relativity"; the child compares stick *D* with each of the others in order to ascertain its correct relative position. But when it comes to the questions about the doll, he has to reconstruct the whole staircase, in order to count how many stairs have been climbed. Like most transitional children, when asked how many stairs are left to be climbed, he is unable to separate out those already climbed from the total.

San (5;0): I. He chose correctly the smallest and biggest sticks then arranged A, B, C. When he came to D, he compared it with each of the others in turn, even the biggest, and put it after C. Sticks E-K were then seriated with some trial and error, the corrections being made in the series itself.

II. He correctly inserted *i* before K, then compared *e* to E, F, D, E, then to all the others in the row before putting it in position. He did the same with *g*. When he had put *h* before G he cried: *"No, that's not right, it's too difficult."*

III. He counted correctly up to 9. Eight elements were left and he counted them correctly.

IV. The sticks were disarranged and San pointed to steps A, *b* and B as having been climbed when the doll had got to C (forgetting *a*). For the steps preceding D he reconstructed the whole staircase, and for the steps still to be climbed he pointed to the whole series.[6]

Despite the fact that transitional children can construct the original series, the difficulty that they have with inserting the new elements proves that they are functioning intuitively rather than logically; they are depending on perceptual comparison rather than mental operation. Here is an excellent example of how rigid and unstable is the solution based on perception and intuition, whereas thinking based on logical operations is flexible, reversible, and stable. Piaget points out that sometimes transitional children can construct a series so efficiently that they seem almost to be operating logically; but when faced with a double series, as in the insertion of a to i, they not only make mistakes but are satisfied with the incorrect results. This, for Piaget, is the proof of the perceptual pudding.

The truly operational child, by contrast, constructs his series with the full understanding that each stick is longer than the one that precedes it and shorter than the one that follows. When faced with the insertion of sticks of intermediate length, he does not regard them as "foreign bodies," but can flexibly assimilate them into his scheme. Most difficult of all, he knows without counting just how many steps the doll has climbed, because he understands the relationship between the doll's Nth position, and the $N - 1$ steps the doll has already climbed. He knows also that the doll's ordinal position, Nth, corresponds to a cardinal number, N, which can be subtracted from the total (T) number of steps $(T - N)$ to give the number of steps remaining to be climbed. All of this indicates, says Piaget, that "the child has reached a level where both logical and numerical operations are possible."[7]

There are more experiments in this series, and they should be read by every primary teacher. Piaget used cards to form a staircase, with equal units marked off on each card to develop the idea of numbers as consisting of units, each integer one unit greater than the preceding one. To dissociate the ordinal number from the cardinal, he devised a succession of hurdles. Each hurdle required a mat before it and a mat after it, for the jumper to land on. This meant that his subjects had to deal with N hurdles and $N + 1$ mats in answering questions about the ordinal number (Nth) of each hurdle which required a cardinal number $(N + 1)$ of mats. For example, if a child were shown the fourth hurdle and could correctly respond that five mats were required to construct the series to that point (one behind and one in front of each hurdle) he would clearly be able to dissociate ordinal (fourth hurdle) from cardinal (five mats) numbers and to handle both series correctly. The results of these experiments, says Piaget, show "the victory of operation over intuition: in both cases the child coordinates beforehand all the relations involved, because operational composition triumphs over perception, or rather, because the latter is from now on controlled by the former."[8]

Piaget's experiments to illustrate the development of arithmetical processes are similar to the ones we have described under the logical groupings of concrete operations. He discusses the stumbling block presented by problems of part-whole relations, such as in the well-known experiment with brown and white wooden beads (see chap. 7). He found his youngest subjects so resistant to the realization that the brown beads were also wooden beads that he devised more experiments of this type. As the following example shows, he found it extraordinarily difficult for the young child to understand the inclusion of classes within larger classes; e.g., poppies and bluebells are flowers.

Arl (5;0): "Look, are there a lot of flowers or a few in this field (a drawing representing 20 poppies and 3 bluebells)? *A lot.* What color are they? *They're red and blue.* The red ones are poppies and the blue ones are bluebells. *Yes.* I want to make a very big bunch. Must I pick the flowers or the poppies? *The poppies.* Show me the poppies. (She pointed correctly.) Show me the flowers. (She made a circular movement to indicate the whole of the drawing.) Then will the bunch be bigger if I pick the flowers or the poppies? *If you pick the poppies.* If I pick the poppies, what will be left? *The bluebells.* And if I pick the bluebells, what will be left? *The poppies.* And if I pick the flowers, what will be left? (Reflection.) *Nothing at all.* Then which will be bigger, the bunch of flowers or the bunch of poppies? *I've told you already.* Think (repeating the question). *The bunch of poppies will be bigger.* And what about the bunch of flowers? *It won't be the same.* Will it be bigger or smaller? *Smaller.* Why? *Because you've made a big bunch of poppies.*"[9]

Only by trial and error, Piaget found, did transitional children come to a full understanding of problems such as this; and it was not until about seven years of age that they could construct what Piaget calls the additive composition of classes: $A + A' = B$, $B - A' = A$.

Here Piaget drew the distinction between logical groupings and mathematical groups. Classes may be grouped inclusively, but numbers are grouped quantitatively. In other words, wooden beads may include brown ones, white ones, red, green, and yellow ones; they all belong to the class of wooden beads. $A + A' = B$ is not a quantitative relationship; it is simply inclusive. We have no way of knowing whether A (brown beads) is greater than A' (white beads). On the other hand, one dozen brown beads plus one dozen white beads equals two dozen wooden beads: $A + A = 2A$. This is a precise quantitative relationship.

In such a relationship, the addition of numbers produces a new number; this process may be reversed by subtraction. Here we see the properties of *combinativity* $(2 + 2 = 4)$, *reversibility* $(4 - 2 = 2)$, and *identity* $(4 + 0 = 4)$ to which we referred earlier. We also referred to *associativity*, the fact that the sum of a series is independent of its order $(4 = 2 + 2$ or $1 + 3)$. Piaget studied children's understanding of this property of numbers by giving them eight candies, some to be eaten in the morning and some in the afternoon. For the first day Piaget gave out the candy in two piles of four candies (I); for the second day he gave the children seven candies for the morning and one in the afternoon (II). Then he questioned them to see if they understood the equivalence of the two sets.

An (6;11): "Is there the same amount there (I) and there (II)? *No. There's 1 there* (II) *and there are 4 there* (I). How many were there before here (II)? (The two sets of 4 were arranged again, then, before the child's eyes, 3 were taken from the first set and added to the 4 of the second.) Aren't they the same, these (II) and those (I)? *No. Now there's only 1 here* (II) *and there are 4 here* (I). Could we make them into 4 and 4 again here (II)? *Yes* (doing so). Will you have the same amount to eat on both days $(4 + 4$ and $4 + 4)$? *Yes.* And now (changing again to $7 + 1$)? *No, because there are less here* (II)."[10]

This youngster obviously did not conserve the quantity of number even when it was constructed before his eyes. Yet a slightly older child, watching the transformations intently, said in astonishment, "They're both the same!" When Piaget asked, "How did you find out?" he said, "I had a good look, and I saw that you could put three of those [7] here [I]," thus mentally reconstructing the 4 + 4 condition. From this stage it is not far to the logical reasoning of the concrete operational stage, which is even capable of correcting its own mistakes:

> Laur (7;3): "Will there be the same amount on both days? *Wait. There* (7 + 1) *they're not arranged the same as here* (4 + 4), *but they're the same, because here* (7) *there are the 3 from there* (I). How many will you eat? *There* (I) *4 and 4, and here, 1 at first and then the 5 others.* Why 5? *Because there are 3 more. Oh no! there are 7 there. There are 8 on both days."*[11]

In studying the multiplicative relations of numbers, Piaget used a number of the correspondence techniques we have already discussed: relating flowers to vases, eggs to egg cups, and so on. For example, he had children put blue flowers in each of ten vases, and then pink flowers in each vase, until they gradually developed the idea of two sets of ten, which could be extended to three or more sets of ten, using the ten vases as the original standard of equivalence. From having to count each set, the youngsters progressed to remembering from one day to the next, "They're the same. . . . I saw yesterday they were the same." Once the sets were seen as equivalent, a given set could be multiplied by any number; three or four or seventeen sets of flowers for the ten vases could be expressed by multiplying 3 or 4 or 17 × 10. Thus the notion of one-to-one correspondence is implicit in multiplication; the child will sooner or later become aware of multiplication as a way of establishing correspondence between several sets.

As we have seen before and shall see again (see chaps. 17 and 18), whenever the notion of equal units emerges, the concept of measurement is not far behind. Whether it be equal classes $(A = B = C,$ which is the same as $A + A + A = 3A$) or equal relations $(A <$

$B < C < D$ by a specified amount X, so that $A + X = B$ and $B + X = C$), once the difference between units is quantified, precise measurement is possible. To illustrate this process, Piaget turned to the various-sized glasses used in the experiments on the conservation of liquid (see chap. 5). Only this time the child was presented with two or three quantities of colored liquid in two or three containers of different shapes, so that he could not tell by looking at them which glasses contained more, less, or the same. There were some empty containers standing by, and Piaget waited to see how long it would take him to use one of them as a standard measure in discovering a solution to his problem.

As a corollary, the child was given a certain quantity of liquid in a wide, low container and asked to put the same amount into a tall, narrow one. While he experimented with pouring from one vessel to another with his standard container, the child discovered various additive and multiplicative relationships. For example, if the container (C) had to be filled twice to fill a wide low glass (L), then $L = 2C$. If only one container of liquid filled the tall thin glass (T), then obviously $C = T$ and $T = \frac{1}{2}L$. The solutions of problems such as these involved all the additive and multiplicative operations required to unite parts into a whole, to divide a whole into parts, to coordinate equivalences, and to multiply relationships. At the end of *The Child's Conception of Number*, Piaget points up again the relationships between logical groupings and mathematical groups. All that is necessary to make the multiplication of classes and relations equivalent to the multiplication of numbers is that the differences between classes, and between relations, be equalized. Once this is done, the differences between them, being equal, can be measured, quantified, added, multiplied, and subjected to all the properties of mathematical groups.

As we shall see once more in the studies of time, speed, and the geometry of space, Piaget feels that experiments in child psychology can often throw light on the logical development of scientific concepts. On the basis of the experiments we have been describing, Piaget takes issue with the famous British mathematician Bertrand Russell. According to Russell, he says, the notions of cardinal and ordinal number develop separately; cardinal number derives from the notion of class (a number would be a class made up of equivalent classes), whereas ordinal number develops from the logical relationships of order. But Piaget has shown that very young children make no distinction between cardinal and ordinal number, and that cardinal number as well as ordinal presupposes a relationship of order. His work in this area should be of great interest to all elementary teachers.

16. Space

In his study of the child's discovery of spatial relationships—his "spontaneous geometry"—Piaget points out that the order of development of geometrical concepts in the child seems to reverse the order of historical discovery. Euclidean geometry (concerned with figures, angles, etc.) was developed by the ancient Egyptians to help them relocate the boundaries of their fields after the yearly flooding of the Nile. Projective geometry, dealing with problems of perspective, appeared in the seventeenth century. Finally, in the nineteenth century, came topology, the study of spatial relationships and forms without size or shape. It deals with open and closed figures such as a simple closed curve that divides a plane into two regions, one inside the curve and one outside. The plane may be twisted, stretched, and distorted like a sheet of rubber, so that squares and triangles lose their shape and become merely rounded polygons. But the distinction between inside and outside, between open and closed figures, is not lost.

Children, says Piaget, grasp topological figures first. At the age of

Figure 22

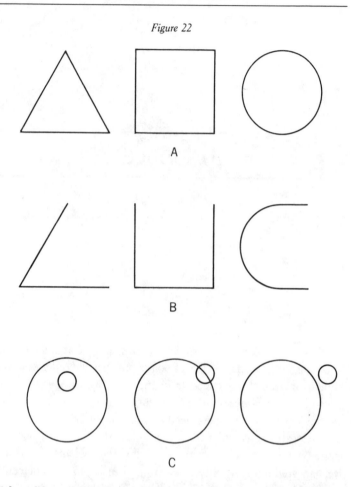

A

B

C

Adapted from Ripple and Rockcastle (eds.), *Piaget Rediscovered*, p.37.

three a child can distinguish between open and closed figures: if you ask him to copy a square or a triangle he will draw a closed circle (as in fig. 22*a*). If you show him open figures (as in fig. 22*b*), he will simply draw open curves. If you give him a circle to copy, with a smaller circle either inside or outside it, or attached to it (as in fig. 22*c*), he can reproduce this relationship quite adequately. But it is not until he is about five that he begins to draw a square and only later that he can copy accurately the number of sides and angles in a rectangle, as Euclidean geometry requires. According to Piaget, the child begins to develop the notions of Euclidean and projective geometry simultaneously, some time after he has mastered topological relationships. "Curiously enough," writes Piaget, "this psychological order is much closer to modern geometry's order of deductive or axiomatic construction than the historical order of discovery was. It offers another example of the kinship between psychological construction and the logical construction of science itself."[1]

To show how children develop projective constructions, Piaget and his associates* set up little sticks stuck into lumps of modeling clay that they called "fence posts." They set two posts on a table about fifteen inches apart and asked their subjects to place other posts in a straight line between them. A young child would approach the problem from a topological point of view. He would set each post next to the preceding one operating on the basis of proximity rather than by the projection of a straight line. The result was a more or less wavy line connecting the two end posts.

At the intermediate stage children tried to make a straight line by depending on some sort of guide. If the end posts were parallel to the edge of the table they would use that as a guide. But if the end posts were placed diagonally across the table, the task became much more difficult. A child might start off parallel to the edge of the table and then curve around to meet the other end post. But Piaget found that by the age of seven, the average child could build a straight fence consistently in any direction across the table. He would shut one eye and project his angle of vision along the line "as a gardener lines up bean poles." The line was still topological, but the child had grasped the projective relationship.

Piaget became interested in the child's ability to coordinate differ-

*It should be noted that from about 1940 on, the experimental studies that Piaget describes were performed by different groups of graduate students, teaching assistants, and doctoral candidates at the University of Geneva. Piaget generated the theory, supervised the work, and wrote up the results, which are published under his own name and sometimes Inhelder's and Szeminska's. The list of collaborators is acknowledged in each volume, but for simplicity's sake I have used Piaget's name as if he himself had performed the experiments. This should be borne in mind by the reader.

ent perspectives when, as we have said (chap. 6), he took his son Laurent for a ride and realized that the boy did not recognize the familiar mountain he could see from his garden when he looked at it from a different perspective. To study this problem a three-dimensional range of mountains was constructed out of papier-maché and set on a table between the child and the experimenter. Naturally, each had a different perspective of the mountain range. The child was then given several drawings from which he was asked to select one that showed his own point of view and one that showed the opposite person's view of the mountains. The youngest children, like Laurent, could pick out only the drawing that depicted their own point of view. Even when a child was asked to change places with the experimenter, so that he now saw the mountains from the opposite side, he still could see only his own present view; he could not reconstruct the opposite view that had so recently been his! This, says Piaget, is "a clear example of the egocentricity so characteristic of children— the primitive reasoning which prevents them from understanding that there may be more than one point of view."[2]

Similar experiments included standing a doll on a table and then placing a pencil lengthwise, diagonally, or crosswise with respect to the doll's line of vision. The child would be asked to draw the doll's view of the pencil or else to select it from several drawings. The results were much the same; it was not until the age of seven or eight that the doll's angle of vision could be correctly reproduced. Furthermore, says Piaget, it is not until a youngster is nine or ten that he can distinguish between and coordinate different possible perspectives accurately.

At the same time that the child is forming the concept of projective space, he is also learning to construct Euclidean space; the two are interdependent, says Piaget. The conservation of length and of distance are both fundamental to the Euclidean concept of space. We have already discussed experiments on the conservation of length (see chap. 5), so let us turn to the study of distance.[3] Piaget set two toy trees perhaps two feet apart on a table and asked his subjects whether the trees were near or far apart. Then he put a cardboard screen between the two trees and repeated his question. Most of the younger children felt that the trees were now nearer together; the introduction of the screen seemed intuitively to have cut down the distance between them. One child said the distance was now less, but it would not be if there were a hole in the "wall." So Piaget obliged by cutting a window in the cardboard screen, which caused one child to respond, "They're further, because there's a hole in it." When Piaget then placed a large cube between the trees, the distance immediately seemed lessened.

Transitional subjects also succumbed to the perceptual illusion of lessened distance, particularly with the cube interposed. One said, "It's nearer because it's thicker"; another explained, "It's nearer because it's more full." A third said, "It makes it nearer when you put the brick there . . . because there's less room." For these children, distance is equated with empty space; space occupied by objects doesn't count! Only near the age of seven, said Piaget, do children realize that intervening objects do not change the distance. Thus, the conservation of length and surface is seen to be fundamental to the construction of geometrical concepts, as we have seen that it is in the construction of number.

Once children have acquired the conservation of length, they spontaneously develop the concept of measurement, as we saw also in studying the idea of number. Piaget and his associates studied the development of measurement by means of the following interesting experiment. They showed each child a tower of twelve blocks on a table, and told him to build another tower, of the same height, on a lower table. Plenty of blocks were provided, of different sizes from those in the model, so that there could be no one-to-one reconstruction of it. There were also sticks and paper strips available to use for measurement should the child so desire, but the rules of the game forbade him to move either tower.

"Children's attempts to deal with the problem," reported Piaget, "go through a fascinating evolution."[4] The four-year-olds, depending on visual comparisons, built their towers to look as tall as the model, often disregarding the difference in the table heights. Given a stick, with the suggestion that they measure, they didn't know how to use it.

Cla (4;1) is given the usual instructions. He spends a long time looking at the model, then carefully makes a tower of his own without looking at the model. When he has finished, he looks back to the model, breaks his up and starts afresh. The same thing happens a third time. "Is yours the same height? *Oh yes.*" He is given a little stick: "You look with that. Can you measure? *I can't use that stick. That one is all right.*" The second stick is a smaller one, and he places this at the top of his tower as an embellishment, saying: *"It's the same height!"*[5]

At a slightly more advanced level, a child might use a long stick to lay across the tops of the two towers—and even if the stick were not horizontal might declare that the two towers were the same. "How can you tell?" Piaget would ask. "Because I've got good eyes!" replied one child.

During the transitional stage, a child would notice that the tables were of different heights, so that the base of the child's tower was lower. Then he would begin to look around for a way to measure the two towers. Interestingly, the first standard that would come to mind was his own body. The child would put one hand at the base of his tower and one on top, and then walk to the model tower, trying to keep his hands the same distance apart. "Children of about the age

Figure 23

of six," remarked Piaget, "often carry out this work in a most assured manner, as if their hands could not change position on the way!"[6] An alternative solution at this age was to measure the height of the tower against the child's own body, and then to walk over to the model tower to compare. Sometimes this led to rather complicated maneuvers, as in the following example:

> Dom (6;5) carries bricks to the model to compare their size. When he has finished he puts one hand over the top of the model and the other against its base. He keeps his hands at this distance and so transfers the height to his copy. Still not satisfied, he goes back to the model and climbs on to a chair: *"I'm not big enough. I got to be the same height to see properly."* He uses his own body as a yardstick, putting one finger against himself at the level of the base and joining his head and the top with a ruler. He then goes across to the other tower and repeats this maneuver: "Could you do it another way? *I could use my arm* (holding it against the two towers in turn). What about this brick?" (He holds the brick at the level of the base of one of the towers, and holding one hand aloft, he transfers this height to the other tower.)[7]

Piaget calls these two approaches *manual transfer* and *body transfer*. They illustrate a first step toward conservation of length, measured with the nearest and most familiar tool of the child—his own body. One little boy simply climbed up on a chair and hugged his tower to see how high it came on him. Then he went over to the model and did the same thing. Other children went through various movements, spreading their fingers or marking their legs. As they realized the unreliability of these measures they looked around for a stable representation of length, and turned to blocks, sticks, or strips of paper. One boy even built a third tower right next to the model, and then carried the blocks over to the lower table and rebuilt it as a standard for his tower. Here we see the beginnings of logical reasoning. If A (the model tower) $= B$ (the movable tower), and C (the child's tower) $= B$, then $A = C$.

The first stages in the evolution of measurement involved the use of rulers in different ways. First the child would use a ruler only if it was the same height as the tower. Then he learned to use a longer one and mark the height of the tower with his finger. One child was even able to take account of the angles of rulers sloping from tower top to tower top, and from base to base, and judge that if the rulers were parallel, the heights were the same.

> Lau (6;1) merely looks at the model to begin with but soon finds this difficult owing to the difference in base levels. He carries bricks across to compare them more closely, and later stretches his arms to span the tops of the towers. But he goes on to say, *"The table comes this high,"* showing the point on the model corresponding with the base level of the copy. He now stands against his tower and looks for a reference point on his own body (his shoulders) but thinks better of it and finds a ruler to measure the two towers. He succeeds because the ruler happens to be the same length as the towers. When asked to measure with a longer ruler, he judges the difference by eye and loses his reference point in the process. He therefore bridges the tops and uses another ruler to bridge the bases, noting that the rulers are parallel: *"It's the same height because they slope the same."* When given a shorter ruler he measures his tower and uses his own hand to make up the difference.[8]

The final step came when the child realized that he could use a rod shorter than the tower, and by repeated applications, measure the height of the tower. This discovery involved two new operations of logic: the division of the tower into parts such that part A = part B = part C; and the displacement of these parts onto the second tower to build a system of units. Thus $A = B = C$, being three equal units, became $A + A + A = 3A$, marking the birth of true measurement.

To study the construction of space in two dimensions, Piaget presented his subjects with two sheets of white paper, one of which had a red dot on it about halfway between the center and the corner on the upper right-hand side. Each child was asked to locate a dot on the blank sheet in exactly the same place. Rulers, strings, and other guides were provided. The youngest children ignored them and just took a guess, using visual approximation. Slightly more advanced children would measure either from the top down or from the side over, and were surprised that this one measurement did not give them the correct position! Then they tried to measure from the corner of the paper, keeping their rulers at the same slant. Finally, at about eight or nine, the youngsters realized that a coordination of two measurements was required ". . . to know where to put the point, in this direction and in that one, too."[9] They had grasped the idea that measurement in two dimensions establishes the axis of coordinates— a central idea of Euclidean space.

Only one more of these geometrical experiments will be described here, although many others can be found in *The Child's Conception of Geometry* by Piaget, Inhelder, and Szeminska. This is the well-known "Cows on the Farm," designed to study the conservation of area and how it is measured. It is based on the Euclidean axiom, "If two equal parts are taken from two equal wholes, the remainders will also be equal." To illustrate this, Piaget and his co-workers produced two identical sheets of green cardboard representing two farmyards. Each farmyard had a little wooden cow placed on it, and the subjects were asked whether the cows had the same amount of green grass to eat. When this was established, the experimenter produced a little farmhouse (wooden cube) for one farmyard, and explained that the farmer needed a place to live. Would the two cows still have the same amount of space for grass? Even the youngest subjects would agree that the farmyard with no house provided more space for the cow to graze. Then a house was produced for the second farmyard, and again the cows had the same amount of grassy space. "The necessary character of Euclid's axiom," wrote Piaget, "seems to be evident at all ages."[10]

Then Piaget kept adding more and more farmhouses, one on each piece of land, and repeating the question. The difference was, however, that on one farm the houses were all placed side by side to form a compact row, whereas on the other they were scattered all over the farmyard, giving it a very cluttered look. Piaget was interested in seeing at what point the children would succumb to the perceptual configuration and declare that the more open-looking farmyard contained more grassy space. Some children would stick to the logical axiom up to fourteen pairs of houses and suddenly fail on the fifteenth, because the appearance of more grassy land in the open farmyard was "somehow irresistible." The children who could hold out against the perceptual appearance of the scattered houses on

Figure 24

From Piaget, Inhelder, and Szeminska, *The Child's Conception of Geometry*, p.262.

logical grounds were usually about seven and a half. The younger ones relied on perception, and beyond that intuitively felt that the two *should* be equal, but could not bring themselves to admit it when the farmyards appeared so different.

Here we have an interesting example of a conservation problem in reverse. It again illustrates how fundamental to all mathematical and scientific thought is the basic notion of conservation. Piaget, through his experiments, has brought forth many unexpected revelations about the development of mathematical concepts and of human knowledge in general.

17. Time

It is an interesting fact that Piaget's studies of time and speed were suggested by Albert Einstein, author of the theory of relativity. At a symposium on the philosophy of science in 1928, Einstein, who was the chairman, became very much interested in Piaget's report of his experiments on the thinking of children. He stimulated Piaget to look into the relationship between time and speed in children's thinking, to see which came first, how they were related, and how one depended on the other. In Einstein's theory of relativity, time and space are relative to the speed of light. In physics, however, time is measured by speed, and speed is defined by time, which sets up a vicious circle. In an effort to discover how these concepts develop in children, Piaget devised experiments to study all aspects of this complex relationship. He published his results in two volumes: *The Child's Conception of Time* and *The Child's Conception of Movement and Speed.*

The concept of time, says Piaget, "is constructed little by little, and involves the elaboration of a system of relations."[1] The baby's first temporal experience is probably a vague feeling of duration; he may be waiting for his bottle and becoming aware of the waiting because he is hungry. Soon he learns that events take place in sequence; when Mother comes into the room, the bottle appears soon afterward. So the child learns to expect a series of events in before-and-after sequence. Many parents have noticed that the hungry infant will stop crying when he hears his mother in the kitchen. This indicates that he anticipates being fed very shortly. When the baby is approximately a year old, if his mother hides his bottle under a pillow while he is watching, he will look for it. In other words, he is aware that the bottle is there even when it is out of sight. This awareness indicates that the baby is taking his first steps toward the construction of object permanence.

But Piaget noticed a curious thing. He was watching his thirteen-month-old nephew chasing a ball one day. It rolled under an armchair and he was able to retrieve it. Then it rolled under a sofa where he couldn't see it—and the toddler ran back and looked under the armchair! Piaget tested this out experimentally and found that if he hid a toy under one cushion and then, very slowly, with the child watching, hid it under another cushion, the child younger than a year old would look for the toy under the first cushion. After about three weeks of this, the child learned to go to the second cushion first, but if he didn't find the toy immediately, he went back to the first cushion. It was not until much later that the child searched only under the second cushion. Piaget explained this by saying that a baby's perception of time—the order in which perceived phenomena occur—is subjective and inaccurate. Babies are "not yet capable of reconstructing the history of external phenomena themselves."[2] By this he meant that a child proceeds rigidly to act out what he has seen in the order in which he experienced the events. He goes to the first place he saw the toy, and when he doesn't find it there, he stops looking. He does not have the memory of sequential events or the flexibility of thought to skip the first cushion and go to the second one until he is older.

But as the child grows, his capacity to retain events in memory increases steadily and is extended to ever more remote happenings.

Figure 25

Jacqueline, before she was two, could remember events from two days before, as the following observation shows.

1;7(27): Jacqueline, on the terrace of a mountain chalet, locates the people I name, taking into account their recent displacement. "Where is Mother?" She points to the chalet. "Where is Grandpa?" She points down to the plain where her grandfather went two days before. "Where is the boy?" She points to the chalet. "Where is Vivianne?" She points to the woods where Vivianne went for a walk.[3]

In the sensory-motor period, the child has learned to order his temporal scheme in relation to that of external things. By the time he is two he is aware of the sequence of events and of the duration of intervals ("It's time for dinner" or "time for bed") in a practical sort of way. But his thinking is still egocentric and centered on his own needs and desires, as Piaget discovered when he began to question four- and five-year-olds about their age. He found that children tend to confuse age with height. The one who is bigger is the elder, regardless of birth order. This has been noticed by many kindergarten and first-grade teachers whose pupils ask them about their "fathers." Usually these are visiting husbands, but at least once for me my "father" was a tall college-age son who came to help with a Christmas play! This confusion of generations comes about, says Piaget, because the child's idea of aging is static and discontinuous; "when growing stops, time apparently ceases to operate."[4] He found that young children didn't know who was born first, their grannies or their mothers, and frequently insisted that they were there when parents or older siblings were born, as in the following interview:

> Bor (4;9): *"I have two brothers, Philippe and Robert.* Are they older or younger than you? *Older than me.* Much older? *Yes.* How old are they? *I don't know.* Do they go to the big school? *Yes, both of them.* Is one older than the other? *No, both of them are the same age* (wrong). Were they born on the same day? *Yes* (wrong). Are they twins? *No.* But they are the same age all the same? *Yes, the same age as myself.* Who was born first then? *Philippe and then Robert* (correct). Who was born first, Philippe or you? *I* (wrong). So who is the oldest of you three? *Nobody.* You told me you were born before Philippe, so you must have been there when Philippe was born? *Oh sure, I was there* (this seems quite evident to him . . .). Who was born first in your whole family? *No one. Philippe came second, then Robert, and I was the fourth because I am four years old."*[5]

Piaget attributes such incomprehensible reasoning to the child's egocentric conception of time, which confuses objective reality with subjective intuition. From the child's point of view, the existence of others begins in his own memory; before he was there they were not there either. Also, a child accepts others as he sees them, with no conception that they were ever once young. One little boy told Piaget that his grandfather was born "old right away." Moreover, since age is equated with size, those who have stopped growing, such as mothers and grandmothers, are often considered the same age or not aging any more because they are "old already." On the other hand, the child who is growing sees himself as able to overtake his forebears and even to catch up with older siblings. A youngster of four and a half confided to Piaget that he had a brother two years older, but he expected to catch up with him "if I eat a lot of soup."

Piaget then describes an intermediate stage in which the child grasps the notions of succession or duration but cannot coordinate the two. In the first case, he may know that his father is older than his mother because he was born first, but does not realize that he continues to remain older. Or he may be aware that age differences persist but be unable to tell in what order people were born, as in the following example:

Dour (7;5): "How old are you? *7½*. Have you any brothers or sisters? *No*. Any friends? *Yes, Gerald*. Is he older or younger than you? *A little older, he's 12 years old*. How much older is he than you? *Five years*. Was he born before or after you? *I don't know*. But think about it, haven't you just told me his age? Was he born before or after you? *He didn't tell me*. But is there no way of finding out whether he was born before or after you? *I could ask him*. But couldn't you tell without asking? *No*. When Gerald will be a father, will he be older or younger than you? *Older*. By how much? *By five years*. Are you getting old as quickly as each other? *Yes*. When you will be an old man what will he be? *A grandfather*. Will he be the same age as you? *No, I'll be five years less*. And when you will be very, very old, will there still be the same difference? *Yes, always*."[6]

Finally, as children reach the operational level, at seven to eight years old, they begin to coordinate the notions of succession and duration, and separate the idea of age from that of size.

Pol (8;3): "*I have two small brothers, Charles and Jean*. Who was born first? *Me, then Charlie and finally Jean*. When you are grown up, how old will you all be? *I'll be the oldest, then Charlie and then Jean*. How much older will you be? *The same as now*. Why? *It's always the same. It all depends on when one was born*."[7]

Piaget says that before the operational stage, thought is not reversible, and therefore the youngster cannot conceive of his parents as having had a past. His understanding of age is based on the obvious perceptual characteristic of size; one is bigger so he must be older. Gradually he develops a primitive intuitive approach, often confused in some aspects, until finally he is capable of reaching an equilibrium among all the factors involved in age and even projecting into the past or the future. These are the familiar three stages that we have met several times before.

Piaget then went on to study more carefully the relationship between age and rate of growth. He presented drawings of an apple and a pear tree that were planted a year apart. At first the apple tree was larger; then the two were the same; but by its fifth year the younger pear tree had surpassed the apple tree in size. This meant that in arranging the drawings the child had to take into account the increasing size of each tree, and then relate the growth of the two trees to each other, with the pear tree always a year behind in age. The child was thus forced to dissociate age from height in answering Piaget's questions about which tree was older during a particular year. The first three years presented no problem, but when the pear tree became larger than the apple tree, the same difficulties arose. The younger children insisted the pear tree was now older because it was bigger; the children in transition vacillated and hesitated between the apple tree, which was planted first, and the pear tree, which was bigger. Finally, in the seven-to-nine age group, one child answered, "The apple tree is always older because it was planted first. The pear tree grows more quickly, but the apple tree is older."[8] Thus, time became divorced from size and acquired "a special structure based on the systematic correlation of durations (ages) and the succession of events (births and anniversaries)."[9]

Piaget found it significant that young children based their judgments of people's ages not on inner criteria (such as that adults know more) but on external characteristics such as size. He therefore proceeded to study introspective estimates of time, based on metronome tests, on fast or slow raps on a table, and on having a child draw quickly or slowly for fifteen seconds. Almost invariably, he found that

Figure 26

younger children thought that quick work must take longer than slow work. A child of four insisted it took him longer to make the rapid drawings because "it went faster when I worked more quickly . . . it took more time."[10] The children here seemed to be relying on the results achieved: more strokes or raps = more time consumed. It was not until they reached more advanced ages that they were able to judge time separately from action. They had to be able to evaluate the length of time that had passed, regardless of how fast they worked. Children above seven said, "I was working more quickly but it took the same time," or "I went more slowly, but I rather think it took the same time."[11]

In other words, the concept of time is dependent on the order of succession of events and on the duration of time intervals; these are two distinct and fundamental systems that must be coordinated. In order to study each one separately, Piaget devised brilliantly simple experiments, some of which will be described here. To study the succession of events, he presented his subjects with two flasks; one an inverted pear-shaped glass (I) with a tap controlling the flow of water into a cylindrical glass (II) underneath it. Piaget would let fixed quantities of colored water run out of I into II so that as the water level fell a certain interval in I, it would rise a corresponding interval in II. Then he gave his watching subjects several sheets of paper on which the apparatus was drawn and had them color in the water levels in the two glasses as they appeared at each successive interval until I was empty and II was full.

The next step in the experimental procedure was to mix up the drawings that each child had made while observing the successive changes in water levels, and ask him to rearrange them in the correct

Figure 27

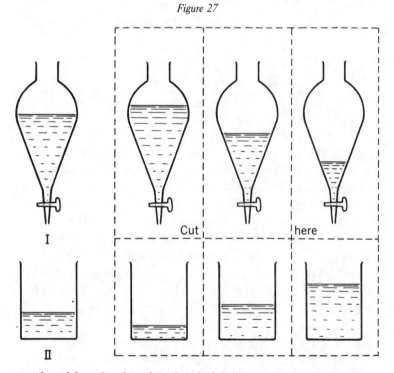

Adapted from Ripple and Rockcastle (eds.), *Piaget Rediscovered*, p.46.

order. Piaget found that the youngest children (around five or six) had difficulty in arranging the sheets in a series even though they had watched and recorded the successive water levels. As he has remarked frequently, "A sequence of perceptions does not in itself constitute a perception of a sequence."[12] These children had obviously not perceived the sequence of events, even though they had observed and drawn the water levels themselves. Older children had no difficulty in arranging the drawings in serial order.

As a final step in the experiment, Piaget cut each child's drawings in half so that Is and IIs were all shuffled together, and then asked him to rearrange them correctly. Here the children from six to nine (mean age seven years, eight months) had great difficulty. Most of them could arrange both I and II in correct order separately but could not correlate them. They might combine pairs of I and II by sheer guesswork, but could not remember or reconstruct a double series based on falling levels of I correlated with rising levels of II. Some children paired low levels of I and II, ignoring the inverse relationships that they had observed. Others paired the extremes correctly —that is, in inverse relationship—but went back to matching the other pairs directly. One boy, when questioned, explained, "The water rises and then it goes down again."[13] Piaget found this surprising, since children of eight and nine can arrange sticks or dolls in a series based on height, as we have seen. He finally concluded, after careful questioning, that the difficulty lay in the simultaneous coordination of two opposite motions—one rising, one falling.

Such an operation would be logically represented by the matrix form previously discussed (see chap. 7). It involves the multiplication of a double series which, unlike the glasses in our previous illustration, has an inverse relationship; as one series increases, the other decreases. The children had an intuitive grasp of the overall order of events but were unable to correlate them two at a time. To do this requires reversibility—the characteristic of operational thought which allows it to go backward in time and reconstruct past events. When only one series is involved, the time sequence is the same as the space series (water levels in this case). But when two different series must be matched in the same time, children have great difficulty in establishing simultaneity (coordination of events happening at the same time). Piaget found that it was not until between eight and nine years that his subjects could arrange events in a series and then correlate that series with another. Through this temporal succession of events, they gradually developed the concept of time. This led Piaget to the conclusion that "the operations of seriation and co-seriation (serial correspondence) are prerequisites of the construction of time (order of co-placements) and not its consequence."[14]

But there is an aspect of time other than that of succession of events, and that is the aspect of duration, of length of time intervals. We have already referred to the youngsters who reported that the faster drawing or rapping or ticking of a metronome took more time than did slower motions. Using the same flask experiment, Piaget studied the development of the realization that velocity is inversely proportional to time—in other words, more rapid = less time. To show how the idea of time becomes divorced from speed or distance, he used the time intervals necessary for water to drop from I to II (expressed as $I_1 II_1$ for the first interval, $I_2 II_2$ for the second, etc.). Now these time intervals were all equal, but because of the pear shape of the upper flask I, the water level fell slowly at first, and more rapidly in the narrow point. But in the lower glass II, the levels rose equally each time because of its cylindrical shape. Piaget marked these intervals (referred to as A, B, C, etc.) clearly on the two glasses and then asked his subjects whether the time required for the changes in water level were the same or different. He found in the youngest subjects that the greater perceptible displacement was considered to take more time (the water in I has "further to go" or "it drops down more quickly"). Again, as in the conservation experiments previously discussed, the children succumbed to the perceptual illusion of greater size or activity, and equated that with longer time.

In the second stage, Piaget found that children began to grasp intuitively that time and speed are inversely proportional. This might have been due, he thought, to experiences such as racing with other children, in which two youngsters starting and stopping simultaneously do not end up at the same point because one child runs faster than the other. As a result of such observations, children learn to

Figure 28

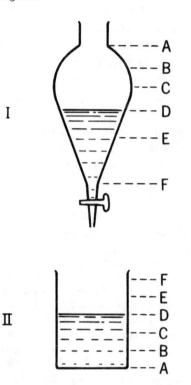

I

II

Adapted from Ripple and Rockcastle (eds.), *Piaget Rediscovered*, p.48.

dissociate the amount of activity from the time interval involved, and realize that time is inversely proportional to speed. Another problem that had to be solved in this second stage, Piaget found, was the equality of the time intervals. The children did not realize that it took the same length of time for the water to drop from gradation I_1 to gradation I_2 in the upper flask, and to rise from II_1 to II_2 in the lower. Since the upper gradations changed with the shape of the flask, while the lower gradations were constant, the younger subjects had much difficulty. Some thought that the lower levels rose more quickly, some that "it drops down much more quickly," or "it takes less time to drop down than to rise." One boy argued that the length of time could be compared only in identical glasses; another that "it wasn't the same time because we didn't go at the same speed." Even when told that equal amounts of water were transferred at each interval, and that the rate of flow was constant, transitional youngsters had trouble understanding that the time intervals in each case were the same. One nine-year-old, guided by Piaget's questions, finally realized, "Oh, it's the same thing . . . because it's the same number"—meaning the amount of water.

Children at the operational level of thinking, however, were able to deduce the equality of the time intervals, either because the amounts of water that ran out were the same or because the starting and finishing points were simultaneous. As one youngster put it, "The water drops and rises at the same time . . . while this one empties, the other one gets filled." The difference in the older children's approach to the problem is illustrated by the following:

> Lad (8;7): "Did these two take the same time (I_1 I_2 and II_1 II_2)? *Yes, they did, because they're divided the same way.* Are they the same height? *No, this one (I_1 I_2) is smaller but that's because it's bigger* (wider). And what about these (I_1 I_3 and II_3 II_5)? *Oh yes, they took the same time because two equal amounts were poured out; it's the same parts of water.* And these (I_2 I_3 and I_6 I_7)? *Oh yes, they took the same time as well.* Why? *Because it's the same amount of water* (points to II_2 II_3 and II_6 II_7). And if we poured this lot (II_6 II_7) into here (I)? *It would make a layer like that one (I_6 I_7)."*[15]

Here Lad is clearly not deceived by the different-sized intervals in I and II. His thinking shows the flexibility and reversibility characteristic of operational thought. He can go back in time and tell what would happen if the water in II_6 II_7 was poured back into I. Children of this age (eight or nine), says Piaget, are now ready to move on to the notion of isochronal *time*, which is measured in equal, recurring intervals. They have accomplished a sequence of logical operations, as follows:

1. The seriation of before and after, or the sequential ordering of events or $A \to B \to C$, $I_1 \to I_2 \to I_3$. Included in this seriation is the co-seriation of simultaneous events, as shown in the flask experiment.

$$I_1 \rightarrow I_2 \rightarrow I_3$$
$$\downarrow \quad\; \downarrow \quad\; \downarrow$$
$$II_1 \rightarrow II_2 \rightarrow II_3$$

2. The inclusive relationship of intervals that constitutes durations.

$$AB < AC < AD$$

3. The coordination of durations as intervals between events with the sequence of succession of such events.

$$A \rightarrow B \rightarrow C$$
$$AB \rightarrow BC$$
$$AC$$

4. Once these operations have been accomplished, the concept of measurement can be attained.

$$AB = BC = CD$$
$$AC = 2AB, \; AD = 3AB$$

The youngster who can logically infer the equality of synchronous durations of time is now ready to construct a time scale. If each unit of water were to equal five minutes of time, an hourglass could be constructed using the equipment in this experiment. Instead of this, however, Piaget used a large sandglass and a laboratory stopwatch. He assigned different activities to the children (i.e., walking around the table, putting marbles in a jar) and found that the youngest ones again equated time with speed. They declared that the sand fell faster when they were more active; therefore more work = more time. Even when they were told to watch the second hand on the stopwatch, which they could see moving at a consistent rate, the little ones declared that the hand moved more quickly than they themselves did. This egocentric thinking showed that the five-year-olds had not yet achieved the notion of constant measured speed; they thought the watch hand moved in time with their movements rather than at a consistent rate.

At around six, however, Piaget's subjects began intuitively to assume the constancy of the watch, but still hesitated about the sand.

Map (6;6): "Did the sand run as quickly or more quickly? *More quickly. . . . No, the same way. . . . No. . . .* As quickly or more quickly? *As quickly.* Why did you think more quickly? *It just slipped out, but it's because I myself was going more quickly.* And the clock? *Always the same way.* It goes for the same time no matter whether you go quickly or slowly? *The same time. "*[16]

Piaget says that it is not until around seven or eight years of age that a child can grasp the concept of successive intervals of time corresponding to equal distances traversed successively on the face of a clock. In other words, children cannot learn to tell time with any real understanding until about second grade. Certainly there is rote learning and the association of numbers on the clock with specific events or TV shows. But the hours that first-grade teachers spend stamping clock faces on papers for their pupils so they can color in the hands correctly might well be spent in more effective ways. I well remember the frustration of trying to teach a class of bright six-year-olds to tell time. They learned to read so quickly; why did they have so much difficulty with hours and minutes? It is a pity that Piaget's research on time was not translated sooner—a lot of it could have been saved!

Piaget describes many more of these ingenious experiments in his book, all leading to the conclusion that the concept of time depends upon speed. Naïve time is just lived; little children deal with time only in the present. But as they learn to order events and to become aware of intervals of time between them, there develops an intuitive understanding of time based on succession of events and duration of intervals. As long as events take place within a given time, they can be ordered by their position in space. The drawings of water pouring from the upper glass into the lower could be arranged on a spatial basis rather than a temporal one. But in order to measure time itself, the length of the interval in which events occur, the time intervals must be related to speeds. So we come back to a fundamental condition. Time can be measured only by the motion of bodies covering equal distances in equal intervals; that is, at a constant rate of speed. Whether it be the swing of a clock pendulum or the earth's motion around the sun, time is dependent on speed. This is Piaget's answer to Einstein's question. Speed is fundamental to the understanding of time and precedes it in the development of children's thinking. Therefore, in the next section we will consider the development of the concept of speed.

18. Movement and Speed

The concept of speed as a relationship between distance traversed and time passed does not begin to appear in children until nine or ten years of age, according to Piaget. It is a relatively sophisticated notion that is not stabilized until the period of formal operations, at eleven or twelve. But very early in life there is a primitive intuition of speed that is based on passing or overtaking. The baby has experienced balls that roll past him or objects that change their position in space, and he has learned to anticipate events that follow each other in serial order. As we saw in the study of time, however, this practical kind of experience is far from being operational thought. The fact that the child has a sequence of perceptions does not mean that he perceives them as a sequence.

This fact Piaget demonstrated very neatly by his experiments to show how the child develops a sense of the order of succession of positions in space. He rolled colored wooden balls through a cardboard tunnel in the order A (red), B (brown), C (yellow), and asked the children to predict in what order the balls would reappear at the

other end (position 2). Then he rolled the balls back again so that
they would emerge in the order *CBA,* and asked the same question.
He found that even the youngest subjects of four or five could predict
the *ABC* order. But when the balls rolled in the opposite direction
(position 1) they could not visualize the reverse order, *CBA,* and were
much surprised when *C* appeared first! There was also confusion
about the middle brown ball *B.* Young children frequently predicted
that the brown ball would emerge first, so it could "have a turn."
They did not understand that the relationship "between" would
persist regardless of the direction of movement.

Next Piaget varied the experiment. He rolled the balls into the
tunnel so they were hidden, and then asked the child to sit on the
opposite side of the table from where he had been sitting, and make
his prediction. He found that younger children confused their position relative to the balls with absolute position, and expected the balls
to emerge in the opposite order from the way they went in—as if the
balls had reversed directions instead of the child! In yet another
variation Piaget would rotate the whole tunnel one half-turn, or 180
degrees. This was done in full view of the children, after the balls had
already been rolled into the tunnel in *ABC* order. Piaget then asked
his subjects to predict in what order the balls would emerge at
position 2. Since the *ABC* order which had been at position 1 was
reversed by the half-turn, the balls came out in *CBA* or inverse order.
When he turned the tunnel a full circle or 360 degrees, there was of
course no change and the balls came out in *ABC* or direct order. But
the younger children became hopelessly confused and muddled by
these changes, as the following illustrates:

Figure 29

An (4 years): "Which will come first out of the tunnel? *The red one* (A). And then? *The brown one* (B) *and the yellow* (C). [Demonstration.] And now they are coming back, which one will come out first? *The red one, the brown, and the yellow one. Look!* [Demonstration.] *Oh, no, it's the yellow, then the brown and the red.* Why? *Because coming back it's the yellow one.* Fine. And now, look, I'm turning the tunnel. . . . Which will be first this time? *The red, then the brown, then the yellow one.* Look! [Demonstration.] *It's the yellow one.* Why? *Because I didn't know.* We'll start again. *It will be the yellow one.* [Demonstration.] Why? *Don't know.* "[1]

Another experiment, using the same techniques, had three little wooden dolls on a wire, passing back and forth behind a screen. The first was blue, the second green, and the third yellow. The results were much the same, with the preoperational youngsters unable to predict the reverse order in which the dolls would appear. The following example shows the firm conviction of a four-and-a-half-year-old that the middle figure (green) would emerge first, despite Piaget's efforts to dissuade her:

Ros (4;6): "Which [one will come out first]? *Blue* (A) *then green* (B) *then yellow* (C). And coming back? *Blue, green, yellow* [going to demonstration]. *No, yellow, green, blue.* Look, now, I'm turning it. . . . Which will be out first? *Blue.* [Demonstration.] Right? *No.* Why not? *Because it's behind the yellow one. The bit of wire turned around.* (New try). *Yellow.* [Demonstration.] *Yes.* Why? *Because it turned the other way.* And after it? *Green.* Why? *Because that's behind the yellow one.* (turning several times) Which will be first? *Blue* (A) *or yellow* (C) *or green* (B). Can the green one be first? *Yes.* How would it do that? . . . (turning five or six times). Which do you think? *Green.* What's that? . . . Look (showing the wire stem and the three dolls). *It can't.* Why? *Because of the wire.* And now (turning more than ten times)? *The green one this time!* Why? *It turned.* Was it at the front? *In the middle.* And if you turn it, can that one come first? *Yes.* Look! *No.* And this time (five more turns). Can the green one be first? *Yes.* "[2]

These experiments show that preoperational children, from four years on, have a primitive intuition of direct order, but that they cannot reverse that order. They simply retrace, in their minds, the events just as they were perceived, instead of imagining an inversion.

This is the rigidity of thought that characterizes preoperational thinking, which we have already seen in the toddler looking for his toy where he first saw it hidden rather than where he last saw it. Even when a child does recognize that he's wrong, he doesn't see why, as shown by the inability to understand that B will always be in the middle.

By the transitional stage, however, children close to or past six can handle the inverse order of the dolls on the return journey and are beginning to understand the invariability of the middle position:

Chri (5;4): "Look at these beads going into the tunnel. How will they come out on the other side? *Red* (A) *first, then black* (B) *and blue* (C) *last.* Good. And now I'm making them come back. So? *Blue* (C) *first, then black* (B) *then red* (A). Why are they the other way? *Because you're coming from the other direction.* Fine. Now, look: I'm sending them in as I did before, as on your drawing, then I'm going to turn the tunnel over. Which is first? *Red* (A). Why? *Because the wire is the other way.* And then? *Black* (B) *and blue* (C). Look: they're going in now and I'm turning the tunnel like that (half turn). Which will be first? *Red* (A). (Exp.). Is that right? *No. It's blue because you made it go the other way.* Let's start again (same explan.). Which first? *Red* (A) *because the wire is this side.* Look (exp.). *Oh, no, blue again because it was turned the other way.* (Start again). And now? *Blue* (correct). And now, listen: I'm going to turn it twice, not just once any more. Which first? *Blue.* Why? *Because it was turned the other way.* Look. (exp.). *Oh, no, red! I thought it would come out on the other side.* (Several turns). Which would it be now? *Red or blue.* Why?

Figure 30

A   B   C

Or else black. Why? *Oh, no, it couldn't because it's in the middle.* "³

There is still difficulty, however, with the effects of rotating the tunnel, even among seven-year-olds. Some can manage three or four half-turns and then become exhausted and make mistakes. Others can manage turns in succession but are lost when the experimenter jumps from one number to another, as in the following:

> Pia (7 years): *"Yellow* (C) *because before it was the blue one* (A). (Two turns or 360°)? *Blue or yellow.* Look. (One turn and one more turn slowly)? *Blue* (A) *because it starts off first and if you turn this once it's yellow* (C) *and if you turn it again it's blue* (A) *once more.* Four times? *Blue* (A) *because it's blue, yellow, blue, then yellow and blue again.* Five times? (He works it out again). *Yellow.* Six times? *Blue.* Three times? *Blue* (wrong). Eleven times? *Blue* (wrong). And black (B)? *No because that's always in the middle: it can't get out because of the others beside it.* "⁴

It is not for some time that children are able to deal operationally with these changes in position. At that point they can generalize that the *ABC* order occurs with even numbers of 180-degree rotations and *CBA* with odd numbers, even though they may not know the categories "odd" and "even." One little boy teased Piaget, telling him, "I can see through the cardboard."⁵

Here we see the typical development of a child's thought from the stage at which the experiment is observed but not understood to the point of abstract generalization and reversibility of thought. Piaget used these experiments as examples of the role of experience in the construction of mathematical relationships. These are experiments the child is really making on himself, on his own actions and sense of direction, rather than on the objects to which his actions are applied. As in the experiment with the colored balls, the child changes his position relative to the objects and then perceives the changes that take place in them. Thus he constructs his notions of order, number, and space.

According to Piaget, the simplest intuition of speed as well as of movement is based on this intuition of order. When a body moving parallel to another body overtakes it, the child notes that the overtaking body is moving faster, because it has changed positions with the body that formerly preceded it. In his characteristically thorough way, Piaget studied this phenomenon in a three-part experiment. First he had two tunnels, a long one and a short one, lined up evenly at one end. He had a little wooden man wired to go through each tunnel; they started at the same time and emerged from the far ends of the tunnels at the same moment. The child, who had already pointed out which tunnel was longer, was now asked whether one of the little men went faster than the other. The little children would say that they went at the same speed because they emerged at the same time. Piaget would say, "Isn't one tunnel longer than the other?" and they would say that it was. "Well, then," Piaget would say, "did they go at the same speed?" And the children would say, "Yes, because they came out together."

Next Piaget removed the tunnels, so the little men were visible to his young subjects. When they could see one overtaking the other, the children agreed that the second one moved faster than the first. Last, Piaget replaced the tunnels and repeated the original experiment. Once again, the young children would return to their original statements: the two men moved at the same speed.

Ios (5;6): "Did they set off at the same time? *Yes.* And stopped at the same time? *Yes.* Did one of the dolls go faster than the other? *No.* Are the tunnels the same length? *No, this one is smaller and this one bigger.* Then was one of the dolls faster? *No.* Watch again (repeat experiment). *Yes, the same speed.* In the smaller tunnel is the road shorter? *Yes.* And they arrive at the same time? *Yes.* Then does one go quicker than the other? *No.* Does it make no difference if one of the tunnels is bigger than the other? *Of course not!* Which is the longer road? *This one.* Then does one of them go faster than the other if they arrive at the same time? *No.* "

(The two paths travelled under the tunnels are marked with chalk and the tunnels removed.) "If they start at the same time and stop at the same time, does one go quicker than the other? *Yes—the first one goes quicker because the path is longer.* (We rub out the chalk and replace the tunnels.) Do they start and finish together? *Yes.* Does one go faster than the other? *No.* Why? *They stop at the same time.* "[6]

Here the child's statement, "the first one goes quicker because the path is longer," sounds like an intuitive grasp of speed based on a relationship between time spent and distance traversed. However, the fact that he returns to his original error when the men are no longer visible indicates that his intuition is of a practical rather than an intellectual relationship. He sees the overtaking simply as an inversion of order; this is the primitive early intuition of speed.

In order to separate the notions of farther or nearer (the order of points of arrival) from the notion of length (the interval between the starting and stopping points), Piaget devised the following experiment with very interesting results. Using string stretched around tacks hammered into a piece of board, he created two "roads," one straight and the other angled as shown in figure 31. On each string was a bead representing a streetcar that could slide along the roads. Piaget moved his bead along the angled road and the child moved his along the straight road. Piaget's directions were: "I'm going to travel along this road, and then you are going to travel along your road exactly the same distance I did. You are to go over just as much road as I do." Piaget would then move his bead two segments as shown in figure 31, and the child would move his opposite Piaget's. When Piaget pointed out that he had gone "all the way," one five-and-a-half-year-old said to him, "It's the same distance because this one is here [i.e., above] and that one is there" (right underneath),[7] Piaget then started over, moved his bead to the next segment, and stopped midway on a right-angle line as in figure 32. Again the child would stop parallel to Piaget's position. Finally, Piaget moved at right angles

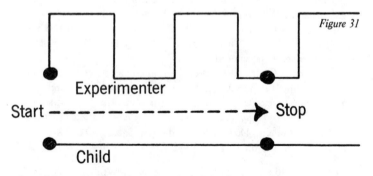

Figure 31

Experimenter

Start ————————————→ Stop

Child

Adapted from Ripple and Rockcastle (eds.), *Piaget Rediscovered*, p.28.

to the child's road and stopped as shown in figure 33. This would confuse the youngster, who would say, "But I'm there," or move just a fraction. When Piaget pointed out that he had moved much farther, or asked, "Have they gone the same distance?" the child would answer, "Yes, because they're opposite."

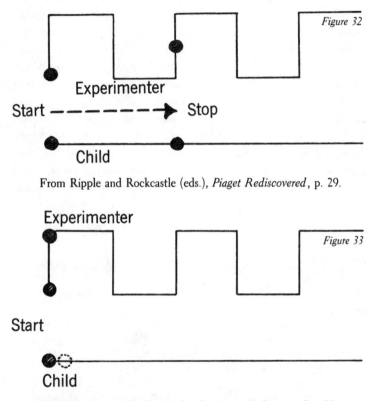

Figure 32

Experimenter

Start — — — — — —➔ Stop

Child

From Ripple and Rockcastle (eds.), *Piaget Rediscovered*, p. 29.

Experimenter

Figure 33

Start

Child

From Ripple and Rockcastle (eds.), *Piaget Rediscovered*, p.30.

In other words, to the children under six, going the same distance meant simply not passing each other. Distance was defined in terms of overtaking rather than of intervals of length. So Piaget tried providing a cardboard ruler, which the transitional children began to use, but inaccurately, most preferring to gauge the distance visually. Gradually, however, the older subjects showed improvement, until between seven and eight they were able to make a comparison of the distances traversed and measure them accurately.

Having studied the effect of order of positions and distances traversed, Piaget turned to a study of relative movements. He used pairs of toy cars moving parallel to each other, but with one car moving up from behind and overtaking the second. The distance between the two cars thus grew smaller and smaller until they were even, and then grew larger and larger. Yet if the two cars stopped at the same time, when they were even with each other, the younger children would say that they traveled at equal speeds. As Piaget remarked, "It is as if the child judged speed by the finishing point alone, regardless of the distance travelled."[8] This experiment indicates once more that the primitive intuition of speed is relative only to the order of positions, not to time spent or distance traveled. Piaget found that if he increased the relative speeds of the cars from the normal ratio of 2 to 1 to a very obvious difference of 4 or 6 to 1, the young child would briefly acknowledge that one car went faster. But a moment later he would slip back into his original error, because it fitted his intuitive logic.

Eri (5;0) (Blue catches up on red): "Was one going harder? *Both the same.* How do you know? *Because one went as fast as the other.* Did one go a longer distance? *Yes, the blue one.* Then was one going harder than the other? *No.*"

(Red overtakes blue): "Was one going harder? *One of them was farther ahead, the red one.* Was that one going harder? *A bit more. It was not going fast, but it was farther ahead.* And the blue one? *Not so hard: it was away behind.*"

(Red almost catches up with blue, travelling almost twice as far in the same time): "*The blue one was farther ahead, the red one was away behind.* Was one of them going harder? *Blue.* Where did it start from? *From here.* Did one do a longer distance? *No, yes, red.* Can you tell if one was faster, going harder? *The red one was slower and the blue one faster.* Why? *Because I can see that it is ahead of the other one.* Which has the longer distance? *The red one.* Which one was faster? *The blue one.* Why? *Because it is ahead of the other one.*"[9]

Here the child's thinking is similar to that observed in the conservation experiments with clay. The child's attention is centered on the stopping points as if they were absolutes; he is unable also to take into account the starting point, or total distances covered. When he is forced, by the dramatic increase of the speed of one car, to turn his attention to the distance covered, he goes through a period of disequilibrium, just like the child who alternately centers on the length, and then the width, of the clay. Finally at around nine or ten he is able to carry both positions—starting as well as stopping—in his mind. If the cars start and stop at the same time, and one covers a greater distance, he can then conclude that it has traveled faster. These experiments make it clear why children cannot handle problems of the Rate $\times$ Time = Distance type, until they are at least in the fourth grade. For slow learners, using toy cars as Piaget did in these experiments would make the relationships much clearer than reading about them in an arithmetic workbook.

Piaget described many more experiments, using bodies with unequal speeds and going in different directions, or bodies that accelerate in speed, to show how children achieve the concept of speed based on a ratio between distance and time. In the concluding chapter of *The Child's Conception of Movement and Speed,* he methodically sums up six different kinds of operations used, beginning with operations of placement and displacement, and culminating in metrical operations. These, through the use of repeatable units, permit measurements of distances and time intervals, leading to the concept of speed $(S = D/T)$.

It is interesting to note that the concepts of both time and speed follow parallel courses in their development. Both are based on a primitive concept of order: order of events in time and order of positions in speed. Piaget points out that in judging speed on the basis of overtaking, or passing, the child has escaped from the chicken-and-egg problem that has plagued the physicists; time measured by speed, and speed defined by time. To the child, time is a coordination of speeds; but speed is independent of time and depends on the order of passing positions in space. When he can take account not only of the order of passing but of the distance covered, the child is ready for the operational concept of speed as a relationship between space (distance) and time.

19. Learning

In the summer of 1959 Piaget's long-time collaborator, Bärbel Inhelder, attended a symposium of scientists at Woods Hole, Massachusetts. Out of the spirited discussions with Jerome Bruner, B. F. Skinner, and others came a renewed interest in learning, in how children move from one cognitive stage to the next, and how knowledge in one field is extended to other closely related fields. After a stay at Bruner's Center for Cognitive Studies at Harvard, Inhelder returned to Geneva, and with Piaget's enthusiastic support and the collaboration of Hermine Sinclair and Magali Bovet, she began a series of learning experiments that lasted over the next ten years. The results were published in 1974 in *Learning and the Development of Cognition*.

Piaget's work had already shown the existence of a succession of stages in cognitive development, but little was yet known about the mechanisms of transition from one major stage to the next. Why was a child at three or four impervious to the fact that a clay sausage could be rolled back into a ball, yet puzzled by it at five or six? As we have said (see chap. 2), Piaget's biological theory had led him to the concept of *cognitive competence*. Just as biological organisms at certain times in their growth are sensitive to specific environmental stimuli, so children at certain stages become competent to grapple with cognitive problems of which they had never before been aware. The mental grappling and the search for a satisfactory solution lead eventually to a higher level of equilibrium, one that regulates and integrates the previously contradictory aspects of a phenomenon such as the length of the clay sausage versus that of the round ball. This is the process of *equilibration*, which we have discussed previously (see chap. 2), the dynamic motivating force that leads to equilibrium between the increasing competence of the child *(maturation)* and his growing range of interactions with objects and people *(physical* and *social experience)*. These are the same four factors that were first mentioned in chapter 2 as stimulating progressive cognitive growth. But exactly how or when or with what effectiveness was not known.

To seek answers to these questions, Inhelder and her associates set up a series of experiments that forced the child to deal with apparent contradictions. One of these had to do with the conservation of continuous quantities such as liquids.[1] It had long been known that preoperational children presented with two equal measures of liquid such as milk, thought that there was more milk in a tall, thin glass than in a short, wide one. Then would come a transitional period of vacillation between height and width, followed by the establishment of true conservation based on the now familiar arguments of quantitative *identity* ("It's the same milk"), *reversibility* ("You can pour it back and it's still the same amount"), or *compensation* ("You didn't put in any more or take out any").

The previous emphasis in Geneva had been mainly on studying the child's responses in terms of his cognitive level without attempting to modify his thinking. This time, however, Inhelder and her associates designed their experiments to "provoke" the child into an earlier understanding of the conservation concept by highlighting the contradictions in his thinking. Thirty-four children between five and seven were selected on the basis of their responses to other conservation tasks as being in clearly preoperational or transitional stages.

Figure 34

From Inhelder, Sinclair, and Bovet, *Learning and the Development of Cognition*, p.42.

They were presented with the apparatus shown in figure 34 in which equal amounts of a colored liquid were poured into the top row of identical jars *A* and *A'*. The children turned the taps on the jars to let the liquid flow into dissimilar jars *B* and *B'*. *B* was the same as *A* but *B'* was narrower (or sometimes wider) so that the liquid would rise higher (or lower) than in *B*. *C* and *C'* were again identical with each other and with *A* and *A'*. The flasks *F* and *F'* were used to pour identical amounts of liquid into *A* and *A'*.

Each child was asked to let the liquid run from the top row into the second one, "so that there will be the same amount to drink" in B and B'. The levels of liquid in both jars were carefully marked with rubber bands, and the child was then asked to predict the amount of liquid there would be in C and C' if he let it run through. The problem he was faced with was that if he let all the liquid in A' run into B', the level of liquid in B' (the narrower glass) would be higher than in B. If he let through a lesser amount of liquid (expecting thus to equalize the heights in B and B') he would be faced with some liquid left in A', and eventually a lower level in C' than in C. If he let through all the liquid from A' into B', he would be forced to realize that B' held the same amount as A' and C', even though it appeared to hold more because of the higher water level.

There were several variations of this procedure, including one in which the second row was concealed and the child was asked to predict the levels of liquid in the hidden middle jars. In all of these tasks the child was confronted with contradictions between his predictions and the objective reality of the jars; they were designed to draw attention to the covariation in their dimensions. It was hoped that the child's curiosity would be aroused and that he might begin to question his naïve perceptual judgments and eventually "interpret reality in a new and different way."[2]

The results of this experiment were very interesting. The most striking was the evidence for the existence of a close relationship between the children's initial levels of development and their reasoning as demonstrated in this experiment. None of the nonconservers on the pre-test acquired conservation, but sixteen out of the nineteen transitional children reached higher levels of reasoning, and ten of them acquired true conservation. Thus their relative levels within the sample remained pretty much unchanged, although all but one child made some progress.

Another interesting finding concerned the instability of the transitional levels: some children who made progress during the experiment regressed between the first and second post-tests, while others showed progress across both post-tests given three weeks apart. These were the ones who were able to generalize their deductions to other areas of conservation, whereas the reasoning of those who regressed appeared to be "strictly local"—unstable, and limited only to the specific areas in which training had been given.

These results seem to support Piaget's hypothesis of cognitive competence. Some children were impervious to the observable features of the levels of liquid (different heights in different jars), while others were able to take account of them only briefly, and still others not only became quickly aware of the contradictions but were able to assimilate them into already coordinated schemes and draw logical inferences from them. Inhelder describes the reactions of one little girl of 6;2 who is bothered by the fact that the levels of liquid in B and B' are unequal. (In this case B' is called N for "narrower.")

> She does not try to explain how equal quantities in A and A' can come to different levels when they are in B and N. Only in the following phase does real conflict occur: Ger continually changes her mind: *"There's more lemonade in N because it's thinner, and there (B) it's fatter,"* she says; then immediately afterward: *"No, it's the same"*— "How do you know?"—*"Because I can see it"*—"How can you see it?" —*"I just know."* She does not yet attempt an explanation based on compensation of the dimensions.[3]

This is a good example of a child being forced, or "provoked," to take account of observable facts for which she does not yet have an explanation. As Inhelder observes, "she does not grasp the crux of the problem and makes no attempt to overcome the conflicts, as do the more advanced children."[4]

Experiments such as this cast light not only on the many regulations and adjustments making up the dynamics of progressive equilibration, but on another important aspect of learning as well. The mechanisms through which learning takes place are *empirical* and *reflective* (or *reflexive*) *abstractions.*[5] *Empirical abstraction* has to do with information extracted from physical objects through observation. A child will observe that a ball is round, red, light, bounceable, rollable, and so on. This is all physical information, which he abstracts through his sensory-motor contacts with the ball. In the case of the experiment just described, the little girl abstracted the physical observation that the liquid looked different in the second row of jars. She was not, however, able to make the necessary abstraction based on reflection and logical inference that would have brought her to an operational concept of conservation.

Reflective abstraction, by contrast, involves reflection about relationships that are not observable but are constructed by the mind. It grows out of logical-mathematical knowledge that, as we have said before (see pp. 141–42), is not inherent in physical objects, and depends not on observation but on logical inferences and deductions. Some of the children who looked at the jars of liquid reflected that while one jar (B') *appeared* to hold more, it must necessarily have contained the same amount because in rows A and C the two jars were identical. That compelling logical necessity arose not out of physical observation of the jars but out of a mental understanding of the relationships between them. Reflective abstraction, according to Piaget, involves projection to a higher level of understanding and reordering at that level. This is the true meaning of learning: knowledge gained at one level is transposed to a higher level and reconstructed at that higher level of abstraction.[6]

In further attempts to study the mechanisms of transition during learning, Inhelder and her associates devised more experiments, most of which set up a conflict between two competing schemes in an effort to find out which scheme would dominate and how the conflict would be resolved. One of these we have already described in chapter 12 (pp. 119–20), in which schemes involving conservation of number and of length were placed in conflict in a configuration of matchsticks (see fig. 19). One variation of this matchstick experiment involved five matches laid out in a zigzag line whose boundaries coincided with a straight line of four matches. Another featured a line of five matches, which the child was asked to duplicate with smaller matches, thus requiring seven short matches to make the boundaries of the lines even (see fig. 35).

The children's remarks during these experiments showed clearly how perplexed and disturbed they were by the number of criteria from which they had to choose in making a decision (number of matches, coincidence of boundaries, length of individual matches, etc.). In general, the younger children were guided by the appearance of the lines and constructed their models so that the boundaries coincided. If they were then asked to count the number of matches used, they became confused and tried different strategies to deal with the conflict, most of them unsuccessful. The most advanced children realized their errors and constructed compromise solutions that, even when they were inadequate, revealed the beginning of a coordination between previously unconnected schemes, such as those of number and length. These experiments, said Inhelder, proved to be "most instructive, highlighting developmental processes in action . . . and provid[ing] impetus for higher-level coordinations leading to new cognitive structures."[7]

The last two studies in this series are of particular interest because they investigate the carry-over from training in one area of knowledge to solutions in another. In this case, Inhelder *et al.* carefully studied the effect on conservation concepts of training in class inclusion tasks (part-whole relationships; see chap. 7). They found that children who made progress in class inclusion, in which they were trained in a series of graded tasks, showed improvement also in conservation tasks in which they received no training, only pre- and post-tests. Then the experimenters reversed the procedure and gave conservation training to another group of children to see whether their class inclusion concepts would improve concomitantly. The results indicated that training in class inclusion was somewhat more effective in promoting conservation than the reverse experiment. This finding, says Inhelder, "supports the postulate of the existence of very general organizational structures."[8] In other words, there seems to be a whole network of operational structures underlying specific concept areas, such that improvement in one area leads to new understanding in other areas as well. This research has only scratched the surface, and

Figure 35

From Inhelder, Sinclair, and Bovet, *Learning and the Development of Cognition*, p.141.

much remains to be done. However, it appears that training can be effective if it is purposefully geared to the child's level of cognitive competence. Children who do not comprehend a given problem make little progress, but the child who is sensitive to newly perceived contradictions can be helped to resolve them through a series of carefully planned training tasks.

Juan Pascual-Leone has referred to this as the method of *graded learning loops*. [9] The structurally related task items are presented in a graded series of difficulty such that if the first task (A_1) is too hard, the child is given A_2, which is easier, or A_3, down to an item so simplified that it is often spontaneously solved. The feedback from that success leads to the use of the same schemes in solving harder items in the series, aided by questions from the experimenter directing the child's attention to crucial aspects of the problem (the method of *critical exploration*). For example, the conservation training begins with discontinuous quantities, which are the easiest to recognize. The child might be asked to put a toy tree in front of each toy house the experimenter places on a table, so that conservation could be easily achieved through one-to-one correspondence. Success at that level would be followed by tasks using less easily observed discontinuous materials, such as beads or marbles. Every time the experimenter drops a marble into a jar, the child would drop one into *his* jar that might be of a different shape, so that the one-to-one correspondence would be harder to follow. For success, perception would have to give way to logic: "We each put in the same number of marbles, so they must still be the same even though they look like more in my jar." Finally, continuous quantities such as clay or water would be used, with questions drawing attention to the covariation between length (or height) and width, as in the first experiment described in this chapter.

The effect of this carefully graded training is to promote the carry-over to harder problems of the operative schemes that are successful in solving easy tasks. Such an approach, it appears, could be adopted by classroom teachers thoroughly familiar with their pupils' developmental levels and able to break down learning tasks into items of gradually increasing difficulty. They should, however, be trained in the Genevan method of critical exploration—of asking questions that point up contradictions, and of requiring logical justification for the subjects' responses. The following excerpt shows how the examiner leads a child through a class inclusion task in which two dolls must each have six pieces of fruit made up of apples *(A)* and other kinds of fruit, such as tangerines or apricots *(A')*. The examiner first gives the boy doll four apples and two other pieces of fruit; then she asks the child to give the girl doll less apples but as many pieces of fruit as the boy doll. The child gives the girl doll two apples and four other pieces of fruit, which is correct, but notice how the child's reasoning is revealed in this conversation. Despite her correct answers, she still has trouble realizing that apples *(A)* and other fruits *(A')* are all subclasses of the inclusive class *(B)* of fruit *(A + A' = B)*.

"How did you work that out?"—*"There are six."*—"Six what?"—*"Six apples . . . no, six fruits."*—"Alright [sic]. How many has the boy got?" —*"Six."*—"And the girl?"—*"Six."*—"Six what?"—*"Six fruits."*— "Yes, that's right. Tell me, does one of them have more *fruits?"*— *"Yes, the boy."*—"You're quite sure? Because, remember that when you gave the fruit you made sure that they both had just as much, so that they'd both be happy! Show me the boy's *fruits."*—(She answers correctly.)—"Good. And now the girl's fruits."—(She answers correctly.)—"Then, one of them has more *fruits?"*—*"Yes, the girl."*— "How many has she got?"—*"Six."*—"And the boy?"—*"Six."*— "One of them has more?"—*"Yes, the girl."*—"Six is more than six?" —*"Yes."*—"You're sure? One of them has more things to eat?"— *"The boy got more, he's got a lot of apples."*—"Yes, but we're not talking about apples, we're talking about things to eat. How many things has the boy got to eat?"—*"Two."* (She points to the two "nonapples.")—"But he can also eat those (apples)! In all, I mean." —*"Six, then."*—"And the girl?"—*"Six."*—"Does one of them have more to eat?"—*"No."*—"What do they both have?"—*"They've got the same."*[10]

This is of necessity a brief and superficial summary of an important series of studies that was undertaken to provide insight into the developmental links between different concept areas, and the transition mechanisms that lead to new modes of thought. Its results seem to support "the epistemelogical conviction that progress in human knowledge results from dynamic processes which imply self-regulatory mechanisms."[11] The clashes and conflicts between different structures of thought lead to new strategies for dealing with them, and for most children, to new and better solutions to the carefully "provoked" problems.

This series of experiments begins to answer some of the many questions about the learning process, or precisely how knowledge is acquired. It shows that many subjects in the different experiments made real progress; in other words, cognitive development *can* be speeded up to some degree under the right circumstances. However, "the nature and extent of the subjects' progress was always, in fact strikingly so, dependent upon their initial developmental level."[12] Clearly preoperational children did not suddenly achieve operational concepts; on the contrary, after the training was over there were some regressions among subjects who had not firmly stabilized the gains made during training. More advanced children showed continuing progress between the first and second post-tests. To quote the authors,

> "In the interval between the two post-tests, progress started during training appears to continue and new coordinations become established. . . . The comparison of pre- and post-tests of all our experiments taken together leads to the conclusion that the findings fit the conception of learning as an integral part of the developmental mechanisms.[13]

There is much more in this seminal study than can be discussed in the present chapter: interested readers are referred to the original source, or to *The Learning Theory of Piaget and Inhelder* by Gallagher and Reid. Suffice it to say that Inhelder and her colleagues have shown the constructive effect upon a child of being confronted with reality in unexpected forms; it arouses his curiosity and starts him experimenting. When things don't turn out as he expected, the child expresses surprise and feelings of conflict that, if he is developmentally ready and competent, will impel him to search for new solutions and to reflect upon the inferences of such phenomena.

These situations have always come about in the course of natural living, but can also, we now know, be set up experimentally; this fact has important implications, particularly for special education. The child learns by dealing with the new, the unexpected, and fitting it into his already existing framework of knowledge through reflective abstraction. "Learning," says Inhelder, "is a constantly renewed process of synthesis between continuity and novelty."[14]

20. Education

In spite of the many areas of cognitive development that Piaget has explored, he has consistently avoided the subject of education. He has been asked so many times how his findings might be used to accelerate learning that he calls it "the American question." Mostly he has left it up to the educators to draw implications for teaching from his work, insisting, "I am not a pedagogue." Yet Piaget is certainly not without opinions on the subject of education, most of which are expressed in *Science of Education and the Psychology of the Child* and *To Understand Is To Invent* (the French title of which is *Ou Va l'Éducation*).

In these books Piaget offers the wisdom garnered from many years of observing children and participating in academic life. There is no mincing of words here, particularly in *Science of Education,* from which much of this chapter is drawn. Piaget feels that many teachers are still using archaic educational methods, and that their students, those who are not actively alienated, are sitting passively in classes that they find meaningless and irrelevant. Learning, far from being interesting and challenging, often means repeating a string of boring facts, completely divorced from thought and feeling. Is it any wonder that our youngsters are resisting traditional methods of education?

Piaget points out that even after all these years we have not clearly answered some of the most fundamental questions about education.

1. *What is the aim of teaching?* Is it to accumulate useful knowledge? If so, "useful" in what sense? How much does the little boy who wants to become an airplane mechanic need to know about the Italian Renaissance? Do we want our students exposed only to certain required areas of the curriculum? Is our aim to have them pass tests on subject matter? To teach them to think creatively and innovatively? To know how to check, verify, and criticize new information? Or to rattle off a string of facts in the order required by the teacher? Is it the aims of the teacher or the aims of the student, or both, that we should be considering?

2. *What should we teach?* What areas of knowledge should be part of the curriculum, and at what level? What areas are necessary and what irrelevant? Should we throw out the classics to make room for women's studies? Should we promote scientific experimentation in the elementary school? Is sex education the school's responsibility or the parents'? How about training in moral values?

3. *How should we teach?* What is the most effective method of teaching basic skills? Should we use computers and visual aids, or concentrate on paper-and-pencil drills? Should we teach reading by the phonetic or the contextual approach? Should we have traditionally structured classrooms, or "activity centers"?

These are only three of the major questions still unanswered in education today. And according to Piaget, they never will be answered until educators turn to experimental research for decisive information. To him, it is shocking and "scarcely believable that in a field so accessible to experiment . . . the pedagogue has not organized sustained and methodical experiments, but has remained content to decide . . . on the basis of opinions whose 'common sense' in fact conceals more affectivity (emotion) than effective reasoning."[1] About the only way we have of judging the effectiveness of our educational methods is to rely on school grades, achievement tests, and examinations. To do this leads us into a vicious circle because much of the work done in school is directed toward preparing for and passing those examinations; how, then, can they be considered a fair criterion of the effectiveness of education? What *should* be done, says Piaget, is to test after several years and see how much of that learning is retained when the examinations are forgotten. Or better yet, "compare the results of schools without examinations, where the students' worth is evaluated by the teachers as a function of work done throughout the year, with those ordinary schools where the prospect of final examinations may be falsifying not only the work of students, but even that of teachers as well."[2]

The fact that on many such fundamental questions educational research "still remains silent" is to Piaget mute testimony to "the terrifying disproportion that still subsists between the scope or importance of the problems facing it, and the means being employed to resolve them."[3] With children's educational and vocational futures dependent on the answers to these and other questions, Piaget sees only the most meager basic research taking place in education, and the prospect appalls him.

Why should this be so? asks Piaget. Why, in an age when sociology, psychology, anthropology, and other social sciences all have a broad basis of scientific knowledge, is education so far behind? The answer rings out clear and honest: education is not considered a science, but rather a second-rate profession. The schoolteacher is lacking in social status and intellectual prestige. It is difficult to get good people into education in many areas, because of relatively low salaries. The teacher is not thought of, by himself or anyone else, as a specialist in techniques and scientific creativity, "but rather as the mere transmitter of a kind of knowledge that is within everyone's grasp."[4]

It is clear that the public (which includes "certain educational authorities" and many of the teachers themselves) does not recognize teaching as a difficult and complex science. Instead of working, as does a doctor, under the jurisdiction of professional associations made up of other doctors, teachers are forced to conform to programs and methods dictated by the school administration or state departments of education. These bodies are generally made up of gentlemen who, if they ever taught inside a classroom, escaped as soon as possible. The teachers, therefore, are extremely restricted, as compared to other professionals, by a bureaucracy that has little time to devote to the research which is education's crying need. Moreover, at professional meetings of educators, as compared with medical or psychological conventions, Piaget says, "one cannot but be struck by the prevailing lack of scientific dynamism . . . when discussing [educational] problems."[5] The author, who has attended many educational conferences, has often dozed off because of this "lack of scientific dynamism."

The last criticism Piaget levels at the teaching profession is also the most serious; it is directed at the teacher-training institutes, which are often isolated from other university facilities and "entirely lack any direct link with . . . research." Although the situation in the United States is somewhat different from what Piaget describes in Europe, it is still true that the traditional system for training teachers has had a "deadly effect" upon educational research. "Cut off from the scientific trends and the atmosphere of research and experiment that could have injected new life into them,"[6] teachers often plug along through their required credits in education and go through the motions of performing a single piece of research, which they hand in with a sigh of relief, never to undertake any more, whereas they should be constantly performing informal experiments and trying out new ideas in their classrooms. Though Piaget has kind words for American "departments of education" as being less isolated than European training institutes, he notes accurately that child psychology is often taught in the education department. This means that the experimental psychology department does its research on rats, "which has often had a somewhat disastrous effect."[7] Another disadvantage which he candidly mentions is the possibility that "mathematicians, physicists, and biologists who have not succeeded in their own fields . . . find outlets in the Departments of Education for teaching the didactics of mathematics, physics, biology, and so on—a state of affairs that is not always of great advantage to the progress of pedagogical research."[8] While no one would deny that there are great and creative

professors in departments of education, there are many more medio-
cre ones who get bogged down in the nitty-gritty of methods and
lesson plans.

The fundamental problem, according to Piaget, is that educators
are more interested in teaching than they are in children. Their
concentration, their training, is upon methods and curriculum. Their
knowledge of child psychology is often sketchy; their interest in the
child's mental and emotional development limited. Teachers want to
teach and have children listen; but this, we have seen, is the antithesis
of how children learn! Over and over, through these pages, we have
heard Piaget saying, "Knowledge is derived from action. . . . To know
an object is to act upon it and to transform it. . . . To know is therefore
to assimilate reality into structures of transformation, and these are
the structures that intelligence constructs as a direct extension of our
actions."[9] From the baby who creeps after his hidden toy, thereby
constructing the notions of space and object permanence, to the
child who counts and seriates and measures, constructing the notions
of number, order, and weight, all knowledge derives from the actions
the child performs on the objects and then organizes and reflects
upon in his mind. Children do not learn by sitting passively in their
seats, listening to the teacher, any more than they learn to swim by
sitting in rows on a dock watching grown-up swimmers in the water.
"If the aim of intellectual training is to form the intelligence rather
than to stock the memory, and to produce intellectual explorers
rather than mere erudition, then traditional education is manifestly
guilty of a grave deficiency."[10]

Even the newer methods of lectures accompanied by demonstra-
tions are not as effective, says Piaget, as having the child discover or
invent ways of dealing with objects for himself. It can be shown that
even the accuracy of the memory of a tower of cubes will differ among
children depending on whether they (a) simply looked at and perceived the tower, (b) observed the tower being constructed by an
adult while the children watched, or (c) reconstructed the tower
themselves. The memories that result from the last treatment are
clearly superior, whereas there is not much difference between the
other two. This shows, says Piaget, "that by carrying out experiments

in the child's presence instead of making the child carry them out, one loses the entire informational and formative value offered by action proper as such."[11]

It is in this kind of basic research that education is woefully lacking, says Piaget. If student teachers were systematically required to observe and question children, they would learn much more about how children's minds develop and how they can be stimulated to think for themselves. But, alas, the student teachers often suffer from the same kind of passive learning as their pupils; they may attend a set of lectures on child psychology and pass an examination without ever having really faced a child. Piaget feels that studying child psychology is not enough—teachers need to actually carry out their own research "to see how difficult it is to make themselves understood by the children, and to understand what the children are saying."[12] Teachers have the illusion, when they stand in front of classes, that they are understanding their students and are making themselves understood. Only performing actual research will make them realize how far they are from the truth. Children are often able to verbalize glibly without having any real comprehension of what they are talking about. This is why the intelligence of the middle-class child is sometimes overestimated by teachers, while that of the inarticulate ghetto child is frequently underestimated.

Piaget feels that all teachers should be active in research instead of just reading about it. He describes the primary school training program in Geneva, which requires that all student teachers take part in a year-long research program. Every afternoon is spent in the schools, working in groups of two or three under the supervision of a trained research assistant. The would-be teachers learn how to question children, how to record their responses, and how to evaluate the success or failure of their experiments. This, says Piaget, is an intellectual training that forces them to understand the complexity of the problems involved, far more than any professor's lecture. "It is by and through research that the teacher's profession ceases to be merely a trade and . . . acquires the dignity of all professions that draw upon both the arts and the sciences."[13]

Piaget is adamant in his insistence that not just primary but all teachers need this kind of training. Secondary school training emphasizes subject matter and methods but often neglects the psychology of the children being taught. The more enthusiastic a teacher is about his specialty, Piaget observes, the less interested he is likely to be in his students. "It often happens that future science teachers display an undisguised contempt for the psychology of development until one can succeed in making them grasp the epistemological bearing of the laws of that development."[14] In others words, science teachers may need to be persuaded that there is an "embryology of intelligence" that develops according to natural laws, just as in other sciences. Once the formative processes involved in the acquisition of knowledge have been understood, they can be related to the teacher's special areas of interest to help him teach more effectively. Thus a mathematician should be interested in how children develop the notions of number or geometry; a chemistry teacher can learn much from observing how youngsters handle the problem of combining chemical elements in Inhelder's and Piaget's experiment with the four flasks. This understanding of the mental processes of their students is just as important for them, Piaget believes, as it is for a nursery school teacher to understand the symbolic meaning of play, or an elementary school teacher to understand the morality of cooperation she sees emerging in her class.

Turning now from teacher training to the state of the schools, Piaget is all in favor of the "new methods of education" as opposed to the traditional approach. He refers frequently to "the active school" as opposed to one in which children experience "cognitive passivity." Through his activities at UNESCO, Piaget has had international influence on public education. His theories are reflected in the British "integrated day," in the "discovery method," "individualized learning," "personalized education," the "inductive method," "activity centers," and a host of other approaches. Basically, what he means by the "active method" is that children should be free to explore, question, and discover for themselves, either on the sensory-motor and symbolic levels for young children or on the basis of internalized action or thought at the operational level. Children need to talk to one another, for that is how they learn. The teacher is not there to lecture and demonstrate, but to observe, question, and bring out contradictions, as we have seen Piaget do in his experiments, in order to make children think and discover new solutions, new structures of thought. At a meeting of the International Bureau of Education in Geneva, Piaget once heard a Canadian say that in his province they had just decided every class should have two classrooms—one where the teacher is, and one where the teacher isn't. Piaget quoted this as the best idea he had ever heard from a teacher! He feels strongly that children need to take a more active part in their own education, because what they most need to learn is not facts, but an independent way of functioning. Much of what we teach children today will be outmoded by the time they graduate, but critical insight and creative ideas will always be needed. Piaget once said:

> The principal goal of education is to create men who are capable of doing new things, not simply of repeating what other generations have done—men who are creative, inventive, and discoverers. The second goal of education is to form minds which can be critical, can verify, and not accept everything they are offered. The great danger today is of slogans, collective opinions, ready-made trends of thought. We have to be able to resist them individually, to criticize, to distinguish between what is proven and what is not. So we need pupils who are active, who learn early to find out by themselves, partly by their own spontaneous activity and partly through material we set up for them; who learn early to tell what is verifiable and what is simply the first idea to come to them.[15]

It is this philosophy of education that has brought about a sweeping revolution in the British "infant schools" (five to seven years), and which is now spreading to this country. On a sabbatical leave in England, I was privileged to visit a number of such schools in Kent, southeast of London, through arrangements made by Joy Gentry, herself a talented teacher and headmistress of a large infant school. In all the schools that I visited, whether they were ancient city buildings or modern, sunny, one-story constructions, there was an air of busy, happy purposefulness. The children were free to choose what materials they wanted to work with, and have a voice in planning the day's program. The "integrated day" means that reading, writing, drawing, science, and social studies may all be taught as part of one unit. As Joy Gentry pointed out, cooking involves reading the recipes and following directions, writing down lists of items to shop for, adding up costs and subtracting to make change, measuring quantities such as flour or raisins, observing the transformations involved in mixing pudding or shaping dough, figuring out the time needed for cooking or baking, and dividing, say, eight gingerbread men among twenty-four children. During the baking, the teacher might read the story of "The Gingerbread Man" and have the children draw pictures or write their own stories to be bound into small, handmade books. Thus many subjects would be integrated into one delightful project in which all the children could take part, according to their individual abilities and interests.

In "active" classrooms such as these, whether in England, the United States, or Switzerland, the children are busily reading, writing, painting, building, caring for pets. The hallways are used for science exhibits, art displays, workbenches, block constructions, and playing store. The children come in and take up whatever they want to do. Some will read quietly or listen to another child in the library alcove. Some will go to the dress-up corner or to the activity tables. Here all kinds of materials await them—on the number tables it might be buttons to count, beads to string, sugar or flour to measure, number lines, rulers, and commercial materials such as Stern blocks or Cuisenaire rods. The children are free to move about and talk with one another. The teacher circulates, listening, asking questions, helping with spelling or reading, "provoking" learning. Her role is much less structured but much more sensitive and creative than that of the traditional schoolmistress. She is responsible for seeing that each child works in each skill area at some time during the day. She must know when to let a child daydream and when to prod him on to something harder. She does not complain about children making a mess, for each child must clean up after himself. There is a great deal of "busy noise" in such a school, but children are not allowed to bother one another. In such an environment children learn quickly, because they *want* to learn. Their activities are their own choice, and they are not forced to sit still at one desk, listening in stultifying boredom while the teacher does all the talking![16]

It is in this kind of setting, where a child's innate curiosity and desire to learn are tapped, that true education takes place, according to Piaget. "The essential functions of intelligence consist in understanding and in inventing; in other words, building up structures by structuring reality."[17] A child, through his own "personal research," organizes objects into series, or classes, or numbers, and thus builds up the logical groupings of classes and relations that we have already discussed. Because he is interested in his own experiments does not mean that they do not involve effort; on the contrary, he is willing to work harder on a project that is his own, as anyone who has watched children is aware. This kind of teaching involves more effort on the part of the teacher, too; ". . . the active methods are much more difficult to employ than our current receptive methods," admits Piaget.[18] The teacher must be able to keep track of many more activities than if she stood at the front of the room, teaching one lesson to all. She has to do a great deal of careful advance planning, and make meticulous records of each child's progress in each skill area. She must be more creative, more experienced, and better trained, with a thorough knowledge of children's emotional and intellectual development. "The heartbreaking difficulty of pedagogy, as indeed in medicine and in many other branches of knowledge that partake at the same time of art and science, is in the fact that the best methods are also the most difficult ones."[19]

Piaget takes a dim view of some of the modern aids to teaching. He feels that many educators with insufficient psychological background tend to confuse "active methods" with "intuitive methods." (We have pointed out that intuitive thinking is based on perception and is subject to error.) Thus the use of audio-visual materials such as films and television is seen as producing "figurative processes" rather than true operational processes. By this Piaget means that they produce perceptions or mental images which are merely a representation of what has been seen, rather than a really flexible, reversible, stable understanding. This is the same kind of rote learning approach that Piaget criticizes in mini-computers and programmed learning machines. Skinner's "teaching machines," he says, are a great success, if by success is meant merely the verbal reproduction of the desired answer.

> The sentimental and the natural worriers have been saddened by the fact that schoolmasters can be replaced by machines. In my view . . . these machines have performed at least one great service for us, which is to demonstrate beyond all possible doubt the mechanical character of the schoolmaster's function as it is conceived by traditional teaching methods: if the ideal of that method is merely to elicit correct repetition of what has been correctly transmitted, then it goes without saying that a machine can fulfill those conditions correctly.[20]

In discussing needed reforms in education, Piaget comes out strongly for the abolition of examinations. He considers them harmful because "they polarize around the pursuit of ephemeral and largely artificial results the majority of the activities that ought to be concentrated upon the formation of the intelligence and good working methods."[21] He feels that examination marks are "variable, relatively arbitrary, and lacking in concrete significance." Good marks on examinations depend on memory and a kind of memory that has little place in real life; in fact it is a "mental artifact." Clearly he feels that current methods of "cramming" are a waste of time. "The only genuine examination," he says, ". . . would be one in which the candidate is free to use his books, notes, etc., and accomplishes a certain amount of work that is merely a continuation of what he has been doing in class."[22]

In his dignified and erudite fashion, Piaget is voicing the same criticisms of the schools that have been raised by John Holt, Jonathan Kozol, Jerome Bruner, George Dennison, Charles Silberman, and a score of others in this country. At a time when the whole world is crying out for more effective ways of educating our children, traditional schools are still stifling the intelligence and creativity of our youngsters, who ingeniously discover ways to revolt against the demands for meaningless obedience. Those schools where newer methods are being tried often find themselves attacked by parents who do not understand "active methods" and dismiss them as "fads" while demanding a return to "the basics." Piaget has clearly stated that he "does not mean that the best method of education is to let children do exactly as they like."[23] But what he *does* mean, and has argued for half a century, is that "if a child is interested in what he does, he is capable of making efforts to the limit of his physical endurance."[24] Only when children become involved in their own learning, "then only will true discipline come into being—discipline that the children themselves have willed and consented to."[25]

This, then, is Piaget's message. The future of education lies in capitalizing on the child's own innate desire to reinvent the world for himself. As Piaget puts it, "to understand is to discover, or reconstruct by rediscovery, and such conditions [active methods] must be complied with if in the future individuals are to be formed who are capable of production and creativity and not simply repetition."[26]

Appendix A
Outline of Piaget's Periods of Cognitive Development

Sensory-Motor Period (First Two Years)

Stage 1 (Birth to 1 month). The newborn's behavior is characterized by inborn reflexes (i.e., rooting, sucking, grasping), which become more efficient and combine with each other to form primitive schemes such as rooting-and-sucking. The infant is "locked in egocentrism," with no awareness of self as such or of the distinction between self and the outer world.

Stage 2 (1 to 4 months). The infant begins to define the limits of his own body through accidental discoveries which prove interesting. He repeats his movements in order to prolong such experiences, combining looking with grasping, for example, to form a more complex organization of behavior called *prehension.*

Stage 3 (4 to 8 months). The baby learns to adapt familiar schemes to new situations, and uses them to "make interesting spectacles last." His interest is focused less on his own body and more on the world about him. He will reach for objects as long as he can see them, but out of sight is out of mind. He uses habitual schemes in a "magical" way, as if he considers his actions capable of causing unrelated external events to happen.

Stage 4 (8 to 12 months). The emergence of intentional behavior is seen as the baby pushes aside obstacles or uses his parent's hand to reach for desired objects. He may search for toys only partly concealed or hidden right before his eyes. He uses familiar schemes in new ways, combining and coordinating them to fit new situations *(mobile schemes).* His anticipatory behavior and his imitation of sounds and actions reveal the beginnings of memory and representation.

Stage 5 (12 to 18 months). The toddler now begins to experiment systematically, varying his schemes in "directed groping." He uses new means such as sticks and strings to attain desired ends, or finds new uses for familiar objects. He is able to follow visible displacements of an object being hidden, and finds it where it was last seen, but cannot infer the results of unseen displacements. He recognizes pictures of familiar persons or objects and can follow simple verbal directions.

Stage 6 (18 to 24 months). This stage marks the transition from sensory-motor to representational activity. The toddler invents new means through mental deduction; trial-and-error "groping" is no longer acted out physically but is carried out symbolically or mentally. The child is now able to deduce the invisible displacements of a hidden object; he clearly knows that it continues to exist even when he does not see it (object permanence). He is beginning to use symbols in language and make-believe play; he remembers past events and imitates them at a later time. He shows purpose, intention, and the beginnings of deductive reasoning, along with a primitive understanding of space, time, and causality. The child is entering the period of symbolic representation.

Preoperational Period (Two to Seven Years)

Preconceptual Stage (2 to 4 years). The child is operating on the level of symbolic representation as evidenced by imitation and memory and shown in drawings, dreams, language, and make-believe play. The first overgeneralized attempts at conceptualization appear, in which representatives of a class are not distinguished from the class itself (e.g., all slugs are "the slug").

While the child manages quite realistically in the physical world, his thinking is still egocentric and dominated by a sense of magic omnipotence. He assumes that all natural objects are alive and have feelings and intention because *he* does. He reasons that things which happen coincidentally have a cause-and-effect relationship. He assumes that the world is as it appears to him; he cannot mentally conceive of another person's point of view.

Prelogical or Intuitive Stage (4 to 7 years). Prelogical reasoning appears, based on perceptual appearances (e.g., half a cup of milk which fills a small glass is more than half a cup which doesn't fill a large glass). Trial and error may lead to an intuitive discovery of correct relationships, but the child is unable to take into account more than one attribute at a time (e.g., blue beads cannot at the same time be wooden beads). Language is used in an egocentric way, reflecting the child's limited experience.

Period of Concrete Operations (Seven to Twelve Years)

During the first and second grades there is a gradual transition into the period of *concrete operations,* which lasts until the age of eleven or twelve. The child in this stage can think logically about things he has experienced and manipulate them symbolically, as in arithmetic operations. He has achieved conservation, and recognizes that a cup of milk is the same amount, whether seen in a tall, narrow glass or a short, wide one. An extremely important development is that he now is able to think backwards and forwards in time. Piaget calls this *reversibility.* It speeds up logical thinking tremendously and makes possible such deductions as "If $2 + 2$ equals 4, then $4 - 2$ must equal 2."

Here we can see the upward spiraling of intellectual development from the knowledge constructed during the concrete experiences of the sensory-motor period to the ability to represent such experiences symbolically, and finally to think about them abstractly. The elementary school child can put things in series, classify them in groups, and perform other logical operations on them. If you show him a stick A which is longer than a stick $B,$ and then a stick C which is shorter than $B,$ he can deduce that A must logically be longer than C without having to see and compare them on a sensory-motor level.

Period of Formal Operations (Twelve Years to Adulthood)

Somewhere around eleven or twelve the youngster becomes able to reason logically about abstract propositions, things, or properties that he has never directly experienced. This ability to hypothesize characterizes the period of *formal operations,* which is the last and highest period in Piaget's developmental model. The student is capable of deductive and inductive reasoning based on the *form* of a given proposition. His knowledge of the problem may be purely hypothetical, yet he is able to reason it through to a logical conclusion. Examples of such thinking include problems in mathematics or chemistry or experiments which manipulate a number of variables in a systematic manner, taking into account all possible permutations and combinations. Not all adults fully achieve this last and highest stage of intellectual development, but certainly such thinking is characteristic of scientists and researchers who work with atoms, quarks, and nuclear fission. Such thinkers are able to cut through masses of material and come up with a clear, encompassing explanation. As Einstein is reputed to have said of Piaget's theory, "It is so simple that only a genius could have thought of it."

Appendix B
The English Translations of Piaget's Works in Chronological Order of French Publication (Including Earliest English Publication Dates)

1923 *The Language and Thought of the Child.* New York: Harcourt, Brace, 1926.

1924 *Judgment and Reasoning in the Child.* New York: Harcourt, Brace, 1928.

1926 *The Child's Conception of the World.* New York: Harcourt, Brace, 1929; London: Routledge & Kegan Paul, 1929.

1927 *The Child's Conception of Physical Causality.* London: Routledge & Kegan Paul, 1930.

1932 *The Moral Judgment of the Child.* New York: Macmillan, 1955; London: Routledge & Kegan Paul, 1932.

1936 *The Origins of Intelligence in Children.* New York: International Universities Press, 1952.

1937 *The Construction of Reality in the Child.* New York: Basic Books, 1954.

1941 With Alina Szeminska. *The Child's Conception of Number.* New York: Humanities Press, 1952.

1942 With Bärbel Inhelder. *The Child's Construction of Physical Quanti-*

ties. *Conservation and Atomism.* London: Routledge & Kegan Paul, 1979.

1945 *Play, Dreams and Imitation in Childhood.* New York: W. W. Norton & Co., 1951; London: Heinemann, 1951.

1946 *The Child's Conception of Time.* New York: Basic Books, 1970; London: Routledge & Kegan Paul, 1969.

1946 *The Child's Conception of Movement and Speed.* New York: Basic Books, 1970; London: Routledge & Kegan Paul, 1970.

1946 With Bärbel Inhelder and Alina Szeminska. *The Child's Conception of Geometry.* New York: Basic Books, 1960; London: Routledge & Kegan Paul, 1960.

1947 *The Psychology of Intelligence.* New York: Harcourt, Brace, 1950; London: Routledge & Kegan Paul, 1950.

1948 With Bärbel Inhelder. *The Child's Conception of Space.* New York: Humanities Press, 1956; London: Routledge & Kegan Paul, 1956.

1951 With Bärbel Inhelder. *The Origin of the Idea of Chance in Children.* New York: W. W. Norton & Co., 1975.

1953 *Logic and Psychology.* New York: Basic Books, 1953; London: Routledge & Kegan Paul, 1953 (out of print).

1955 With Bärbel Inhelder. *The Growth of Logical Thinking from Childhood to Adolescence.* New York: Basic Books, 1958.

1959 With Bärbel Inhelder. *The Early Growth of Logic in the Child.* New York: Harper & Row, 1964; London: Routledge & Kegan Paul, 1964.

1961 *The Mechanisms of Perception.* New York: Basic Books, 1969; London: Routledge & Kegan Paul, 1969.

1964 *Six Psychological Studies.* New York: Random House, 1967.

1965 *Insights and Illusions of Philosphy.* New York: World Publishing Co., 1971.

1966 With Bärbel Inhelder. *The Psychology of the Child.* New York: Basic Books, 1969.

1966 With Bärbel Inhelder. *Mental Imagery in the Child.* London: Routledge & Kegan Paul, 1971; New York: Basic Books, 1971.

1967 *Biology and Knowledge.* Chicago: University of Chicago Press, 1971.

1968 With Bärbel Inhelder, et al. *Memory and Intelligence.* New York: Basic Books, 1973; London: Routledge & Kegan Paul, 1973.

1968 *Genetic Epistemology.* New York: Columbia University Press, 1970. (The Woodbridge Lectures, given at Columbia University in 1968; not published in French.)

1968 *Structuralism.* New York: Basic Books, 1970.

1969 *Science of Education and the Psychology of the Child.* New York: Orion Press, 1970.

1970 *Psychology and Epistemology.* New York: Grossman, 1971.

1970 *The Principles of Genetic Epistemology.* London: Routledge & Kegan Paul, 1972; New York: Basic Books, 1972.

1970 *Main Trends in Interdisciplinary Research.* Mouton/UNESCO, 1970; New York: Harper & Row, 1973.

1971 With R. Garcia. *Understanding Causality.* New York: W. W. Norton & Co., 1974.

1972 *To Understand Is to Invent: The Future of Education.* New York: Grossman, 1973.

1972 *The Child and Reality: Problems of Genetic Psychology.* New York: Grossman, 1973.

1974 *The Grasp of Consciousness.* Cambridge, Mass.: Harvard University Press, 1976.

1974 *Success and Understanding.* London: Routledge & Kegan Paul, 1978; Cambridge, Mass.: Harvard University Press, 1978.

1975 *The Development of Thought: Equilibration of Cognitive Structures.* New York: Viking, 1977.

1976 *Behavior and Evolution.* New York: Pantheon, 1978.

Notes

Chapter 1: Piaget: A Profile

1. Jean Piaget, "Autobiography," in Richard I. Evans, *Jean Piaget: The Man and His Ideas* (New York: E.P. Dutton & Co., 1973), p. 106.
2. Ibid.
3. Ibid., p. 111.
4. Jeanette Gallagher, "Reflexive Abstraction and Education," in Jeanette McC. Gallagher and J. A. Easley, Jr. (eds.), *Piaget and Education*, vol. 2 of *Knowledge and Development* (New York: Plenum Publishing Corp., 1978), p. 9.
5. David Elkind, *Children and Adolescents: Interpretive Essays on Jean Piaget* (New York: Oxford University Press, 1970), p. 9.
6. Reproduced in *À Jean Piaget*, a commemorative volume put out by the Centre de Télévision in Geneva for Piaget's eightieth birthday, p. 38.

Chapter 2: A Biological Theory of Knowledge

1. Jean Piaget, "Phenocopy in Biology and the Psychological Development of Knowledge," in Howard E. Gruber and J. Jacques Vonèche (eds.), *The Essential Piaget* (New York: Basic Books, 1977), pp. 803–13.

2. Jeanette Gallagher, "Piaget's Concept of Equilibration," in Marilyn H. Appel and Lois S. Goldberg (eds.), *Equilibration: Theory, Research, and Application*, vol. 1 of *Topics in Cognitive Development* (New York: Plenum Publishing Corp., 1977), p. 22.
3. Jean Piaget, *Six Psychological Studies* (New York: Random House, 1967), p. 3.
4. D. Kim Reid, "Genevan Theory and Education," in Gallagher and Easley (eds.), *Piaget and Education*, p. 200.
5. Constance Kamii and Rheta DeVries, *Physical Knowledge in Preschool Education: Implications of Piaget's Theory* (Englewood Cliffs, N.J.: Prentice-Hall, 1978), p. 16 note.
6. Gallagher, "Piaget's Concept of Equilibration," p. 27.

Chapter 3: The Beginnings of Intelligence

1. Jean Piaget, *The Origins of Intelligence in Children* (New York: W. W. Norton & Co., 1963), p. 110.
2. Jean Piaget, *Six Psychological Studies*, p. 4.
3. See ibid., and Jean Piaget, "Development and Learning," in Richard E. Ripple and Verne O. Rockcastle (eds.), *Piaget Rediscovered: A Report of the Conference on Cognitive Studies and Curriculum Development, March, 1964* (Ithaca, N.Y.: School of Education, Cornell University, 1964).
4. Piaget, *Six Psychological Studies*, p. 9.
5. Ibid., p. 10.
6. Piaget, *Origins of Intelligence in Children*, p. 52.
7. Ibid., p. 159.
8. Ibid., p. 217.
9. Ibid., p. 291.

Chapter 4: An Overview of Development

1. Described by Gallagher in Gallagher and Easley (eds.), *Piaget and Education*, pp. 14 ff.

Chapter 5: Conservation and Identity

1. Reported in a series of articles in *Scandinavian Journal of Psychology* (1961), some of which have been reprinted in Irving E. Sigel and Frank H. Hooper (eds.), *Logical Thinking in Children: Research Based on Piaget's Theory* (New York: Holt, Rinehart and Winston, 1968), pp. 265–95.
2. Jean Piaget, "Development and Learning," in Ripple and Rockcastle (eds.), *Piaget Rediscovered*, p. 11.

3. Elkind, *Children and Adolescents*, p. 18.
4. Jean Piaget, Bärbel Inhelder, and Alina Szeminska, *The Child's Conception of Geometry* (New York: Basic Books, 1960), pp. 95–101.
5. Piaget, "Development and Learning," p. 17.
6. Jean Piaget, *Play, Dreams and Imitation in Childhood* (New York: W. W. Norton & Co., 1962), p. 224.
7. Jean Piaget, "Identity and Conservation," in Bärbel Inhelder and Harold H. Chipman (eds.), *Piaget and His School* (New York: Springer-Verlag, 1976), p. 92.

Chapter 6: The Preoperational Child

1. Jean Piaget, *The Language and Thought of the Child* (Cleveland: World Publishing Co., 1955), chap. 5.
2. Jean Piaget, *The Moral Judgment of the Child* (New York: Free Press, 1965), p. 24.
3. Jean Piaget, *The Child's Conception of the World* (Totowa, N.J.: Littlefield, Adams & Co., 1965), p. 9.
4. Wayne Dennis, "Piaget's Questions Applied to a Child of Known Environment," *Journal of Genetic Psychology* 60 (1942): 307–20.
5. Piaget, *Play, Dreams and Imitation in Childhood*, p. 258.
6. Elkind, *Children and Adolescents*, p. 12.
7. See Beryl Geber, "Toward a Developmental Social Psychology" in Geber (ed.), *Piaget and Knowing: Studies in Genetic Epistemology* (Boston: Routledge & Kegan Paul, 1977), chap. 8.
8. Piaget, *Child's Conception of the World*, p. 220.
9. Roger W. Russell and Wayne Dennis, "Studies in Animism: I. A Standardized Procedure for the Investigation of Animism," *Journal of Genetic Psychology* 55 (1939): 389–400.
10. Piaget, *Child's Conception of the World*, p. 64.
11. Ibid., p. 94.
12. Ibid., pp. 110–11.
13. Piaget, *Play, Dreams and Imitation in Childhood*, p. 231.
14. Ibid., p. 225.
15. Ibid.
16. Ibid., pp. 229 f.
17. Ibid., p. 270.

Chapter 7: Concrete Operations

1. John H. Flavell, *The Developmental Psychology of Jean Piaget* (Princeton, N.J.: D. Van Nostrand Co., 1963).
2. Alfred L. Baldwin, *Theories of Child Development* (New York: John Wiley & Sons, 1968).

3. Bärbel Inhelder and Jean Piaget, *The Growth of Logical Thinking from Childhood to Adolescence* (New York: Basic Books, 1958); idem, *The Early Growth of Logic in the Child* (New York: W. W. Norton & Co., 1969).
4. Flavell, *Developmental Psychology of Jean Piaget*, p. 187.
5. Inhelder and Piaget, *Early Growth of Logic in the Child*, p. 22.
6. Ibid., p. 55.
7. Jean Piaget and Alina Szeminska, *The Child's Conception of Number* (New York: W. W. Norton & Co., 1965), p. 164.
8. Ibid., p. 176.
9. Jerome S. Bruner et. al., *Studies in Cognitive Growth* (New York: John Wiley & Sons, 1966), pp. 154 ff.
10. Flavell, *Developmental Psychology of Jean Piaget*, p. 192.

Chapter 8: Formal Operations

1. Inhelder and Piaget, *Growth of Logical Thinking*, p. xxiii.
2. Ibid., pp. 174–75.
3. Flavell, *Developmental Psychology of Jean Piaget.*
4. Baldwin, *Theories of Child Development.*
5. Inhelder and Piaget, *Growth of Logical Thinking*, p. 111.
6. Ibid., pp. 114–15.
7. Ibid., p. 117.
8. Ibid., p. 121.
9. Ibid., p. 338.
10. Ibid.

Chapter 9: Imitation and Play

1. Thomas G. R. Bower, *A Primer of Infant Development* (San Francisco: W. H. Freeman, 1977), pp. 28 ff.
2. Ina Uzgiris, "Patterns of Vocal and Gestural Imitation in Infants," in L. Joseph Stone, Henrietta Smith, and Lois B. Murphy (eds.), *The Competent Infant* (New York: Basic Books, 1973), pp. 599–604.
3. Ibid., p. 600.
4. Piaget, *Play, Dreams and Imitation in Childhood*, p. 10.
5. Ibid., p. 51.
6. Ibid., p. 63.
7. Ibid., p. 93.
8. Ibid., p. 94.
9. Ibid., p. 97.
10. Ibid., p. 125.

11. Ibid., p. 121.
12. Ibid., p. 131.
13. Ibid., p. 132.
14. Ibid., pp. 133–34.
15. Ibid., p. 134.
16. Ibid., p. 136.
17. Ibid., p. 138.
18. Ibid., p. 139.
19. Ibid., p. 141.
20. Ibid., p. 142.
21. Ibid., p. 154.
22. Ibid., p. 166.
23. Ibid., p. 168.
24. Ibid., p. 289.
25. Dorothy G. Singer and Jerome L. Singer, *Partners in Play* (New York: Harper & Row, 1977), p. 10.

Chapter 10: Language

1. Ruth Formanek and Anita Gurian, *Why? Children's Questions: What They Mean and How to Answer Them* (Boston: Houghton Mifflin, 1980).
2. Cited in Hermine Sinclair, "Developmental Psycholinguistics," in Inhelder and Chipman (eds.), *Piaget and His School*, p. 194.
3. See chapter 4 in Bärbel Inhelder, Hermine Sinclair, and Magali Bovet, *Learning and the Development of Cognition* (Cambridge, Mass.: Harvard University Press, 1974).
4. Piaget, *Play, Dreams and Imitation in Childhood*, p. 216.
5. Piaget, *Language and Thought of the Child*, p. 32.
6. Ibid., p. 37.
7. Ibid., p. 59.
8. Cited in Geber (ed.), *Piaget and Knowing*, p. 220.
9. Jean Piaget, *The Child and Reality* (New York: Grossman, 1973), p. 119.

Chapter 11: Perception

1. A. Ames, Jr., "Visual Perception and the Rotating Trapezoidal Window," *Psychological Monographs* 65, no. 7 (1951).
2. Jean Piaget, *The Mechanisms of Perception* (New York: Basic Books, 1969), p. 84.
3. Ibid., p. 71.

4. Ibid.
5. Flavell, *Developmental Psychology of Jean Piaget*, p. 231.
6. Piaget, *Mechanisms of Perception*, pp. 315 ff.
7. Piaget, Inhelder, and Szeminska, *Child's Conception of Geometry*, pp. 95 ff.
8. Piaget, *Mechanisms of Perception*, p. 359.
9. For reviews, see Eleanor Gibson and Vivian Olum, "Experimental Methods of Studying Perception in Children," in P. Mussen (ed.), *Handbook of Research Methods in Child Development*, chap. 8 (New York: John Wiley & Sons, 1960); and Joachim Wohlwill, "Developmental Studies of Perception," *Psychological Bulletin* 57 (1960): 249–88.
10. Gloria Wolinsky, "Piaget's Theory of Perception," in *Training School Bulletin* 62 (1965): 20.
11. Jean Piaget and Bärbel Inhelder, *The Psychology of the Child* (New York: Basic Books, 1969), p. 32.
12. J. McV. Hunt, *Intelligence and Experience* (New York: Ronald Press, 1961).
13. F. H. Hooper, "Piagetian Research and Education," in Sigel and Hooper (eds.), *Logical Thinking in Children*, p. 424.

Chapter 12: Imagery and Memory

1. Piaget, "Mental Images," in Gruber and Vonèche (eds.), *The Essential Piaget*, p. 653.
2. Jean Piaget and Bärbel Inhelder, *Mental Imagery in the Child* (New York: Basic Books, 1971), p. 90.
3. Bärbel Inhelder, "Memory and Intelligence in the Child," in Inhelder and Chipman (eds.), *Piaget and His School*, p. 105.
4. See Lynn S. Liben, "Memory from a Cognitive-Developmental Perspective: A Theoretical and Empirical Review," in Willis E. Overton and Jeanette McC. Gallagher (eds.), *Advances in Research and Theory*, vol. 1 of *Knowledge and Development* (New York: Plenum Publishing Corp., 1977), pp. 149–99.

Chapter 13: Morality

1. Piaget, *Moral Judgment of the Child*, p. 55–56.
2. Ibid., p. 66.
3. Ibid., p. 111.
4. Ibid., p. 180.
5. Ibid., p. 133.
6. Ibid., p. 144.

7. Ibid., p. 191.
8. Ibid., p. 198.
9. Ibid.
10. Ibid., p. 201.
11. Ibid., p. 213.
12. Ibid., p. 256.
13. Ibid., p. 261.
14. Ibid., pp. 319–20.
15. See the review by Thomas Lickona, "Moral Development and Moral Education: Piaget, Kohlberg, and Beyond," in Gallagher and Easley (eds.), *Piaget and Education,* pp. 21–67.
16. Piaget, *Moral Judgment of the Child,* p. 366.

Chapter 14: Emotional Development

1. Jean Piaget, *The Psychology of Intelligence* (Totowa, N.J.: Littlefield, Adams & Co., 1960), p. 6.
2. Jean Piaget, "The Relation of Affectivity to Intelligence in the Mental Development of the Child," *Bulletin of the Menninger Clinic* 26 (1962): 129–37.
3. Piaget, *Play, Dreams and Imitation in Childhood,* p. 207.
4. Piaget, *Six Psychological Studies,* part I.
5. Inhelder and Piaget, *Growth of Logical Thinking,* p. 349.
6. Piaget, *Six Psychological Studies,* p. 36.
7. Ibid., pp. 54–55.
8. Ibid., p. 59.
9. Inhelder and Piaget, *Growth of Logical Thinking,* p. 349.
10. Piaget, *Six Psychological Studies,* p. 69.
11. Ibid., pp. 68–69.
12. Stanley I. Greenspan, "Intelligence and Adaptation: An Integration of Psychoanalytic and Piagetian Developmental Psychology," *Psychological Issues,* monograph 47/48, vol. 12, nos. 3, 4 (New York: International Universities Press, 1979).
13. R. D. Tuddenham, cited in Sohan Modgil, *Piagetian Research: A Handbook of Recent Studies* (New York: Humanities Press, 1974), p. 370.
14. Jean Piaget, *The Child and Reality,* pp. 31–32.

Chapter 15: Numbers

1. L. G. Marsh, *Approach to Mathematics* (London: A. & C. Black Ltd., 1969), p. 19.
2. Piaget, *Six Psychological Studies,* p. 53.

3. Piaget and Szeminska, *Child's Conception of Number,* p. 47.
4. Ibid., p. 64.
5. Ibid., pp. 124–25.
6. Ibid., p. 127.
7. Ibid., p. 134.
8. Ibid., p. 149.
9. Ibid., p. 167.
10. Ibid., p. 187.
11. Ibid., p. 189.

Chapter 16: Space

1. Jean Piaget, "How Children Form Mathematical Concepts," in Richard C. Anderson and David P. Ausubel (eds.), *Readings in the Psychology of Cognition* (New York: Holt, Rinehart and Winston, 1965), p. 409.
2. Ibid., p. 410.
3. See Piaget, Inhelder, and Szeminska, *Child's Conception of Geometry,* chap. 3.
4. Piaget, "How Children Form Mathematical Concepts," p. 412.
5. Piaget, Inhelder, and Szeminska, *Child's Conception of Geometry,* p. 34.
6. Piaget, "How Children Form Mathematical Concepts," p. 412.
7. Piaget, Inhelder, and Szeminska, *Child's Conception of Geometry,* pp. 45–46.
8. Ibid., pp. 52–53.
9. Ibid., p. 168.
10. Ibid., p. 263.

Chapter 17: Time

1. Jean Piaget, *The Construction of Reality in the Child* (New York: Basic Books, 1954), p. 320.
2. Ibid., p. 335.
3. Ibid., pp. 346–47.
4. Jean Piaget, *The Child's Conception of Time* (New York: Basic Books, 1970), p. 202.
5. Ibid., p. 204.
6. Ibid., p. 209.
7. Ibid., p. 210.
8. Ibid., p. 223.
9. Ibid., p. 224.

10. Ibid., p. 234.
11. Ibid., p. 240.
12. Ibid., p. 13.
13. Ibid., p. 16.
14. Ibid., pp. 26–27.
15. Ibid., pp. 64–65.
16. Ibid., pp. 179–80.

Chapter 18: Movement and Speed

1. Jean Piaget, *The Child's Conception of Movement and Speed* (New York: Basic Books, 1970), p. 6.
2. Ibid., p. 7.
3. Ibid., pp. 16–17.
4. Ibid., p. 24.
5. Ibid., p. 28.
6. Ibid., p. 123.
7. Ibid., p. 61.
8. Ibid., p. 163.
9. Ibid., pp. 157–58.

Chapter 19: Learning

1. See Inhelder, Sinclair, and Bovet, *Learning and the Development of Cognition*, chap. 1.
2. Ibid., p. 48.
3. Ibid., p. 55.
4. Ibid.
5. Jeanette Gallagher, "Reflexive Abstraction and Education," in Gallagher and Easley (eds.), *Piaget and Education*, chap. 1.
6. Ibid., p. 9.
7. Inhelder, Sinclair, and Bovet, *Learning and the Development of Cognition*, p. 166.
8. Ibid., p. 211.
9. Cited in Gallagher and Easley (eds.), *Piaget and Education*, pp. 230 f. and 284 f.
10. Inhelder, Sinclair, and Bovet, *Learning and the Development of Cognition*, p. 205 f.
11. Ibid., p. 242.
12. Ibid., p. 244.
13. Ibid., p. 245.
14. Ibid., p. 272.

Chapter 20: Education

1. Jean Piaget, *Science of Education and the Psychology of the Child* (New York: Orion Press, 1970), p. 7.
2. Ibid., p. 8.
3. Ibid.
4. Ibid., p. 11.
5. Ibid., p. 13.
6. Ibid., p. 14.
7. Ibid., p. 17.
8. Ibid.
9. Ibid., pp. 28–29.
10. Ibid., p. 51.
11. Ibid., p. 36.
12. Jean Piaget, "Relations Between the Notions of Time and Speed in Children," in Ripple and Rockcastle (eds.), *Piaget Rediscovered,* p. 40.
13. Piaget, *Science of Education and the Psychology of the Child,* p. 130.
14. Ibid., p. 132.
15. Ripple and Rockcastle (eds.), *Piaget Rediscovered,* p. 5.
16. For more about the British infant schools, see Mary Brown and Norman Precious, *The Integrated Day in the Primary School* (New York: Agathon Press, 1969), Donald V. Erger, *Understanding British Infant Schools* (Farmingdale, N.Y.: Carley Publications, 1972) or Mary Sime, *A Child's Eye View* (New York: Harper & Row, 1974).
17. Piaget, *Science of Education and the Psychology of the Child,* p. 27.
18. Ibid., p. 69.
19. Ibid.
20. Ibid., p. 77.
21. Ibid., p. 108.
22. Ibid.
23. Piaget, *Moral Judgment of the Child,* p. 366.
24. Ibid., p. 365.
25. Ibid., p. 364.
26. Jean Piaget, *To Understand Is to Invent: The Future of Education* (New York: Grossman, 1973), p. 20.

Glossary

ABSTRACTION. Information gained through observation and reflection, which can then be generalized to other objects and situations. *Empirical* abstraction has to do with information extracted from physical objects through observation (i.e., color or size). *Reflective* (or *reflexive*) abstraction has to do with logical-mathematical relationships constructed by the mind (i.e., series or classes).

ACCOMMODATION. *See* Adaptation.

ADAPTATION. A biological mode of functioning that characterizes all forms and levels of life. It consists of the dual processes of assimilation and accommodation, which go on continuously. *Assimilation* is the process of taking in from the environment all forms of stimulation and information, which are then organized and integrated into the organism's existing forms or structures, thus creating new structures. *Accommodation* is the process of reaching out and adjusting to new and changing conditions in the environment, so that preexisting patterns of behavior are modified to cope with new information or feedback from external situations.

AFFECT. The emotional aspect of behavior that includes feelings, motivation, interest, and values.

ANIMISM. The child's belief that everything in nature is endowed with life and purpose, like himself (e.g., the sun follows him to watch over him, the wind blows to keep him cool).

ARTIFICIALISM. The child's belief that human beings created natural phenomena such as the sun, the moon, lakes, rivers, and mountains.

ASSIMILATION. *See* Adaptation.

CENTRATION. The first, immediate aspect of perception, which involves *centering* or focusing upon the most compelling features of that which is perceived, to the exclusion of other aspects. (*See also* Decentration.)

CIRCULAR REACTION. The repetition of a sensory-motor pattern of response until it becomes strengthened and consolidated into a new scheme. Later, it may be repeated with variations in order to produce varied effects.

COGNITION. Refers to all the intellective activities of the mind, such as thinking, knowing, remembering, perceiving, recognizing, or generalizing.

COGNITIVE COMPETENCE. A state of being sensitive to new problems and possibilities and capable of finding new ways of dealing with them.

COLLECTIVE MONOLOGUE. The egocentric conversations of preoperational children who talk to each other but pay little attention to what other children are saying and pursue their own lines of thought.

COLLECTIVE SYMBOLISM. Play in which children take different roles and act them out with full awareness of each other and of their separate roles.

COMPENSATORY PLAY. The child's "make-believe" play in which he acts out fear, anger, and other emotions in gradual degrees so that he can cope with them (e.g., children who face a feared operation play "hospital").

CONCRETE OPERATIONS. *See* Operations.

CONSERVATION. The ability to understand that objects or quantities are "conserved" and remain constant despite changes in their appearance (e.g., one cup of milk is the same amount whether poured into a tall, thin glass or a wide, shallow bowl).

DECENTRATION. The secondary and continuing aspect of perceptual activity, by means of which errors or distortions of perception are corrected. Perception focuses first upon the most compelling aspect of a stimulus to the exclusion of others; decentration, or focusing on secondary aspects and incorporating them into the total percept, leads to modified and more accurate perception.

DEFERRED IMITATION. *See* Imitation.

DIRECTED GROPING. The experimental variation of a familiar behavior pattern in order to observe what will happen. This begins to occur during the second year of sensory-motor development.

EGOCENTRISM. Lack of awareness of anything outside the realm of one's immediate experience. It is evidenced most clearly in infants, who are unaware even of their own hands and feet as being parts of their bodies and do not realize that objects exist when they can no longer be seen. Egocentric thinking persists throughout childhood, as shown by the child's unawareness of points of view other than his own, and his projection of his own wishes, fears, and desires onto the world around him.

ELEMENTARY ERRORS. Errors of perception that lead to overestimation of stimuli under certain conditions.

EQUILIBRATION. The dynamic, continuously self-regulating process of balancing the changes brought about by constant assimilation and accommodation in order to arrive at a "steady state" or *equilibrium*. It is the organizing factor underlying all biological and intellectual development. (*See also* Adaptation.)

FIGURATIVE. Refers to aspects of knowledge that are static, focused on the configurations of objects, on their perceived appearances. Figurative and operative knowledge represent different aspects of the same knowing process. (*See also* Operative.)

FORMAL OPERATIONS. *See* Operations.

GENETIC EPISTEMOLOGY. The developmental study of the nature of knowledge: what it is, how it begins, and how it develops.

GROUPINGS. Organized structures of thought that are reversible and logical in the sense that every element is related to every other element. They include the logic of classes and relations and are characteristic of the period of concrete operations.

HYPOTHETICO-DEDUCTIVE THINKING. Inferential thinking which follows a hypothesis through to all possible logical conclusions. It is based on theory, and is characteristic of the period of formal operations.

IDENTITY. The understanding that people and objects retain their identity despite changes in appearance. (*See also* Conservation.)

IMAGERY. Arises out of imitation and consists of internalized representations functioning in the absence of the imaged objects. Piaget refers to *reproductive* (past) imagery and *anticipatory* (future) imagery.

IMITATION. Represents the child's attempt to adjust to the environment. It is based primarily upon the accommodation of the child to what he observes around him, whether he understands (i.e., has assimilated) it or not. *Deferred imitation*—imitation of something observed in the past, which indicates the child's emerging ability to remember.

INNATE OR NEONATAL REFLEXES. Behavior patterns that are present at birth, such as sucking and grasping.

INRC GROUPS. Logical-mathematical groups characterized by four kinds of transformations: *I*dentity, *N*egation, *R*eciprocity, and *C*orrelation. They characterize the thinking of the period of formal operations.

INTERIORIZATION. The gradual dissociation between external actions and the mental representations that replace them (e.g., the action of counting aloud while touching each of five blocks becomes interiorized as a numerical experience of a series of five).

INTUITIVE REASONING. Characteristic of the preoperational child between four and seven. It is based on immediate perception but through trial and error may lead to correct conclusions.

LOGICAL-MATHEMATICAL KNOWLEDGE is contrasted with physical knowledge in that the former depends upon relationships constructed in the mind (i.e., number or class), rather than physical characteristics observed in the object (i.e., size or color).

LUDIC SYMBOLISM. The playful symbolism of children's "make-believe" games in which objects are used to represent other objects not present (e.g., a stick is used as a gun, or a rag doll becomes a baby).

MATURATION. The emergence of a condition of possibilities, not simply for the content of knowledge, but also for the development of the form it takes.

MORALITY OF CONSTRAINT. Based on a sense of moral realism (see below). Punishment is meted out according to the amount of damage done, regardless of intention. The harshest punishment is the fairest. Characteristic of preoperational children.

MORALITY OF COOPERATION. Takes into account the motives and degree of responsibility of the offending child. Punishment is not based just on the amount of damage done. Characteristic of the period of concrete operations.

MORAL REALISM. The young child's view that the severity of punishment should depend on the amount of damage done, regardless of intention (e.g., it is worse to break six glasses accidentally than one glass deliberately because six glasses cost more than one).

OBJECT PERMANENCE. An intellectual achievement of the sensory-motor period in which the baby learns that objects and people exist independently of his perception of them.

OPERATIONS. The interiorized activities of the mind, as opposed to the sensory-motor or physical activities of the body. Characterized by logical thought processes that are organized, structured, reversible, and can be generalized. *Concrete operations* are concerned with concrete, existing objects and include ordering, serial arrangements, and classification, as well as mathematical processes. *Formal* or *second-order operations* are concerned with logical propositions and hypothetical reasoning, and may be based on theoretical constructs rather than concrete experience.

OPERATIVE. Relating to actions; the dynamic, transformational aspect of knowledge at any level, from sensory-motor to formal. (*See also* Figurative.)

ORGANIZATION. The innate tendency of all living organisms to organize and integrate experiences and activities into physical or psychological structures *(schemes)*. Organization goes hand in hand with *adaptation;* they are the functional invariants of all biological behavior.

PERCEPTION. The direct and immediate first impression of objects or situations perceived. (*See also* Centration.)

PERCEPTUAL ACTIVITY. The continuing aspect of perception that modifies and corrects the often inaccurate first perception by focusing on other aspects of the stimulus and incorporating all perceptions into a more accurate whole. (*See also* Decentration.)

PERCEPTUAL CONSTANCY. The ability to perceive objects as constant in size, shape, color, etc., even when seen in changing settings that make them appear different (e.g., a man is perceived as life-sized even when seen from a block away so that he actually appears much smaller).

PERCEPTUAL REASONING. Based on immediate appearances. Characteristic of the preoperational child who focuses on only one aspect of a stimulus at a time (i.e., the length of a clay "sausage"). (*See also* Intuitive reasoning.)

PRECONCEPTS. The child's first, fuzzy attempts at generalization, in which he confuses representatives of a class with the whole class. Preconceptual thinking characterizes the child between two and four years old.

PREOPERATIONAL. Refers to the period of early childhood preceding the emergence of logical, reversible operations. Characterized by egocentric thinking, symbolic representation, and illogical intuitions based upon perception.

REALISM. The child's belief that whatever is real to him, such as dreams, feelings, or symbols, has objective reality, which is shared by other people.

REPRESENTATION. The process by which an image, a sign, or a symbol comes to represent an external reality. In symbolic play, a child may use acorns to represent nonexistent dishes. Memories are interiorized images, whereas words are verbal signs that represent complexes of socially shared meanings.

REVERSIBILITY. A characteristic of logical operations that permits the mind to reverse its activity and go backward in thought in order to coordinate previously observed phenomena with present circumstances (e.g., if 2 and 2 make 4, then 4 less 2 leaves 2 once more).

SCHEME. A cognitive structure or pattern of behavior or thought arising out of the integration of simpler, more primitive units into an enlarged, organized, and more complex whole (e.g., sensory-motor reflexes and activities gradually become coordinated into more complex behaviors such as prehension; the understanding of number is constructed out of experiences of one-to-one equivalence).

SENSORY-MOTOR. Refers to knowledge based on information received through physical exploration and sensory stimulation; also to the earliest developmental period.

SOCIAL TRANSMISSION. A form of learning that depends on interpersonal relations, verbal instruction, and experiences of a social or cultural nature.

STAGES. Levels of development characterized by successively differentiated, more complex, and more highly integrated patterns of thought or behavior. Usually characteristic of certain chronological age ranges.

SYMBOLIC PLAY. The child's "make-believe" fantasies in which assimilation predominates, as the child uses objects to represent in his play other objects that are not present, but that he is seeking to understand or familiarize himself with (e.g., the child uses leaves and twigs to represent papers and pencils as she "plays school").

SYMBOLIC REPRESENTATION. Refers to the use of symbols to represent external reality as in *symbolic play* (above). (*See also* Representation.)

SYNCRETISM. The reasoning of the preoperational child that explains cause and effect in terms of contiguity. Things that happen together cause each other (e.g., the road causes the bicycle to go).

TOPOLOGY. The study of spatial relationships and forms without size or shape. Deals with open and closed figures such as a simple closed curve that divides a plane into inside and outside.

TRANSITIVITY. The ability to transpose differences between items in a series (e.g., if $A > B$, and $B > C$, it follows that $A > C$).

References

Ames, A., Jr. "Visual Perception and the Rotating Trapezoidal Window." *Psychological Monographs* 65, no. 7 (1951).

Anderson, Richard C., and Ausubel, David P., eds. *Readings in the Psychology of Cognition.* New York: Holt, Rinehart and Winston, 1965.

Anthony, E. J. "The System Makers: Piaget and Freud." *British Journal of Medicine and Psychology* 30 (1957): 255–69.

Appel, Marilyn H. and Goldberg, Lois S., eds. *Equilibration: Theory, Research, and Application,* vol. 1 of *Topics in Cognitive Development.* New York: Plenum Publishing Corp., 1977.

Baldwin, Alfred L. *Theories of Child Development.* New York: John Wiley & Sons, 1968.

Bower, Thomas G. R. *A Primer of Infant Development.* San Francisco: W. H. Freeman, 1977.

Brown, Mary, and Precious, Norman. *The Integrated Day in the Primary School.* New York: Agathon Press, 1969.

Bruner, Jerome S. *The Process of Education.* New York: Vintage Books, 1960.

Bruner, Jerome S., et al. *Studies in Cognitive Growth.* New York: John Wiley & Sons, 1966.

Dennis, Wayne. "Piaget's Questions Applied to a Child of Known Environment." *Journal of Genetic Psychology* 60 (1942): 307–20.

Elkind, David. *Children and Adolescents: Interpretive Essays on Jean Piaget.* New York: Oxford University Press, 1970.

Erger, Donald V. *Understanding British Infant Schools.* Farmingdale, N.Y.: Carley Publications, 1972.

Evans, Richard I. *Jean Piaget: The Man and His Ideas.* New York: E. P. Dutton & Co., 1973.

Flavell, John H. *The Developmental Psychology of Jean Piaget.* Princeton, N.J.: D. Van Nostrand Co., 1963.

Gallagher, Jeanette McC., and Easley, J.A., Jr., eds. *Piaget and Education,* vol. 2 of *Knowledge and Development.* New York: Plenum Publishing Corp., 1978.

Gallagher, Jeanette McC., and Reid, D. Kim. *The Learning Theory of Piaget and Inhelder.* Monterey, Calif.: Brooks/Cole, in press.

Geber, Beryl A., ed. *Piaget and Knowing: Studies in Genetic Epistemology.* Boston: Routledge & Kegan Paul, 1977.

Gibson, Eleanor, and Olum, Vivian. "Experimental Methods of Studying Perception in Children." In *Handbook of Research Methods in Child Development,* edited by Paul Mussen, pp. 311–73. New York: John Wiley & Sons, 1960.

Gouin-Décarie, Thérèse. *Intelligence and Affectivity in Early Childhood.* New York: International Universities Press, 1965.

Greenspan, Stanley I. "Intelligence and Adaptation: An Integration of Psychoanalytic and Piagetian Developmental Psychology." *Psychological Issues,* Monograph 47/48, vol. 12, nos. 3, 4. New York: International Universities Press, 1979.

Gruber, Howard E., and Vonèche, J. Jacques, eds. *The Essential Piaget.* New York: Basic Books, 1977.

Hunt, J. McV. *Intelligence and Experience.* New York: Ronald Press, 1961.

Inhelder, Bärbel, and Chipman, Harold H., eds. *Piaget and His School.* New York: Springer-Verlag, 1976.

Inhelder, Bärbel, and Piaget, Jean. *The Early Growth of Logic in the Child.* New York: W. W. Norton and Co., 1969.

———. *The Growth of Logical Thinking from Childhood to Adolescence.* New York: Basic Books, 1958.

Inhelder, Bärbel; Sinclair, Hermine; and Bovet, Magali. *Learning and the Development of Cognition.* Cambridge, Mass.: Harvard University Press, 1974.

Kamii, Constance, and DeVries, Rheta. *Physical Knowledge in Preschool Education: Implications of Piaget's Theory.* Englewood Cliffs, N.J.: Prentice-Hall, 1978.

Laurendeau, Monique, and Pinard, Adrien. *Causal Thinking in the Child.* New York: International Universities Press, 1962.

———. *The Development of the Concept of Space in the Child.* New York: International Universities Press, 1970.

Marsh, L. G. *Approach to Mathematics.* London: A. & C. Black Ltd., 1969.

Modgil, Sohan. *Piagetian Research: A Handbook of Recent Studies.* New York: Humanities Press, 1974.

Mussen, Paul, ed. *Handbook of Research Methods in Child Development.* New York: John Wiley & Sons, 1960.

Overton, Willis E. and Gallagher, Jeanette McC. eds. *Advances in Research and Theory,* vol. 1 of *Knowledge and Development.* New York: Plenum Publishing Corp., 1977.

Piaget, Jean. *Behavior and Evolution.* New York: Random House, 1978.

———. *Biology and Knowledge.* Chicago: University of Chicago Press, 1971.

———. "The Child and Modern Physics." *Scientific American* 196, no. 3 (1957): 46–51.

———. *The Child and Reality.* New York: Grossman, 1973.

———. "Children's Philosophies." In *Handbook of Child Psychology,* edited by C. Murchison, pp. 534–47. 2d ed. Worcester, Mass.: Clark University Press, 1933.

———. *The Child's Conception of Movement and Speed.* New York: Basic Books, 1970.

———. *The Child's Conception of Physical Causality.* Totowa, N.J.: Littlefield, Adams & Co., 1960.

———. *The Child's Conception of Time.* New York: Basic Books, 1970.

———. *The Child's Conception of the World.* Totowa, N.J.: Littlefield, Adams & Co., 1965.

———. *The Construction of Reality in the Child.* New York: Basic Books, 1954.

———. "The Definition of Stages of Development." In *Discussions on Child Development,* edited by J. M. Tanner and B. Inhelder, vol. 4, pp. 116–35. New York: International Universities Press, 1960.

———. "Development and Learning." In *Piaget Rediscovered: A Report of the Conference on Cognitive Studies and Curriculum Development, March, 1964.* Edited by Richard E. Ripple and Verne N. Rockcastle. Ithaca, N.Y.: School of Education, Cornell University, 1964.

———. "The Development of Time Concepts in the Child." In *Psychopathology of Childhood,* edited by P. H. Hoch and J. Zubin, pp. 34–44. New York: Grune & Stratton, 1955.

———. *Genetic Epistemology.* New York: Columbia University Press, 1970.

———. "How Children Form Mathematical Concepts." In *Readings in the*

Psychology of Cognition, edited by Richard C. Anderson and David P. Ausubel, pp. 406–14. New York: Holt, Rinehart and Winston, 1965.

———. *Judgment and Reasoning in the Child.* Totowa, N.J.: Littlefield, Adams & Co., 1959.

———. *The Language and Thought of the Child.* Cleveland: World Publishing Co., 1955.

———. *The Mechanisms of Perception.* New York: Basic Books, 1969.

———. *The Moral Judgment of the Child.* New York: Free Press, 1965.

———. *The Origins of Intelligence in Children.* New York: W. W. Norton & Co., 1963.

———. "Peering into the Mind of a Child." *UNESCO Courier* 12 (1959): 4–7.

———. "Perceptual and Cognitive (or Operational) Structures in the Development of the Concept of Space in the Child." *Proceedings of the Fourteenth International Congress of Psychologists* (1954), pp. 41–46.

———. "Piaget's Theory." In *Carmichael's Manual of Child Psychology,* edited by P. Mussen, vol. 1, pp. 703–32. 3d ed. New York: John Wiley & Sons, 1970.

———. *Play, Dreams and Imitation in Childhood.* New York: W. W. Norton & Co., 1962.

———. "Principal Factors Determining Intellectual Evolution from Childhood to Adult Life." In *Outside Readings in Psychology,* edited by E. L. Hartley and R. E. Hartley, pp. 43–55. 2d ed. New York: T. Y. Crowell, 1958.

———. "The Problem of Consciousness and Symbolic Processes." In *Problems of Consciousness: Transactions of the Fourth Conference* (March 24–31, Princeton, N.J.), edited by H.E. Abramson. New York: Josiah Macy Foundation, 1954.

———. *The Psychology of Intelligence.* Totowa, N.J.: Littlefield, Adams & Co., 1960.

———. "The Relation of Affectivity to Intelligence in the Mental Development of the Child." *Bulletin of the Menninger Clinic* 26 (1962), 129–37.

———. "The Right to Education in the Modern World." In UNESCO, *Freedom and Culture.* New York: Columbia University Press, 1951, pp. 67–116.

———. *Science of Education and the Psychology of the Child.* New York: Orion Press, 1970.

———. *Six Psychological Studies.* New York: Random House, 1967.

———. *Structuralism.* New York: Basic Books, 1970.

———. *To Understand Is to Invent: The Future of Education.* New York: Grossman, 1973.

————. "Understanding and Verbal Explanation Between Young Children of the Same Age." In *Readings in Social Psychology,* edited by G. E. Swanson, T. M. Newcomb, and E. L. Hartley, pp. 54–66. New York: Holt, 1952.

Piaget, Jean, and Inhelder, Bärbel. *The Child's Conception of Space.* New York: W. W. Norton & Co., 1967.

————. *Memory and Intelligence.* New York: Basic Books, 1973.

————. *The Psychology of the Child.* New York: Basic Books, 1969.

————. *Mental Imagery in the Child.* New York: Basic Books, 1971.

Piaget, Jean; Inhelder, Bärbel; and Szeminska, Alina. *The Child's Conception of Geometry.* New York: Basic Books, 1960.

Piaget, Jean, and Szeminska, Alina. *The Child's Conception of Number.* New York: W. W. Norton & Co., 1965.

Piaget, Jean, and Weil, A. "The Development in Children of the Idea of the Homeland and of Relations with Other Countries." *International Social Sciences Bulletin* 3 (1951): 561–78.

Pulaski, Mary Ann S. "Play as a Function of Toy Structure and Fantasy Predisposition." *Child Development* 41 (1970): 531–37.

————. "Play Symbolism in Cognitive Development." In *Therapeutic Uses of Child's Play,* edited by Charles E. Schaefer. New York: Jason Aronson, 1976.

————. "Toys and Imaginative Play." In *The Child's World of Make-Believe,* edited by Jerome L. Singer. New York: Academic Press, 1973.

————. *Your Baby's Mind and How It Grows: Piaget's Theory for Parents.* New York: Harper & Row, 1978.

Ripple, Richard E., and Rockcastle, Verne O., eds. *Piaget Rediscovered: A Report of the Conference on Cognitive Studies and Curriculum Development, March, 1964.* Ithaca, N.Y.: School of Education, Cornell University, 1964.

Russell, Roger W., and Dennis, Wayne. "Studies in Animism: I. A Standardized Procedure for the Investigation of Animism." *Journal of Genetic Psychology* 55 (1939): 389–400.

Sigel, Irving E., and Hooper, Frank, H., eds. *Logical Thinking in Children: Research Based on Piaget's Theory.* New York: Holt, Rinehart and Winston, 1968.

Sime, Mary. *A Child's Eye View: Piaget for Young Parents and Teachers.* New York: Harper & Row, 1974.

Singer, Dorothy G., and Singer, Jerome L. *Partners in Play.* New York: Harper & Row, 1977.

Smedslund, Jan, "The Acquisition of Conservation of Substance and Weight in Children." In *Logical Thinking in Children,* edited by Irving E. Sigel and Frank H. Hooper, pp. 265–95. New York: Holt, Rinehart and Winston, 1968.

Uzgiris, Ina. "Patterns of Vocal and Gestural Imitations in Infants," in *The Competent Infant,* edited by L. Joseph Stone, Henrietta T. Smith, and Lois B. Murphy. New York: Basic Books, 1973.

Weiner, Melvin L. *The Cognitive Unconscious.* New York: International Universities Press, 1975.

Wohlwill, Joachim. "Developmental Studies of Perception." *Psychological Bulletin* 57 (1960): 249–88.

Wolff, Peter H. "The Developmental Psychologies of Jean Piaget and Psychoanalysis." *Psychological Issues,* Monograph 5, vol. 2, no. 1. New York: International Universities Press, 1960.

Wolinsky, Gloria. "Piaget's Theory of Perception: Insights for Educational Practices with Children Who Have Perceptual Difficulty." *Training School Bulletin* 62 (May 1965): 12–25.

Index

Grateful acknowledgment is given to the following:

International Universities Press, Inc., and Delachaux & Niestle, Neuchâtel, Switzerland, for *The Origins of Intelligence in Children,* by Jean Piaget.

Longman Group Limited and The Viking Press, Inc., for *Science of Education and the Psychology of the Child,* by Jean Piaget. Translated by Derek Coltman. Copyright © 1969 by Editions Denoel, Paris. English translation copyright © 1970 by Grossman Publishers, Inc. Reprinted by permission of Grossman Publishers.

Routledge & Kegan Paul Ltd. and Humanities Press Inc. for *The Child's Conception of the World* and *The Child's Conception of Number,* by Jean Piaget.

Routledge & Kegan Paul Ltd. and Basic Books, Inc., Publishers, for *The Growth of Logical Thinking from Childhood to Adolescence,* by Bärbel Inhelder and Jean Piaget. Translated by Anne Parsons and Stanley Milgram. Basic Books, Inc., Publishers, New York, 1958.

Routledge & Kegan Paul Ltd. and Basic Books, Inc., Publishers, for *The Child's Conception of Time,* by Jean Piaget. Translated by A. J. Pomerans. English translation copyright © 1969 by Routledge & Kegan Paul Ltd. and Basic Books, Inc., Publishers, New York.

Routledge & Kegan Paul Ltd. and Basic Books, Inc., Publishers, for *The Child's Conception of Movement and Speed,* by Jean Piaget. Translated from the French by G. E. T. Holloway and M. J. MacKenzie. English translation copyright © 1970 by Routledge & Kegan Paul Ltd. and Basic Books, Inc., Publishers, New York.

Routledge & Kegan Paul Ltd. and Basic Books, Inc. Excerpts from *Mental Imagery in the Child: A Study of the Development of Imaginal Representation* by Jean Piaget and Bärbel Inhelder. Copyright © 1971 by Routledge & Kegan Paul. Published in the U.S. by Basic Books.

Routledge & Kegan Paul Ltd. and W. W. Norton & Company, Inc., for *Play, Dreams and Imitation in Childhood,* by Jean Piaget. Translated by C. Gattegno and F. M. Hodgson. All rights reserved. W. W. Norton & Company, Inc. Norton Library Edition 1962.

Routledge & Kegan Paul Ltd. and The Free Press for *The Moral Judgment of the Child,* by Jean Piaget. Reprinted with permission of the Macmillan Company, first published 1932.

Routledge and Kegan Paul Ltd, London, for two figures and quotes from *Learning and the Development of Cognition* by Inhelder, Sinclair and Bovet. Reprinted by permission of the publisher.

Springer-Verlag New York, Inc., for four figures from *Piaget and His School,* edited by Inhelder and Chipman. Reprinted by permission.

Cornell University Press for portions of *Piaget Rediscovered,* 1964. Adapted from Ripple and Rockcastle, editors. Reprinted by permission of Verne N. Rockcastle.

Appendix A "Outline of Piaget's Periods of Cognitive Development (pp. 185–189) revised from *Your Baby's Mind and How It Grows* by Mary Ann Spencer Pulaski. Copyright © 1978 by Mary Ann Spencer Pulaski. By permission of Harper & Row, Publishers, Inc.

Mary Ann Spencer Pulaski is a psychologist educated at Wellesley College and the City University of New York, where she received her Ph.D. She has taught at levels from the elementary grades through graduate school, served for many years as a school psychologist for the Herricks (Long Island) public schools, and has conducted numerous symposia, lectures, and workshops. A charter member of the Jean Piaget Society, she has been a member of its Executive Committee and its International Advisory Board. She serves on the Council of Representatives of the New York State Psychological Association and the Executive Board of its School Psychology Division. She is a Fellow of the American Psychological Association, and past president of the Nassau County Psychological Association.

Dr. Pulaski, who lives in Port Washington, New York, is also the author of *Your Baby's Mind and How It Grows: Piaget's Theory for Parents,* published by Harper & Row in 1978.